MAX

CONTRACTION

TRAINING

The Scientifically Proven Program for Building Muscle Mass in Minimum Time

JOHN LITTLE

Contemporary Books

Chicago   New York   San Francisco   Lisbon   London   Madrid   Mexico City
Milan   New Delhi   San Juan   Seoul   Singapore   Sydney   Toronto

The McGraw-Hill Companies

Library of Congress Cataloging-in-Publication Data

Little, John R., 1960–
    Max contraction training : the scientifically proven program for building muscle
mass in minimum time / John Little.
       p.   cm.
    ISBN 0-07-142395-8
    1. Bodybuilding.   2. Bodybuilding—Psychological aspects.   I. Title.

GV546.5.L54   2003
613.7'1—dc21   2003010553

2 3 4 5 6 7 8 9 10 11   VLP/VLP   0 9 8 7 6 5

ISBN 0-07-142395-8

The advice presented within this book requires a knowledge of proper exercise form and a
base level of strength fitness. Although exercise is very beneficial, the potential for injury
does exist, especially if the trainee is not in good physical condition. Always consult with
your physician before beginning any program of progressive weight training or exercise. If
you feel any strain or pain when you are exercising, stop immediately and consult your
physician. As all systems of weight training involve a systematic progression of muscular
overload, a proper warm-up of muscles, tendons, ligaments, and joints is mandatory at
the beginning of every workout.

McGraw-Hill books are available at special quantity discounts to use as premiums and
sales promotions, or for use in corporate training programs. For more information, please
write to the Director of Special Sales, Professional Publishing, McGraw-Hill, Two Penn
Plaza, New York, NY 10121-2298. Or contact your local bookstore.

This book is printed on acid-free paper.

To Mike Mentzer (1951–2001), a friend and mentor who taught me not only much of value about the science of bodybuilding, but also that without the added meaning other activities such as family and love provide, a muscular physique would be worthless. And to Terri Little, and our wonderful children Riley, Taylor, Brandon, and Benjamin, who taught me that the greatest "titles" a man can have are those of "husband" and "father."

CONTENTS

FOREWORD

I first met John Little several years back during a *PowerTalk!* interview session I arranged. I had approached John to discuss a training protocol that he had innovated and, with his friend Peter Sisco, written a book about (*Static Contraction Training*). John's theory made perfect sense to me, as I always listen to whatever I'm hearing from what I call the "common sense corner" of my brain—and I was keen to try his novel approach to training for myself.

After our on-camera interview, John put me through a workout in a nearby gym—and I became a believer in his strength training methods right away. I was never a big bench presser or leg presser, but John explained that my muscles were actually incredibly strong if I would overcome the "weak link" in my approach to exercise. That workout saw me bench press 500 pounds—which was phenomenal in comparison to my previous range in that exercise (165–175 pounds), and my legs pressed over 2,000 pounds, when conventionally I had only done 400 pounds. The secret to such staggering results was maximum muscular contraction.

Recently, when I learned that John had created another—even more potent—training system that only took between 10 seconds and 1 minute to perform, my interest was again piqued. After one mini-workout (a total 10 seconds in length), I felt great, and the amount of weight I lifted was phenomenal! I didn't feel "beat up" or "dead," and the muscular development I experienced, just in this first little exposure to Max Contraction Training was amazing. It was clear that John was onto something. This form of exercise is so efficient—as insane as it may sound—that 10 to 20 seconds of exercise per week can yield better results than workout protocols that send people to the gym for an hour a day!

We all know people who spend hours and hours working out each week, but after a few months, when their progress tends to drop off, get frustrated and quit. They're not getting the results they're after, and their drive for a more fit and healthy body starts to dwindle. Who in their right mind is going to continue going to the gym for an hour a day three days a week, investing 180 minutes of their life each week in working out, when they aren't seeing any results? With Max Contraction Training, all you have to invest is 10 seconds to 1 minute, and even at 1 minute (the long version of the workout program in this book), you're still getting results many times more efficient than the conventional 180-minute program (and that's just once a week). Included in the book are John's own personal experiences with the program and the results he's achieved, data from the hundreds of clients he's trained on the program, as well as a full explanation of the program's scientific basis—Max Contraction Training is a truly revolutionary approach to building strength and lean body mass.

And while strength training may lack the appeal that other physical disciplines possess, such as yoga and aerobics, I find the benefits of strength training incredibly appealing. It's an absolutely essential component of anyone's health and wellness program. You can make all kinds of changes to your emotions and your relationships, but if you're physically unable to follow through on your decisions, it's all for naught. After more than a quarter of a century working with 3 million people from 80 different countries, I have learned that most people, unfortunately, don't truly realize how interconnected physical fitness—including strength training—is to fulfilling one's potential at the highest level.

Simply put, health and physical wellness are integral components in *all* aspects of not only the quality but also the length of our lives. Strength training in particular helps to stave off the aging process. Each of the 10 biomarkers of aging—and the quality of each in our lives—is directly affected by strength training. Specifically, these biomarkers are as follows:

1. *Bone density*: as people age, their bones tend to lose calcium, making the skeleton weaker, less dense, and more brittle, which typically leads to osteoporosis.

2. *Body temperature regulation*: the body is supposed to maintain an internal temperature of 98.6 degrees, but as people grow older they tend to lose muscle and the heat that muscle provides. Their body temperature becomes more vulnerable to hot and cold, which often leads to illness.

3. *Basal metabolic rate*: our rate of energizing, or determining how many calories our bodies require to sustain their internal processes, declines by 2 percent per decade after the age of 20.

4. *Blood sugar tolerance*: the body's ability to use glucose in the bloodstream declines with age and thereby raises the risk for type 2 diabetes, which is the third or fourth most common disease in this country.

5. *A decline in muscle strength*: older people are less strong because of the gradual deterioration of the muscles and motor nerves, which typically begins at the age of 30.

6. *The fat content of the body*: between the ages of 20 and 65, the average person doubles his or her ratio of fat to muscle. This process is exacerbated by a sedentary lifestyle and overeating. (Exercise often retards appetite and, conversely, a lack of exercise can cause one to be hungrier and thus to eat more often.)

7. *Aerobic capacity*: the body's ability to use oxygen efficiently declines by 30 to 40 percent by the time people reach the age of 65.

8. *Cholesterol and HDL ratios*: around age 50 people see a decrease in their HDL (high density lipoproteins, the "good cholesterol," which protects the body against heart disease) levels and an increase in their LDL (low density lipoproteins, the "bad cholesterol") levels, a phenomenon that dramatically greatens the risk of heart attack.

9. *A decline in muscle mass*: the average American loses 6.6 pounds of muscle with each decade after young adulthood, and the rate of loss increases after the age of 45 (but only if one doesn't do anything to replace it).

10. *Blood pressure*: the majority of Americans show a steady increase in blood pressure with each decade of age.

Strength training is the *only* activity that's been proven scientifically to positively affect all 10 of these biomarkers! No other activity even comes close, not even aerobics! And just imagine how much you could achieve physically if you were to find a way to make your strength training program even more efficient. John has done just that and presents his training program to you in *Max Contraction Training*. In such a short period of time in comparison to conventional workouts, you can increase the quality of your life, look good, feel good—and as John points out—even reduce your stress levels and your overall amount of body fat.

History has indicated that those who succeed are those who question. Great thinkers such as Aristotle, Plato, and Galileo, whose teachings have endured for centuries, have served as the impetus for many great thinkers to follow. While they were honored as brilliant in their time, consider all that we wouldn't know had their knowledge and tradition been left unquestioned. Human progress hinges on the commitment of a select few to not accept current knowledge as a final truth, but to continue striving to improve their methods, their knowledge base, and their skill set. John Little questioned conventional strength training methods and has created a system that takes traditional results to the next level.

John is a well-established innovator in fitness and strength training, and his methods have been employed by hundreds of thousands of individuals around the world. In fact, they have been touted as the impetus for "physiol-ogy books to be rewritten," and *Max Contraction Training* fulfills this necessity. By following the methods outlined in this book, you will save hours of unnecessary time in the gym and open your eyes to the most up-to-date research and information available in the bodybuilding industry. *Max Contraction Training* provides you with a truly revolutionary approach to strength training that, when properly applied, will result in real, meaningful, and sustainable physical results, and will help build a confidence in your own abilities that will permeate into all areas of your life.

—Anthony Robbins
Chairman,
The Anthony Robbins Companies

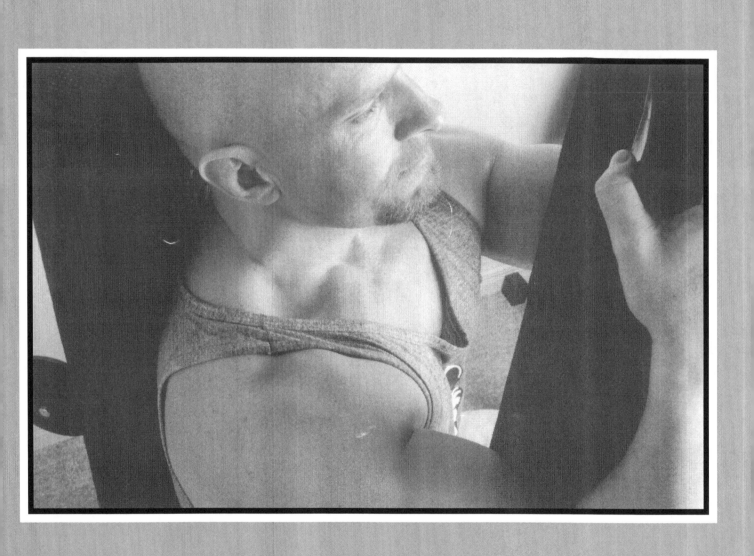

PREFACE

For decades people desiring to build muscle, lose weight, tone up, or become healthier have tried every sort of diet, infomercial product, and training approach available. Perhaps you have been among those who have joined a gym and attempted to build your body by pumping up, pulling, pressing, and supersetting. From there it was on to the high-volume routines of the various bodybuilding champions, trying one routine after the other, only to ultimately feel that no matter how much iron you pumped, how many days per week you trained, and how many supplements you consumed, your muscles had ceased to respond. In fact, if you're like most people, you've done every exercise in the book and, when you still didn't get the results you wanted, you got more books and did all the exercises in those, too. Add it all up and you've invested thousands of hours lifting millions of pounds during thousands of sets of dozens of exercises—and you're still not satisfied with your results.

So what would you think if I said you could get better results doing one set that requires no motion at all and from a workout that requires no more than a handful of exercises, that lasts a mere ten seconds, and is performed a mere one or two days a week? I've spent the past 19 years researching and refining a method that will make your muscles bigger,

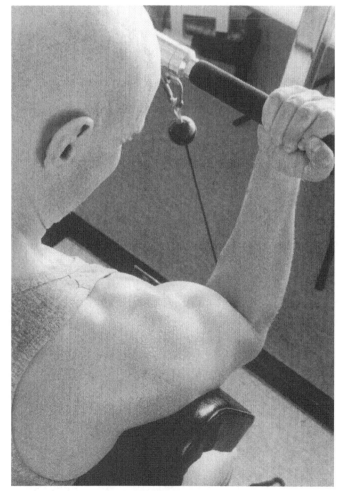

Max Contraction Training requires that a muscle be taken into a position of full contraction and overloaded with ample resistance on a progressive basis.

leaner, and stronger than they've ever been. I call it Max Contraction Training, and I think it's the safest and most productive way you'll ever find to build your muscles and become stronger without spending the rest of your life in a weight room.

Max Contraction Training is based on one simple premise: there is one position in any muscle's range of motion that is more productive than any other. This one position involves a muscle's greatest amount of fibers—and when sufficient resistance is applied to a muscle when it's in this position, more muscle fibers will be recruited and stimulated to grow bigger and stronger. Using a training approach that follows this premise will produce results many times greater than the growth stimulation imparted by conventional bodybuilding protocols, such as lifting a weight up and down.

Why is the Max Contraction Training program the most effective way to build muscle? The unique secret is in the protocol. Where, for instance, is it etched in stone that one must lift a weight up and down in order for a resistance exercise to be productive? What studies have proven the superiority—or even the necessity—of even lifting (i.e., raising) a weight at all? Where is it ordained that a series of sets of such lifts must be performed, or that a typical set of resistance exercise must last more than 1 to 6 seconds? The answers to these questions are as follows: nowhere, none, and nowhere.

The vast majority of bodybuilders, and no small number of personal trainers, simply train the conventional way because "everybody else trains that way." But what if the conventional approach to training is flawed and grossly inefficient? What if there exists a better way to build muscle? And just what is this better way? This book is an attempt to provide answers to these important questions.

Within the pages of this book I will reveal to you the most important lessons I've learned after some 23 years of independent research and experimentation in the field of bodybuilding training. I will also reveal the crucial insights and discoveries of noted exercise physiologists and disciplined thinkers on the subject of muscle building, in addition to sharing with you extensive excerpts from dialogues that took place over a 21-year association and friendship with the late Mike Mentzer, one of the greatest bodybuilders in the history of the sport and a true pioneer in the field of high-intensity training. You will find that Max Contraction Training provides reasons for each of its conclusions—from how many sets to perform, to why the position of maximum contraction is the most desirable and productive, to why the stress of training must be applied with caution and sparingly—reasons that are well grounded in the science of human physiology. I propose with this book to expose a few deceptions within bodybuilding as it is currently being practiced and promoted to the public, the perpetuation of which over many years has resulted in bodybuilding killing its own market—and not a few of its competitors.

And while I'm destroying certain idols with the one hand, with the other I will be constructing a far more rewarding alternative—a new, safe, and incredibly potent muscle-building program.

INTENSITY, NOT DURATION

Ever since the public became seriously interested in bodybuilding during the fitness boom of the 1980s, hundreds of theories have been advanced on how best to proceed with the prospect of growing bigger and stronger muscles.

Unfortunately, almost all of these approaches made the cardinal error of assuming that muscle building and strength training must be performed with an eye toward conditioning the body to tolerate longer and longer exercise sessions. However, science has revealed that it is not the duration but the intensity of the exercise that is solely responsible for effecting an increase in muscle strength and size and, hence, personal appearance. (Muscle is what gives both sexes their desirable shape, fat being formless.) Intensity and duration exist in an inverse ratio to each other; thus, the higher the intensity, the briefer the workout must be.

My training hundreds of individuals with this method and discussing the principles of this protocol with both exercise scientists and champion bodybuilders has resulted in some rather startling, if not revolutionary, conclusions:

- That only one set lasting a mere 1 to 6 seconds is required to effect increases in muscle size and strength (i.e., you do not need multiple sets of an exercise for any given bodypart).
- That this same 1- to 6-second time of contraction (TOC) is more important than repetitions.
- That movement through a full range of motion is less valuable for size and strength increases than is a full or maximal contraction that is sustained for the TOC indicated.
- That only two workouts per week are required to make optimal (not minimal) progress—and even *less* training is required as you become bigger and stronger.
- That an increase in lean body tissue will result in a substantial raise in your basal metabolic rate, allowing you to burn more calories at rest, and lose more fat, thereby negating the need for deprivation dieting and hours of aerobic exercise each week.
- That a well-balanced diet will provide all the nutrition your body requires to allow you to lose fat, build muscle, and have more energy (i.e., you do not need supplements; supplements have been overemphasized for commercial reasons and do nothing to stimulate muscle growth, nor will they allow the body to build muscle or strength faster).
- That a productive workout requires no more than 1 minute (maximum) and 10 seconds (minimum) of total training time to complete.
- That you can improve "problem" bodyparts and build impressive levels of muscle size and strength on virtually any type of progressive resistance equipment (from machines to free weights)—if you correctly employ this new protocol and its principles.
- That you need only perform a 1-second maximum contraction once every two weeks to maintain the gains you make on this new system.
- That you do not need to spend hours a day and multiple days per week in the gym to build a muscular body and to dramatically increase the size and strength of your muscles.

There are a host of ancillary benefits that attend training with Max Contraction apart from its power to dramatically increase muscle size and strength, including a reduction in body fat levels, stress release, and a huge savings in the time required to realize all of the above. In this hectic world, few working people and parents have the luxury of a lot of time to spend on going to the gym for many hours each week. Many trainees mistakenly believe that they must slavishly devote up to six hours a week (or more) in order to realize their desire of building bigger and stronger muscles; some even venture out to the gym twice a day for two hours at a crack, six days a week. This represents a total of 1,248 hours per year—hours irretrievably spent—in the hopes of building more muscle, or otherwise effecting a positive change in one's appearance. This is a considerable time investment, particularly when carried on over years and years—and the worst part is that very few of these dedicated souls ever see much in the way of progress.

Fortunately, a more effective way does exist—a way that will deliver better results from a workout lasting a mere 10 seconds and performed but once or twice a week and, rather than having to workout for *longer* periods of time as you become stronger, even *less* training time will be required. Think for a moment what you could accomplish—or suddenly find the time for—if you didn't "have to work out" (for many hours) several days each week! You would probably be able to take a college course, or start building financial independence, or even begin studying philosophy

Many individuals looking to increase their size and strength head to the gym to perform many sets and reps of many different exercises; such practices are no longer necessary. Training your muscles in a more efficient manner leaves you more time to devote to other equally important aspects of total development, including the building of your mind.

to balance the building of your body with the building of your mind—or, perhaps most importantly, if you're a parent, you would now have "extra time" to spend with your family. And all of these "extra" activities could be accomplished while still doing all that is required to maximally improve the way you look, feel, and perform.

What I've just revealed is already happening with hundreds (perhaps now even thou-sands) of trainees from all walks of life. People are gaining from 12 to 30 pounds of muscle per year; others are dropping from 10 to 40 pounds of fat—and all of them from work-outs lasting a mere 10 seconds to 1 minute in length. Max Contraction Training has proven not only that you don't need to spend hours each week in the gym to build an incredibly fit and muscular body, but also why such approaches are doomed to fail.

Inside the pages of this revolutionary book you will learn all the specifics of this ground-breaking new protocol (fully supported by science) that maximizes muscle fiber stimula-tion and that has proven to be far more effi-cient than conventional training methods for building muscle. In addition, you will learn how to optimally space your workouts apart and how to structure your workouts year-round for continuous gains, and you will also come to understand the crucial role of "off days"—and why you need *more* of them. You will also learn the best bodypart specialization exercises and the ideal routines required to develop problem or lagging bodyparts—in short, everything you need to know in order to build muscle and strength in your arms, chest, back, shoulders, and legs without spending your life in a gym. In summary, the book you are now holding in your hands contains a new and powerful technology, a technology that required the better part of two decades of research, experiment, and refinement to perfect and that has resulted in the first legitimate twenty-first-century approach to bodybuild-ing exercise.

Never before has a concerted effort been made to determine just what type (or how *little*) exercise is actually required to effect positive change in one's health and physique. That has all changed now with Max Contrac-tion Training. I noted earlier that few people these days have a lot of time to devote to body-building. The good news is that "a lot of time" is no longer required.

Keeping your bodybuilding training in proper perspective to other life issues will result in your living a more balanced and rewarding life.

ACKNOWLEDGMENTS

The author wishes to thank photographer Laura Bombier for her artistry, and models Joe Ostertag, Irwin Heshka, Leslie Cockwell, and Jesse Jones for their assistance in demonstrating the Max Contraction exercises. Additional acknowledgment is made to Gold's Gym (Venice) and The Big Buddy Gym (Bracebridge) for permission to shoot photos for this book at their gyms; to photographer/publisher John Balik for his images of Mike Mentzer; and to the Steve Reeves International Society for providing the images of Steve Reeves. In addition, the author would like to acknowledge the work of Joanne Sharkey (mikementzer.com) for her efforts in preserving and perpetuating the teachings of my friend Mike Mentzer, whose contributions to the science of bodybuilding should never be forgotten.

Part I

PRELIMINARIES

Chapter 1

BODYBUILDING: A BETTER APPROACH

Bodybuilding, as it is presently practiced, is one of the most mindless, least healthy, and unscientific disciplines on the face of the earth. I recognize that this is quite an indictment for an author of a "bodybuilding" book to make, but we must face facts.

It's an irony too seldom noted that few people these days will admit to being "bodybuilders" without an apologetic preface. One would assume that people who spend many hours per week engaged in an activity such as bodybuilding would have reasons for doing so, and that such reasons would reflect the values that such people hold or seek to obtain. Yet, unlike the student who spends comparable time in obtaining a college degree, or an athlete training diligently to compete in the Olympic Games, there is little pride of purpose evident in these people who willingly spend upwards of 12 hours a week in a bodybuilding gymnasium —and with good reason: such an expenditure of time is entirely irrational when equal or even better results can be obtained by training a mere 10 to 20 seconds a week. However, the issue of training efficiency, while a contribut-

ing factor, is not in itself sufficient explanation for the reticence, if not downright embarrassment, of these people when it comes to admitting that they are "bodybuilders."

So why is bodybuilding no longer an activity to be celebrated or, at the very least, admitted to? Why is the discipline not embraced the way it used to be? Why have organizations such as the International Olympics Committee repeatedly denied requests from the main bodybuilding organizations to accept it as a legitimate competitive sport, and why are its champions never given endorsements on par with the champions of tennis, football, or baseball?

Part of the reason for bodybuilding's fall from grace can be attributed to the influx of anabolic steroids and other growth drugs into the sport, which resulted in the creation of ultrahuge, grotesquely defined physiques that have turned off more members of the general public than they have attracted. Steroids came into the bodybuilding scene in the 1950s, escalated in use during the 60s, 70s, and 80s, and metastasized out of control throughout the

1990s until the present. Steroids grew in appeal largely due to an inherently attractive desire within most bodybuilders to take "the quick and easy way." There was a hidden cost to the use of these drugs, however, that made the lives of most of these bodybuilders anything but easy; this cost came in the form of a very real threat to their overall health and well being. Many champion bodybuilders from the 1970s and 80s have suffered mental illness (sometimes resulting in incarceration), many more have suffered serious heart trouble, others have had kidney failure, and still others have died. All of this can be attributed—directly or indirectly—to their use of what are commonly referred to as "bodybuilding drugs."

The look of today's professional bodybuilders has been off-putting to the general public.

In addition, bodybuilding has become such a huge commercial bonanza that it has been infiltrated over the years by no shortage of unscrupulous characters and corporations whose business it is to convince the innocent and naïve that they needed to purchase their products (usually supplements) in order to build muscles. Even the contests are not above suspicion; there have been many allegations of "fixed" contests and not all of them are without merit. Also there are many bodybuilders who are so one-dimensional that they would engage in any activity—and I mean *any* activity—that remunerated them sufficiently to cover the cost of their contraband expense (one pro bodybuilder told me that he spent more than $40,000 in drugs in preparation for one contest!), and, when they fail to place or be featured in a magazine, they are lost, having nothing—no vocation or other interests—to fall back on and lack the self-esteem to do anything else. One of the most pathetic examples was a former gym owner from Missouri who went down the wrong path with drugs, lost his business, his marriage and—now in his autumn years—is scraping out a living trying to scare up "personal training" clients. He had it all; now he has only the memories of when he had it all—and no means of regaining it.

This brings us back full circle to the issue of training efficiency. The bodybuilding establishment, inclusive of the magazines that help to support it, has long been promulgating the high-volume/high-frequency training approaches of the drug users as "the only way" to build bigger muscles. "If you want to look like a bodybuilder, then you must train like a bodybuilder," they say—omitting to mention that such high volume (up to 30 sets or more per bodypart) and frequent training routines (up to 24 hours of training per week) only work in conjunction with nightmarish quantities of so-called "bodybuilding drugs."

In truth there is no such thing as a "bodybuilding drug"—only drugs that bodybuilders consume indiscriminately, from amphetamines, thyroid hormones, blood platelet aggregation inhibitors, and blood viscosity conditioners, to estrogen antagonists, anabolic steroids, growth hormones, insulin,

"To look like a bodybuilder, you must train like a bodybuilder," says a popular bodybuilding adage. However, there's another component that figures prominently into this "look" that such adages fail to mention.

and others. If the average trainee isn't willing (and most with an intact, functioning brain are not) to risk cancer, kidney failure, leukemia, liver damage, testicular atrophy, chromosome damage, and heart disease by taking these substances, then his body will never be able to tolerate the chronic, gross overtraining that the magazines so often recommend. Bodybuilding has deservedly lost the affection of the general public because what was once a bona fide pursuit of health, well-being, and the aesthetic appeal of a well-developed physique (physical culture) has, over time, given way to illegal drugs, questionable lifestyles, atrophied character, and chronic health maladies. Ironically, it's probably safe to say that many bodybuilders who win contests in this era are the unhealthiest men on the stage.

Such a dilemma has left many of us who recognize that bodybuilding can (and should) be a health-promoting activity confused by the turn of events. After all, it wasn't that long ago when bodybuilders were considered to be

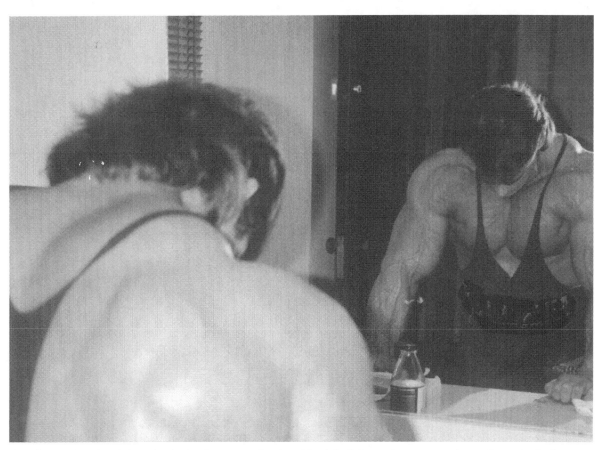

Creating and maintaining the look of most professional bodybuilders takes an exacting toll on the body.

among the healthiest people on the planet. The bodybuilders of the mid-twentieth century—men such as John Grimek and Steve Reeves—successfully altered the then prevailing notion that lifting weights was somehow bad for you, correcting the misconception to more accurately reveal that it is a superior activity to promote fitness and health. The impression among members of the general public that all bodybuilders were cerebrally challenged hulks was also disproved with the emergence of competitors such as Arnold Schwarzenegger and Mike Mentzer. But somewhere along the line

the bodybuilding train slipped off the tracks; bloated muscle size became its sole criterion, and the mindless pursuit of it became the standard. Health and fitness became subordinate to puffy, swollen tissue—so much so, in fact, that, over time, health and fitness disappeared from the sport altogether, and a preponderance of low-grade mentalities who were willing to wink at ethics if it meant having their picture in a magazine toed the corporate line and rose to the top. The conclusion had to follow from the premises: soon the old criticisms that should have long ago been put to rest returned,

John Carl Grimek, one of the greatest bodybuilders of all time. Grimek was every bit as strong as he looked; he represented the United States as a weight lifter at the Olympic Games. Also an accomplished gymnast, he built his body and strength in an era when steroids were unheard of.

specterlike, to haunt the sport—and justifiably so, as they had now been proven valid.

Rather than taking these criticisms as a long overdue wake-up call, the bodybuilding establishment chose to ignore them. Some magazines actually reveled in the fact of rampant drug use among bodybuilders, going so far as to publish articles on which drugs they took and how much—never minding that neither the writers of these articles nor the bodybuilders featured in them were medically trained and had no concept of what damage their advice would wreak on those who followed it. And the damage was (and continues to be) extensive indeed.

REDISCOVERING THE BENEFITS OF PROPER BODYBUILDING

All this being what bodybuilding has become, and should not be, it remains to say what bodybuilding *is*, or ideally might be. Can we restore this once-noble discipline to its ancient scope and power? Bodybuilding, ideally, is the strengthening and aesthetic development of one's body to the full measure of its genetic capacity. It does not require drugs, it does not require posing trunks. The approach to bodybuilding I'm advocating here is not intended for competitive bodybuilders (although even competitive bodybuilders will benefit from the protocol), but for all those who earnestly desire to become bigger and stronger but who have no desire to become one-dimensional misfits and who believe there is a life outside of the gym. There are a host of benefits that attend this approach to bodybuilding that extend far beyond the mere development of an attractive physique, including a reduction in stress and enhanced circulation—which can often serve

Arnold Schwarzenegger proved to the masses that bodybuilding can be a helpful adjunct to a spectacularly successful life.

Bodybuilding, ideally, is the strengthening and aesthetic development of one's body to the full measure of its genetic capacity.

as a tonic to the brain and to one's emotional well-being. As philosopher/historian Will Durant once put it, "To an organism in a fair condition of health, every sense and organ of the body is an answer to the pessimist and a justification of life."

An Aegean Interlude

The ancient Greeks first posited the idea of a strong body's direct relationship to sound mental health; the Greeks glorified the building of the body and mind simultaneously, and were the first to combine their academic institutions with their gymnasiums for the express purpose of cultivating "a healthy mind in a healthy body." Athletics, more than anything else, served to frame the constitution of the Greek character. As Durant points out:

> Religion failed to unify Greece, but athletics—periodically—succeeded. Men went to Olympia, Delphi, Corinth, and Nemea not so much to honor the gods—for these could be honored anywhere—as to witness the heroic contests of chosen athletes, and the ecumenical assemblage of varied Greeks. Alexander, who could see Greece from without, considered Olympia the capital of the Greek world. Here under the rubric of athletics we find the real religion of the Greeks—the worship of health, beauty, and strength. . . . We must not think of the average Greek as a student and lover of Aeschylus or Plato; rather, like the typical Briton or American, he was interested in sport, and his favored athletes were his earthly gods. . . . To the Greek the best life [was] the fullest one, rich in health, strength, beauty, passion, means, adventure, and thought. Virtue is *arete*, manly . . . excellence . . . precisely what the Romans called *vir-tus*, man-liness. The Athenian ideal man is the *kalokagathos*, who combines beauty and justice in a gracious art of living that frankly values ability, fame, wealth, and friends as well as virtue and humanity; as with Goethe, self-development is everything.[1]

From the isle of Ceos, the Greek poet Simonides (ca. 556–468 B.C.) announced: "To be in health is the best thing for man; the next best, to be of form and nature beautiful; the third, to enjoy wealth gotten without fraud; and the fourth, to be in youth's bloom among friends."[2] And the legendary Homer reminded the ancient Greeks in his *Odyssey* (which was virtually the bible of the Greeks), "There is no greater glory for a man as long as he lives, than that which he wins by his own hands and feet."[3]

The era in which Simonides wrote is commonly referred to by historians as the "Golden Age" of our human heritage; it was truly ideal in many respects, giving us everything from democracy, literature, philosophy, science, schools, universities, gymnasiums, and stadiums, to trial by jury, drama, and engineering and medical science (to name but a few of their gifts). Although we "moderns" are inclined to think of the body as something separate from the mind, the ancient Greeks fully grasped the concept that the two are interrelated and, indeed, that a well-developed body was a precondition to a well-developed mind. In fact, the Greek soldier and historian Xenophon (430–354 B.C.) reported that the great philosopher Socrates was among the strongest advocates of this concept, as evidenced in the following exchange between the old philosopher and his young friend Epigenes:

Socrates: You're out of training, Epigenes.

Epigenes: I don't do physical training, Socrates.

Socrates: But you ought to. . . . In the first place, those who keep themselves fit are healthy and strong; and this means that many of them come through the conflicts of war with honor, and escape from all its dangers; many help their friends and do service to their country, and so earn gratitude and win great glory and achieve the most splendid honors, and consequently live out their lives with greater pleasure and distinction, and leave behind them a better start in life for their children. . . . You can take it from me that there is . . . no activity of any kind in which you will be at a disadvantage

Bodybuilding legend Steve Reeves was the epitome of the Grecian ideal.

from having your body better prepared. The body is valuable for all human activities, and in all its uses it is very important that it should be as fit as possible. Even in the act of thinking, which is supposed to require least assistance from the body, everyone knows that serious mistakes often happen through physical ill-health. Many people's minds are often so invaded by forgetfulness, despondency, irritability and insanity because of their poor physical condition that their knowledge is actually driven out of them. On the other hand, those who are in good physical condition have ample cause for confidence and run no risk of any such misfortune through debility. Their physical fitness is likely to contribute towards results that are contrary to those of unfitness— results which a sane man would surely endure any hardships to secure. Besides, it is a shame to let yourself grow old through neglect before seeing how you can develop the maximum beauty and strength of your body.[4]

It is a shame that the insights of many of these ancient Greek sages aren't given much attention in our bodybuilding magazines these days, and the result is that bodybuilding is increasingly coming to be viewed as something merely cosmetic, rather than essential, to our daily life. The ancient ideal of a "healthy mind in a healthy body" is all but forgotten and certainly is no longer actively championed (save, perhaps, for the writings of this author and the late Mike Mentzer). However, as Durant pointed out, health and strength were necessary to the realization of the ideal of *kalokagathos*, being necessary and vital adjuncts to living a fuller, more rewarding life.

Many bodybuilding authorities are content to dismiss the "mind" as something ephemeral and separate from the body, and, therefore, when they speak of "total fitness," they confine themselves solely to issues of strength, flexibility, and endurance, with little or no indication of the mental benefits or even the mental connection that attends physical training. The truth is that "total health" must, by definition, include both the physical and mental, that is, the body and mind. Also, the mind, rather than being something detached from the body, is actually a function of the brain—which is just as much a physical part of the body as the biceps. The mind and body *are* interrelated—after all, the muscles contract via impulses from the central nervous system, of which the mind (and personality) are a part—and both require exercise to grow stronger.

The Physiology of Stress

To this end, the stronger and healthier the body, the stronger and healthier the mind. This is most obviously manifest in the potential for exercise for relieving or even staving off certain psychosomatic disorders caused by the accumulation of maladaptive factors such as stress. Stress can be mental or physical; however, given the interrelationship of mind to body, if stress is left unchecked, its symptoms are typically expressed physically.

The late Dr. Hans Selye, a pioneer in stress research, wrote at length about how unchecked mental stress can quickly lead to bodily malfunctions. Selye maintained that things such as heart attacks, migraine headaches, neck pain, alcoholism, and obesity can be caused by stress, and that the relief of stress can go a long way toward eradicating these problems. Wilhelm Reich later concluded that other physical problems such as asthma, rheumatism, hypertension, and ulcers were often also the result of chronic mental anxiety. People today are taking more and more antidepressants and other "stress medications," and there is a concomitant rise in visits to overcrowded doctors' and psychiatrists' offices; there is little doubt that the stress of life is increasing for most people and causing problems for them in their day-to-day existence.

Stress, as defined by Selye, is "the nonspecific response of the body to any demand." The body's reaction to this is what Selye called the General Adaptation Syndrome, or GAS, a three-tiered response that begins with an alarm stage, followed by a stage of resistance, and finally a stage of exhaustion. The stress itself can cause internal chemical reactions that include the release of adrenaline, increased heart rate, faster reflex speed, muscle tension, and accelerated thought processes. Selye's research indicates that our bodies react exactly the same way to stress—whether it comes in the form of pleasure, success, failure, or depression. Evidently, both good and bad life situations cause what the body perceives to be stress, and everyone is under some degree of stress, even when asleep.

Stress, then, is the rate of daily wear and tear on our existence. Its effects, however, depend on how we adapt to it and how we're able to dissipate its accumulation of repressed energy. The General Adaptation Syndrome is always in operation in our bodies, often on an emergency basis, but the physical outlets for its dissipation are not built in. And it's becoming clear that these dammed-up emotions have to be released on a regular basis if we are to stay mentally healthy.

Here is where bodybuilding qua bodybuilding can reassert its significance and value with some authority. Bodybuilding exercise is probably the most productive means of releasing stress; while almost any active exercise can reduce tension levels in the body, bodybuilding training appears to be unique in that it can be pinpointed to the precise area where the stress is located—for example, in the neck, stomach, shoulders, or back. Bodybuilding exercise can provide immediate relief of tension in these areas, as well as remove the general feeling of lethargy that results from our daily wear-and-tear encounters.

Reducing Body Fat

Another benefit afforded by proper bodybuilding training is the loss of body fat—without dieting. To many people, the notion that an individual can actually lose body fat and become leaner by working out with weights is nonsensical. After all, bodybuilding training simply builds bigger muscles, right? To lose body fat, the general advice is to start jogging, go on a diet, or enroll in an aerobics class. However, it is this very "muscle-building" feature of bodybuilding training that is responsible for the fat loss.

The reason is that muscle cells, unlike fat cells, are designated as "active" tissue, meaning that a certain number of calories are required simply to sustain their existence. In fact, for every pound of muscle you gain, between 50 and 100 calories are required daily simply to sustain its cellular activity. If, for example, you could add even one pound of muscle to your body, your resting metabolism would increase by roughly 75 calories a day—even if you did no exercise at all. That may not sound like much, but, given the fact that there are 3,500 calories in a pound of fat tissue, if you were able to keep that new pound of muscle tissue for an entire year, you would lose approximately eight pounds of fat. If you try to picture in your mind what eight pounds of butter looks like, you will begin to appreciate just how radical a change in appearance an eight-pound fat loss truly is. However, the converse is also true: if you lost a pound of muscle tissue (whether through atrophy, overtraining, or severe dieting), you would also lose that pound

of muscle's calorie-burning potential. Thus, a certain percentage of the calories you took in on a daily basis would now end up being stored as fat—with the net result, again, being a rather profound change in your appearance, this time for the worse.

Bodybuilding, though for years considered the weak sister of health and fitness exercise, has actually been proven to be more effective than aerobics in reducing the level of body fat in the body. Wayne Wescott, an exercise physiologist and strength-training consultant to the YMCA, conducted a study in which he compared two groups of 36 men and women who had completed an eight-week program. All of them consumed a reduced caloric diet made up of 20 percent fat, 20 percent protein, and 60 percent carbohydrates. In addition, the subjects were required to exercise three times per week for 30 minutes a session. One group combined a 15-minute total bodyweight training program with 15 minutes of aerobic exercise. The other group did 30 minutes of aerobic activity only. The results were fascinating: the aerobics-only group lost an average of 3.2 pounds of fat, but the weight training/aerobic exercise group ended up losing an average of 10 pounds of fat—almost three times more fat loss than the aerobics-only group! It's significant to note that this group also gained two pounds of muscle per person, compared to a loss of a half a pound of muscle per person among the aerobic exercise–only group.

Another study conducted by researchers at Emory University in Atlanta revealed similar findings, this time with overweight women as their subjects. The women, who either did 20 minutes of aerobics three times a week or nothing at all, lost only 72 percent of fat per pound of weight lost. Mary Ellen Sweeney, M.D., of the Emory Health Enhancement Program, reported that those who did 20 minutes of strength training three times a week retained more muscle mass—which parlayed into 85 percent of every pound they lost being fat tissue.

In light of this research, an effective bodybuilding program would appear to be the most efficient route to obtaining a lean, muscular body and, perhaps more importantly, maintaining it.

HGH Production

HGH is an acronym for human growth hormone, a naturally occurring substance in the human body. Dr. Mary Lee Vance, an endocrinologist who conducted a hormone replacement study at the University of Virginia School of Medicine in Charlottesville, told *Men's Journal* magazine, "Our bodies make less growth hormone in our fifties, sixties, and seventies than they do in our twenties—a lot less. We know growth hormone helps to burn fat and build muscles, and to improve metabolism." She went on to state that, in small doses, the hormone would prove to be basically safe and even beneficial. However, she cautioned that the results of the present investigations going on around the country would first have to be analyzed before any conclusive statements regarding the compound could be accurately drawn.

Kinesiologist Terry Todd, interviewed in the same issue of *Men's Journal*, stated that higher-than-normal levels of growth hormone may result in what he termed "substantial benefits." These include a healthier heart, since HGH lowers cholesterol levels in the blood and may further serve to keep fat from collecting around the abdomen, thereby reducing the risk of heart disease. Todd also pointed out that HGH further serves to build "a stronger immune system, quicker healing response, and an increased sex drive. But it is the growth hormone's ability to build muscle mass and reduce fat that is especially striking. Research reveals that the hormone rewires the body's metabolic engine, causing it to burn fat to meet energy demands while converting the building block proteins to muscle."

As with most drugs, however, there exists a dark side to this "wonder drug." The problems associated with HGH injections center around determining just where the fine line exists between *ideal* dosage and *over*dosage. This appears to be a highly individual matter, as too much of this apparently "good" thing can produce problems ranging from carpal tunnel syndrome and osteoporosis, to diabetes, arthritis, and heat intolerance. Such problems, scientists report, result from receiving overdoses of

Intense bodybuilding exercise, if performed regularly, can boost the body's natural production of HGH by as much as 50 percent.

the *synthetic* version of this hormone via injections—but what if we could produce more of this powerful hormone naturally? What if we could have the benefits of an increased amount of HGH coursing through our bodies—which would serve to burn fat and build muscle mass—without any of the problems associated with potential overdoses and injections of synthetic compounds? Well, obviously it would be great. And greater still is the fact that we can accomplish this. How? Well, again, according to Todd, "High intensity exercise . . . done two or three times a week, handling loads you can lift only a maximum of 6 repetitions (versus lighter weights lifted 15 times or more) appears to stimulate significant HGH production." High-intensity training—the kind that would see you unable to squeeze out more than 6 repetitions' worth of effort—would obviously involve the use of a heavy resistance; if we can extrapolate, the heavier the resistance and the greater the intensity of our muscular contractions, the more HGH we should be able to secrete naturally.

This view is corroborated by Dr. Mauro Di Pasquale, from the University of Toronto, who has gone on record as stating that the physical stress of bodybuilding workouts, if performed regularly, can boost the body's natural production of HGH by as much as 50 percent. Again, it is evident that the body increases the production of growth hormone in direct response to the intensity of the exercise performed.

The supreme importance of high-intensity muscular contraction in building and reshaping the human body has, as we shall see, been established beyond question over the past five decades—both clinically in the lab and by individuals in the gym. And while various training systems deliver various degrees of intensity and, consequently, various degrees of muscle stimulation, until the arrival of Max Contraction Training, no training system has ever existed that allowed for the highest possible intensity of muscular contraction. The results this system has produced thus far have been absolutely astounding, even to those who are highly experienced in bodybuilding, strength training, and physical fitness.

In the following chapters, you will learn of the evolution of this revolutionary new form of bodybuilding, and of the scientific reasons underpinning its viability. All of the

previously cited benefits to mind and body are available to anybody who is willing to embrace (or re-embrace) "bodybuilding," properly defined. What I will outline in this book is bodybuilding in the purest sense of the term and bodybuilding that is engineered toward results—and not results that require drugs, deceit, or the selling of one's soul to obtain, but rather "results," as our old friend Socrates once pointed out, "which a sane man would surely endure any hardships to secure."

Max Contraction Training—the results are worth the effort.

The ancient Greeks believed in the power of human reason to obtain valid knowledge on all subjects they set their minds to—including training.

Chapter 2

THE EVOLUTION OF MAX CONTRACTION TRAINING

The concept of Max Contraction Training came to me in, of all places, a Greek history class at McMaster University in Hamilton, Ontario, Canada. I even know the date and time—2:00 P.M. on Monday, January 10, 1984—I jotted down the framework of the theory and system in my class notebook that day. As the professor spoke about the Greek love for physical beauty, health, form, athletic training, competition, dialogue, and wisdom (i.e., philosophy), it struck me that this ideal of a "well-tempered man" was a fair one for any individual to strive for. It would, if one attempted to pursue it consistently, lead to a deeper appreciation of the arts, enhanced physical well-being and attractiveness, heroic achievement in all arenas (for competition is a broad abstraction that isn't simply restricted to athletics), more intriguing and often scintillating conversation, and a keener desire and means (logic) to understand ourselves and the universe we are a part of.

As the fount and promoters of these ideals, the Greeks believed in the power of human reason to obtain valid knowledge on all subjects they set their minds to—including training. This concept of intellectual efficacy was euphorically stimulating to this young student (and remains so to the older student he has become). Ironically, the philosophy professors there at that time did not teach this philosophical perspective; this job fell to the history professors. And believing that my (or anyone else's) mind had within it the means by which to discern answers to important issues, I turned my mind to a topic that was of immense personal interest to me—bodybuilding training. Immediately a series of questions formed in my mind: Why did most bodybuilders train the same way? Why was it that most of them could not offer sound reasons for why they trained in the manner that they did? Why did they usually fall back on the stock reply of "so-and-so trained this way, and if it was good enough for him, it's good enough for me." That most bodybuilders trained as other bodybuilders did before them relied on the logical fallacy of appealing to tradition or custom, not a criterion of truth; tradition and custom, unlike truth, are subject to change depending upon what social caprice happens to be in vogue.

People who employ custom as their standard are engaged in "weather vane" thinking—allowing other people's ways (regardless of whether they are right or wrong, helpful or harmful, true or false, etc.) to hold sway over their own ability to decide for themselves whether or not an act or thought is true or false. It is, for example, a custom in some primitive countries to avoid bathing, as water is believed to cause pregnancies. Whenever people dress as others dress, use slang expressions that are in vogue for the moment, or "do as others do"—in other words, do whatever is "popular"—they are suspending their own critical faculty, turning off their minds, and following the herd. However, a public opinion poll can never be the best way to determine scientific truths.

Besides, what if "so-and-so's" training was grossly inefficient? Most of the current training practices employed by bodybuilders have been predicated on steroid use, which renders the protocols impotent to the non–steroid user. Yet while steroids allow gains to occur with these types of training methods, humankind built bigger and stronger muscles long before the advent of anabolic steroids. In truth, if you took steroids all day long but didn't train your muscles, you wouldn't gain any additional muscle mass. Steroids by themselves are inert; they have to be combined with training to become potent (and dangerous) muscle builders. So if training—not steroids—is the key, what aspect of training, what one factor about lifting weights, can be isolated as being solely responsible for turning on the muscle growth mechanism of the body? Such were the nature of the thoughts running through my mind that day in Greek history class.

Science—not tradition—will point the way to rapid increases in muscle mass and strength.

I knew from the scientific literature that in order to make muscles grow bigger and stronger they had to be subjected to a progressive overload, and that the higher the intensity of muscular contraction, the greater the growth stimulation. But what specifically about the actual act of contracting a muscle against resistance was the key to the whole thing? It wasn't the volume of sets; if this were true, the biggest muscles would be found on those who were willing to train eight, ten, or more hours a day. Anyone who trained that much usually ended up looking like a distance runner—not a bodybuilder. Moving in the other direction, I considered the actual repetition itself: was there one position in a given muscle's range of motion that stimulated more fibers than any other position—and, if so, what was it? It was then that I recollected a particular statement of former Mr. Universe winner Mike Mentzer (who was for a very long time the embodiment of the ancient Greek ideal of "a healthy mind in a healthy body"):

Certainly the name of the game is contraction. To induce maximum levels of growth stimulation, as many as possible of the available fibers must be made to contract. As muscle fibers work, or contract, by becoming shorter and reducing their length, it appears obvious that a muscle would have to be in a fully contracted, or peak, position if all the fibers were to be contracted at the same time.

I should digress here for a moment to confess that all high-intensity training theorists are brought to their particular vantage point (however new or revolutionary) by standing on the shoulders of—i.e., building on, or extrapolating from, the efforts and insights of—those who went before. For me, it was Mike Mentzer who

Former Mr. Universe winner Mike Mentzer displays how a muscle—in this case, his biceps—"would have to be in a fully contracted, or peak, position if all the fibers were to be contracted at the same time."

provided a very strong pair of shoulders to stand upon and who, in turn, stood upon the shoulders of other giants: men such as Dr. Hans Selye, a pioneering researcher in the physiology of stress and its effects on the body (touched on in Chapter 1); Dr. Arthur Steinhaus, one of the leading exercise physiologists of the twentieth century; and Arthur Jones, the man considered the father of high-intensity training. Jones, though not a degree-holding physiologist, might be said to have hailed from what philosopher Will Durant once referred to as "the islanded aristocracy of thought," as many lettered exercise scientists are only now beginning to grasp the truths he first pointed out over thirty years ago. Mentzer recognized immediately the significance of Jones's contributions to the field of bodybuilding science. After communicating with (and for a time working with) Jones over the course of his life, Mentzer came to share these insights with bodybuilders. Later he revised Jones's theories based upon his own insights and experiences, thus advancing the science of bodybuilding still further. In the quotation cited on page 17, Mentzer was, in fact, echoing an observation made by Jones in Chapter 2 of his first *Nautilus Bulletin*, which Jones had self-published in the early 1970s:

> It should be plain that the muscle could be in no position except its shortest, fully-contracted position if all of the muscle fibers were contracted at the same time; the individual fibers must grow shorter in order to perform work, and if all of the fibers were shortened at the same time, then the muscle as a whole would have to be in a position of full contraction—no other position is even possible with full muscular contraction. . . . But it does not follow that even a position of full contraction will involve the working of all of the individual fibers; because only the actual number of fibers that are required to meet a momentarily imposed load will be called into play. Thus, in order to involve 100 percent of the fibers in a particular movement, two conditions are prerequisites; the muscle (and its related body part) must be

in a position of full contraction—and a load must be imposed in that position that is heavy enough to require the work of all of the individual fibers.

The logic of the statements of these two men resulted in a flash of insight. If, as Jones pointed out, "the muscle could be in no position except its shortest, fully-contracted position if all of the muscle fibers were contracted at the same time," the question arose: of what value would any exercise be for building muscle that did not involve this position of full or maximum contraction? The answer: obviously very little. Moreover, if, as Mentzer indicated, "as many as possible of the available fibers must be made to contract" in order "to induce maximum levels of growth stimulation," then —equally as obvious—the position of full or maximum contraction was the only position where this was possible. In which case, why move out of it? And if a load or resistance was then imposed that was, as Jones recommended, "heavy enough to require the work of all of the individual fibers," then these were the two requisite conditions for maximum stimulation of 100 percent of any given skeletal muscle.

This concept held immense appeal. After all, we were not endurance athletes but bodybuilders; our objective was not to see how many sets and reps we could perform, how exaggerated a range of motion we could make our muscles move through, nor how long we could make a workout last, but rather to direct our training efforts by a specific method that would stimulate the greatest muscle growth. And if a position of maximum or full contraction coupled with sufficient overload were the two most important considerations in the recruitment and stimulation of muscle fibers, then all other training considerations were superfluous and unessential and, most certainly, less efficient for this purpose. According to Jones, 100 percent of a muscle's fibers could be recruited if two preconditions were met: that the muscle be placed in a position of full contraction and that the load or resistance imposed be of sufficient weight to activate all of the fibers. As 100 percent is as high as it gets —that is, *all* available fibers within a given muscle group—no other training consideration was necessary. These two preconditions removed the alleged "need" for any other training consideration. Training protocols such as multiple sets, angle training with different exercises, and a host of others that had become accepted by the bodybuilding orthodoxy over the years were now open to question.

Ironically, neither Jones nor Mentzer went on to make what seemed to me the logical deductive conclusion, that is, that a new training protocol could (and should) be created that would take as its premise the two preconditions elucidated by Jones some 30 years previously. Indeed, while Jones went on to create a whole line of Nautilus exercise machines that incorporated an offset cam in order to provide maximum resistance in the position of full

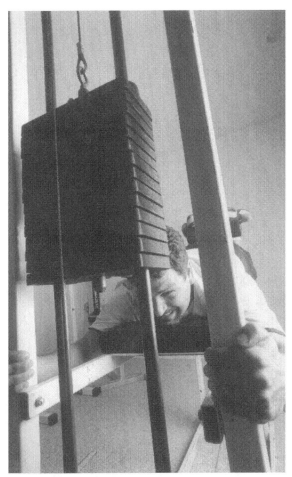

The two requirements for maximum muscle stimulation are placing the muscle group you are training in the fully contracted position and providing a sufficient overload to activate as many muscle fibers as possible.

muscular contraction, he then advised trainees not to keep the muscle in this position, but to utilize a full range of motion, in effect, compromising fiber involvement with each repetition performed. Mentzer, to his credit, while advocating a full range of motion for many years, was, by the mid-1990s, starting to make the logical connection and even began a limited implementation of the maximum contraction protocol with many of his personal clients with great success. However, even he was not entirely willing to countermand Jones's advocacy of full range training. (Jones, it must be pointed out, had by the 1980s shifted his focus away from bodybuilding qua bodybuilding. He had begun focusing instead on the athletic and rehabilitation communities—both of which required a full range of motion, whether as suppleness for their respective sports or in rebuilding range into an injured limb.)

To anyone with an eye toward creating a more potent form of bodybuilding, however, it stood to reason that a system comprising exercises performed in this fully contracted position and under sufficient load would be far more efficacious than any other method; it was a physiologically more efficient manner in which to recruit muscle fibers and stimulate them to grow. Perhaps others could have made this connection; however, no one did. And thus it fell to me to take the next logical step.

I recall spending the remainder of my Greek history class that day considering which exercises would best lend themselves to such a protocol. Compound exercises were out, owing to the fact that none of them provided effective resistance in the position of full contraction. Exercises such as squats and bench presses (both long-time staples in the bodybuilding world), owing to their physics, provided no effective resistance in the fully contracted position of the quadriceps or pectoral muscles; once the bones were "locked out," so to speak, the resistance—which was provided linearly— fell solely on the bones rather than the muscles. Isolation exercises, however, fit the bill perfectly for this new method of training, and I quickly composed a list of the exercises that would result in the best stimulation of each muscle group of the body.

Next I began to pore over anatomy and physiology textbooks; I realized that the muscle magazines and professional bodybuilders, on the whole, could teach me nothing of substance in this regard—the former were in the business of selling products (usually nutritional supplements) and so had a vested interest in distorting bodybuilding reality; the latter owed the majority of their muscular gains to some Hercules in their family tree and/or the contents of a syringe rather than to their knowledge of human physiology. My focus now shifted from what the magazines preached to what science had to say about what was really required to build muscle; doing so, I reasoned, would determine whether or not my classroom epiphany had any support from actual exercise physiology studies that had been conducted on the ways and means of muscle growth. Simply taking the matter on faith from either Jones or Mentzer would not be sufficient (for reasons already outlined). Although I knew that a theory was supposed to represent an accurate representation of the facts of reality, I also knew that I would not have any tangible proof of my theory's validity without testing it. I needed to see for myself what practical results such a theoretical approach might yield.

I quickly sought out trainees (myself included) who had spent years working with weights (as opposed to newcomers to bodybuilding who would grow on just about any system of progressive resistance exercise owing to the novelty of the training stress) to take part in a training experiment to test the potency of this new system. After many months of training individuals, note taking, and additional research into muscle physiology, I was frankly stunned at the potency of the new protocol. People were gaining anywhere from 12 to 30 pounds of muscle (we utilized fat calipers to determine that the muscle gains were in fact muscle gains, rather than merely bodyweight gains).

My own strength and size gains utilizing this method skyrocketed, with my strength increasing upwards of 110 percent in some exercises and 70 percent overall. More impressive was the effect this type of training was having on my physique: my arms went from 15 to 16¼ inches, my chest from 43 to 47 inches, and my bodyweight from 172 to 195 pounds—a gain of 23 pounds. All of these gains took place over a span of eight weeks on the new system—and after more than 10 years of training on conventional methods with little or no progress to show for it.

A few years after this breakthrough, I was asked to write articles for the British version of *Flex* magazine by longtime friend and ace bodybuilding photographer Chris Lund. As we had often talked bodybuilding, he knew of my experimentation with the new protocol and, indeed, had witnessed the change in my own physique over the months that I was training on the new system. He encouraged me to pen a series of articles revealing the fundamental principles of the method I had developed and also to draft several specialization routines based on the system that would allow bodybuilders to apply the new technology to problem bodyparts or bodyparts that they particularly wanted to beef up. I did so and christened the system Static Contraction Training. For reasons I will elaborate on below, I recognize now that the name was ill chosen. Nevertheless, the response to these articles was unprecedented. At this point—in 1988—I decided that I would publish my findings and make the training system available to bodybuilders who earnestly desired a more efficient and productive way to build muscle.

James Wright, Ph.D., then the science editor of *Muscle and Fitness* magazine, had, unbeknownst to me, read my series of articles with great interest and tried out the protocol for himself. He then wrote an article about "motionless exercise," in which he pointed out his own incredible experiences with the method. The article was published in *Muscle and Fitness* and resulted in hundreds of letters filling my mailbox from all corners of the world. People wanted to know more about the mechanics of the new system and when I would be writing a book on the topic. Approximately one year later, I was offered a job in California to work for Joe Weider's *Flex* magazine as a senior writer. I accepted, and shortly after arriving in the *Flex* offices I bumped into Dr. Wright and told him I had completed a rough draft of the manuscript. He graciously agreed to check over my conclusions from a scientific standpoint to ensure that I had correctly interpreted the data from the various physiology studies on hypertrophy (muscle growth) that I cited.

This book would have been published then, in 1992, had I not been sidetracked and, during the detour, cowrote *Power Factor Training* (Contemporary Books, Chicago) with longtime friend Peter Sisco. When the results of this system got out in 1992, we both found that our time was quickly taken up solely in answering questions and responding to the public's demand for more information on this method of training. When things slowed down somewhat, I had intended to return to my original book on the maximum contraction protocol, and, having worked well with Peter before on publishing a book on training, had asked him

if the idea of motionless exercise and shorter workouts held appeal. In a peripheral manner it did, but Peter indicated that he was more interested, as an evolution of the Power Factor Training concept, in the question as to whether or not the heavy compound movements we had used to such great effect in Power Factor Training could produce similar or better results with a zero range of motion.

Peter devised a study that would test just such a method, and many of our clients who were training with *Power Factor Training* took part in it. Lo and behold, their results were terrific! As the method we employed was based on my Static Contraction system protocol (i.e., static holds performed for the most part in a muscle's fully contracted position), we decided to use the original name for my system, Static Contraction. The public reception to *Static Contraction Training* (Contemporary Books,

The author (background) supervises the training of bodybuilder Paul DeMayo during a photo shoot demonstrating the Power Factor Training protocol, circa 1992.

Chicago) was tremendous, and soon we were inundated with calls. Renowned Peak Performance coach, Anthony Robbins, tracked us down to take part in one of his *PowerTalk!* videos which he dedicated entirely to the new system, and *Ironman* magazine even went so far as to state that our book could "cause physiology books to be rewritten."

Despite the obvious success of *Static Contraction Training*, I had begun to note certain elements of inherent impracticality in the modified version of the protocol. For one thing, no conventional equipment could accommodate the weight demands that resulted from the phenomenal increases in strength our subjects were experiencing—with the result that trainees were quickly maxing out the machines in their gyms and there was no means by which to provide additional overload on a safe and progressive basis. Training in such a fashion at home was potentially dangerous, as home gym equipment is not typically of the gauge of professional gym equipment. This type of training necessitated nothing less than heavy-duty power racks, Smith machines, and leg presses —all of which had to be of commercial gym standard. Such equipment was almost always prohibitively expensive, which made it impractical for the average home gym trainee.

I also noted that the compound movements that Peter and I had incorporated into Power Factor Training and the modified version of Static Contraction Training, while very effective for stimulating general growth in the muscles of the body owing to their involving many different muscle groups, were ineffective for maximally stimulating specific bodyparts for the same reason. With isolation movements such as those advocated in Max Contraction Training, the growth stimulus is not compromised at all, as 100 percent of the training stress goes directly to the intended muscle group. If in the bench press, for example, 60 percent of the stress is borne on the triceps and deltoids, that leaves only 40 percent for the pectoral muscles. Isolation exercises (and even a select few compound movements) could, when properly employed, stimulate 100 percent (or as near to that figure as possible) of the targeted muscle group without any chance of any

percentage of the stimulus being dissipated through several ancillary muscle groups. Bodybuilders seeking to stimulate maximum growth in their pecs, then, would therefore benefit more from having the ability to direct 100 percent of the possible stimulation directly to the pecs, effectively bypassing the smaller and weaker muscle groups (such as the deltoids and triceps).

Ray Mentzer, Mike's younger brother, had pointed out to me back in 1990 that many compound movements, such as the bench press—which we had recommended in the *Power Factor Training* and *Static Contraction Training* books—were, in his opinion, next to useless as they did not incorporate the proper kinesiology for maximum muscle stimulation. The primary function of the pectoral muscles, for example, is to draw the arm across the midline of the torso (as on a Pec Deck machine), not extend the forearms (as in the bench press movement); that was the function of the triceps muscles. And while there could be no question that the pecs received stimulation from heavy partial bench presses, there was also no question that this exercise would not allow the pecs to fulfill their primary function, and, therefore, the pecs were never contracting maximally against the resistance. Ray had advised selecting exercises for the pecs "that bring your elbows across your sternum, things that bring the elbows across the chest bone. The more you can find exercises that can induce that, the more fiber you're going to work in your pecs."

When I returned to my anatomy and physiology textbooks, it became obvious that compound movements would provide direct resistance to only a handful of bodyparts, such as dips for the triceps (as dips fulfilled both of the functions of this muscle group, i.e., the extension of the forearm and the drawing of the arm behind the body), shrugs (as it is pure trapezius that lifts the weight), and toe presses on the leg press machine (which directly hit the calf muscles without ancillary muscle groups absorbing the bulk of the training stress). However, simply because certain exercises allowed you to hoist more weight, this didn't necessarily mean that the muscles you were

The bench press exercise, though long considered the king of chest developers, is not as efficient for stimulating growth in this region as had previously been supposed.

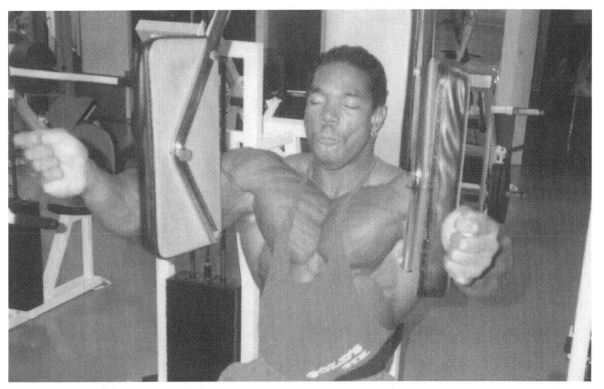

Exercises that draw the arms across the midline of the body more closely parallel the primary function of the pectoral muscles. Here, bodybuilding legend Flex Wheeler works his chest muscles on the Pec Deck machine during a workout in Gold's Gym in Venice, California.

hoping to stimulate were *contracting* against more weight, as the 60–40 split of triceps/shoulders-to-chest ratio previously cited would indicate. The muscle groups that were not being hit directly with compound movements would never receive maximal growth stimulation.

I had been blinded by the notion of "work per unit of time" and equated the supporting of heavy weights with maximal muscle contraction—when they were not necessarily the same thing. For example, when Peter and I were testing various exercises for our *Power Factor Specialization: Chest & Arms* book (Contemporary Books, Chicago), we found that

How much weight you can support is not as important for muscle building purposes as how much weight your muscles actually contract against.

"Work per unit time" is not as important for muscle building as the intensity of muscular contraction; in one study, push-ups—a low-intensity calisthenics movement—were shown to have the highest work-per-unit-time measurement.

push-ups—where only a portion of one's body-weight registered as effective resistance—provided far and away more "work per unit of time" than any other exercise, despite the fact that push-ups (performing, say, 65 or 70 repetitions in a minute) were a calisthenics movement—not noted for building massive muscle. And yet, the work-per-unit-time component was satisfied and it proved—by that application—to be the "best" pec exercise. We noted that something was askew about this and subsequently did not include the exercise in the book, making a mental note to revisit the issue when time permitted more experimentation and abstract thought on the matter. Obviously there was something inappropriate about the measurement or, more specifically, what it was that we were attempting to measure. There needed to be a more precise definition of "work," physiologically speaking, that would have a direct bearing on muscle growth.

Even walking—by this definition—whereby you transfer your bodyweight from one leg to the other in a limited range activity, would translate into a huge "work per unit of time," if you walked as quickly as you could over the course of, say, one minute and then stopped to compute your weight × "reps" (steps) and divided by time. But again, how much weight you can support and how much weight your muscles can contract against are not necessarily synonymous, and intensity—long considered by physiologists to be the sole requisite of muscle growth stimulation—only had a bearing in relation to the contractile tension it generated within a given muscle. The heavier the weight, the greater the contractile tension within the muscle, providing that it was the muscle itself—rather than the bones—that was bearing the brunt of the resistance. Weight was important, obviously, but only weight that your muscles were made to fully contract against—not weight that was merely supported by the bones. As Mike Mentzer had pointed out, it was contraction that was the name of the game.

Moreover, apart from factors influencing the maximum stimulation of specific muscle groups, there were safety concerns with both Power Factor Training and Static Contraction

Training that troubled me. Whenever heavy compound movements are employed—particularly in exercises such as squats—the compression factor on spinal vertebrae and joints is not desirable. Further, limited range compound movements such as leg presses and squats do not provide peak stimulation to muscle groups such as the hamstrings and glutes, as the training stress is borne almost entirely by the hip flexors and the quadriceps. This leaves the antagonistic muscle groups largely unstimulated, resulting in a disproportionate development of the frontal thigh to the rear thigh, which could result in injury if not corrected by direct hamstring work. The other concern was that you were always restricted—for safety reasons—to using a heavy-gauge power rack; this restricted your exercise options and in time made training a boring, pedestrian affair for those of a creative bent. Then there was the issue of spotters; with such heavy compound exercises, you almost always required a couple of very strong training partners (once the weights began mounting up). This was not always practical for reasons of scheduling or the fact that hoisting hundreds of pounds of weights on and off bars (particularly when doing so for two or three trainees) can nearly exhaust you prior to your actual workout!

And this is not to impugn our previous work, nor to imply that strongest range partials or motionless exercise won't produce gains in muscle mass. They do; our studies proved that. The perennial question, however, is, Were the gains "maximum"? Or was there a still better way? Was there a more efficient protocol that might even reduce the in-the-gym training time still further (by being more intense) yet result in even more muscle growth being stimulated? I was more interested in finding out the truth of the matter than merely resting on the laurels of having contributed to the innovation and publication of two highly regarded and successful bodybuilding books.

I decided to revisit my original training system. It stood to reason that if what the exercise physiologists had said was true, i.e., that muscle only grows in proportion to the intensity of the training stress and that the higher the intensity the briefer the workout, then a

If work per unit time were the sole criteria for muscular hypertrophy, then walking would be all you'd ever need to do to build huge legs.

set of the highest intensity would have to be of the briefest duration. I began to wonder if even briefer workouts might yield even more impressive gains. In my original Static Contraction system, I had trainees hold the resistance in the position of full-muscular contraction for 30 to 60 seconds. In the modified version I tested with Peter, we had reduced the contraction times to 15 to 30 seconds; both yielded good gains for trainees.

However, according to the scientific literature, the element of duration contributed nothing to the muscle growth process. Indeed, it was the intensity factor alone (i.e., the intensity of the muscular contraction) that stimulated increases in muscle mass and strength. I also knew that intensity and duration existed in an inverse ratio to each other and that the greater the intensity, the greater the muscle growth stimulation, but the briefer the workout. I knew it would be hard to cut back on the number of exercises in the workout if I wanted

Engaging in workout protocols such as Power Factor Training requires commercial gym-caliber equipment to support the kind of tonnage advocated in the workout program.

to stimulate all of the body's major muscle groups—but what if the load the muscles were made to contract against was made heavy enough to make a long contraction impossible? Wouldn't that represent an increase in intensity? The physiology studies further revealed that maximum strength (which has a direct correlation to maximum muscle size) had been stimulated in subjects with as little as a 1-second contraction—if that contraction was a maximum effort. Now things were really getting interesting!

I quickly gathered a new group of trainees to retest the protocol and incorporate the scientific data of reduced contraction times to the training protocol. Almost immediately the strength and size gains of the trainees skyrocketed! This revealed that, for the purpose of building muscle size and strength, a contraction lasting 15 to 30 seconds represented overkill; it was unnecessary to subject the muscles

to any more than 1 second of maximum stimulation. In our Static Contraction study, the most successful subjects had performed two sets per bodypart. Scientific studies (some modern, some dating back 50 years) had categorically concluded that one set was all that was required, while Mentzer had likewise indicated through his research with thousands of clients that one set was plenty; also, most of Mentzer's clients—and the subjects taking part in the physiologists' studies—were training with full-range exercises, which were not nearly as intense as exercises performed solely in the fully contracted position. A set performed through a full range of motion only hit the fully contracted position briefly and it was seldom, if ever, sustained at this point. A Max Contraction set, by contrast, took the muscle into its fully contracted position, where all of its fibers were activated, and made it contract against the heaviest weight possible, with the

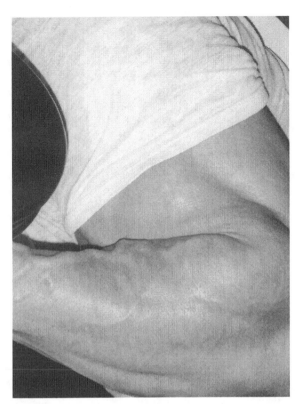

The position of Max (full) Contraction is the single most important point in a muscle's range of motion for involving as many muscle fibers as possible.

1. The new name more accurately reflects the protocol.
2. It removes any confusion with the existing Static Contraction system, which incorporates exclusively compound exercise movements and calls for supporting extremely heavy weights in optimal leverage configurations via the bones or levers (which make it inadequate for generating the highest possible intensity or tension within the targeted muscle group), along with the use of a split routine wherein the whole body is not trained in a single workout, longer hold times, and exercises that are not always performed in a given muscle's position of maximum contraction.

result that the duration of the set had to be the briefest possible. And as only one set was required to have a workout at all, one set was what was employed—with great success. I then decided to rechristen the training protocol Max Contraction Training. The reason for the name change is twofold:

It is then with the belief that there does exist a more efficient way for bodybuilders to train and that, properly employed, such a method will produce increases in lean body mass far quicker than any other training system presently known that this book is now finally being published. It represents, in my opinion, a quantum step forward in the actual science of bodybuilding; so large a step, in fact, that it rightfully may be called the "new science of bodybuilding." It contains powerful new information that will be of immense benefit to any bodybuilder seeking greater gains in muscle mass and strength, and it will deliver these gains in the shortest possible time.

Part II

THE SCIENTIFIC FOUNDATION

The man with perhaps the greatest bodybuilding genetics of all time—Steve Reeves. Reeves had it all: great skeletal formation, superb muscle fiber density, tremendous muscle belly length, and a metabolism that allowed him to develop large muscles.

Chapter 3

THE GENETIC FACTOR IN THE MUSCLE BUILDING EQUATION

Anatomists tell us that more than four hundred muscles are responsible for allowing us to go about our daily activities. It's also common knowledge that if we don't make an effort to keep them strong and balanced in relationship to one another, they'll slowly wither away with the passage of time. Ironically, while all of us possess the same number of muscles, not all of us will be able to develop them to championship proportions.

The champion bodybuilders of yesterday, today, and, for that matter, tomorrow possessed one quality that the vast majority of us do not—exceptional genetics. There simply can be no downplaying the importance of heredity in laying the foundations for building massive muscles and developing a championship physique. I remember once asking former Mr. America Ray Mentzer (Mike's brother) how important genetics were in determining one's bodybuilding success. His answer was brief but telling: "Genetics are everything." It's hard to place a percentage on the importance of genet-

ics or even to attempt to quantify it but, were we to do so, the figure might well be close to 90 percent.

This may read like an overstatement, as obviously a champion bodybuilder's training and nutritional (and often drug) practices play supporting roles in his superb development, but, in all candor, not more than 10 to 20 percent. While it is true that the physiological principles involved in stimulating muscle growth are universal and, as such, common to everyone, it is also true that certain genetic factors serve to enhance or even militate against any given individual's response to bodybuilding exercise. Factors such as age and sex, for example, are important, but even they are not the predominant indices of an individual's muscular potential. Aside from the motivational traits—which are necessary to pursue any goal to its fulfillment, there also exist certain other more tangible traits. These are far and away the most important considerations in your quest to develop bigger and stronger muscles. These traits are skeletal formation, muscle fiber density, muscle belly length, and metabolism.

SKELETAL FORMATION

Perhaps the most important factor on the aforementioned list of genetic traits is that of skeletal formation. The size and formation of

Professional bodybuilding champion Shawn Ray, displaying the perfect bone structure for bodybuilding success.

an individual's bones dictates how much muscle can be carried or supported by those bones, in addition to determining muscle shape and density, two factors that impart an aesthetic quality to a physique. I well recall visiting Mike Mentzer at his apartment in Hollywood back in 1986. Mentzer had a business appointment and was putting his papers in order when suddenly his watchband snapped, causing his wristwatch to fall to the floor. He attempted to reconnect the band, but, after several minutes with no success, he placed his watch on his desk and headed for the door. As he was leaving, I offered him the use of my wristwatch. "Thanks anyway," Mike replied, "but it won't fit." I was incredulous—my watch had a large band; so large in fact that I had to slide it in four notches in order to prevent it from falling off my wrist. I protested to Mike that he couldn't possibly know that my watch wouldn't fit around his wrist—and that he could if necessary extend it to the last notch.

Mike smiled a "forgive him for he knows not what the hell he's talking about" look and said, "Okay, John. Let me see your watch for a minute." I handed it to him and watched him attempt to fasten it to his wrist. He could not do it. His wrist circumference was so large that the ends of the watchband barely touched at all! "See?" Mike said. "I told you it wouldn't fit." This really brought home to me the fact that those with particularly thick musculature also have a particularly thick bone structure.

MUSCLE FIBER DENSITY

Another trait that is genetically predetermined is muscle fiber density, i.e., the number of fibers packed within a given cross-section of muscle. One whose calf muscles have one-third the number of fibers of his training partner's will still appear to have smaller calves—even if he doubles their size while his partner's remain the same (provided, of course, that his calves were proportionately smaller to begin with). The more muscle fibers an individual has packed into each square inch of his muscles, the bigger the growth potential of those muscles.

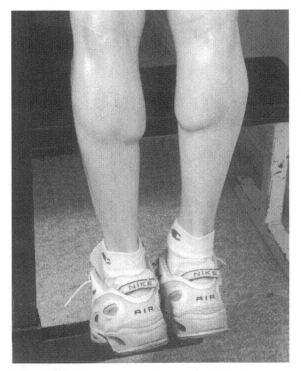

This bodybuilder does not have a particularly high percentage of muscle fibers in his calves. Nevertheless, he has developed impressive shape through proper training.

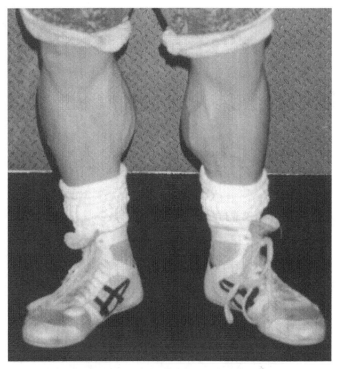

This bodybuilder has incredible muscle fiber density in his calves, allowing him to develop them to an extraordinary degree.

MUSCLE BELLY LENGTH

Interestingly, while it's the size of one's skeleton that enables an individual to support massive muscles with great contractile power, the ultimate size to which a muscle will grow is determined primarily by its length. A muscle's width will never exceed its length, which means that the longer the muscle, the greater its potential for acquiring mass. The length of the bone to which the muscle is attached is not as important as the length from where the tendon attaches to the muscle at one end to the point where the tendon attaches at the other end; this is what determines how much mass a muscle will appear to have.

METABOLISM

For the same reason that not all of us are six feet tall with a face like a movie star, not all of us have the metabolic capability that allows for the creation of larger than normal levels of

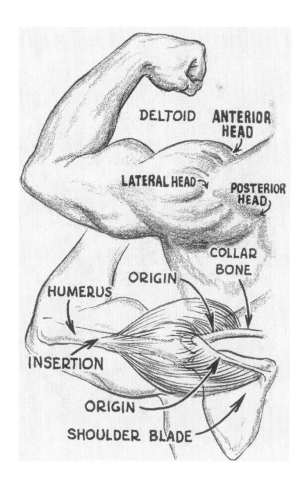

A bodybuilder with a good metabolism for developing impressive muscularity in his shoulders and back.

A bodybuilder with an excellent metabolism for developing his back and shoulder muscles.

muscle mass. We have all witnessed the fruitless efforts of the hardcore bodybuilding zealot who seems to train harder than anyone we've ever seen, yet never shows any visible signs of improvement. If you have been training hard for a couple of years on a high-intensity training program and have made only minimal gains in muscular mass, the odds are that you're probably not geared metabolically to the development of large muscles. Many, however, could gain more than their present rate of growth might indicate if they were to adopt a more efficient training program.

While none of the genetic traits previously described are subject to alteration by training, proper bodybuilding training will allow people with an abundance of these requisite genetic materials to fully (and more quickly) realize their genetic potential. However, even those select few, the "thoroughbreds" of our species, who possess a superabundance of the required traits will improve faster and develop further if they train properly. And, in this respect, both the thoroughbred and the genetically bereft—ironically—achieve parity.

The individual with the greater complement of the above indicated genetic factors does have a better chance of achieving bodybuilding success. However, unless he cultivates the philosophical, scientific, and motivational (i.e., intellectual) skills necessary to understand (philosophical) the best way to proceed with his training (scientific) and the willingness to implement them (motivational) in his training on a progressive basis, he will not develop his physique to its full potential, whereas the less genetically gifted individual who does implement the above intellectual skills will.

In fact, it is not uncommon for those with lesser genetic potential to develop more impressive muscles than those with superior genetic potential simply because they trained intelligently enough to realize close to 100 percent of their potential, whereas the genetic marvel trained improperly and only realized 50 percent of his. However, potential is only the expression of a latent possibility that will not be realized unless all of the correct factors are present; in bodybuilding these are as fol-

Genetic potential can only be realized through dedicated and purposeful training.

No matter what your potential, you will develop quicker and further with an intelligent training approach.

lows: the correct training stimulus, adequate recovery time, and proper nutrition. While not everyone is going to become Mr. Olympia, with proper training all of us can improve on the size, strength, and appearance of our physiques.

Chapter 4

THE SCIENCE OF MUSCLE GROWTH

The use of logic or reason leads us away from the comfort of traditional belief systems and toward the realm of science. Science, in fact, can quite rightly be called "applied logic," as science concerns itself wholeheartedly with the amassing and interpretation of noncontradictory data. And whenever new data seem contrary to the belief or model that has been the paradigm or standard, the paradigm is reevaluated and, if found to be in error, is amended or, if no longer tenable, discarded and a new paradigm is created.

To this end, traditions such as those so rampant in bodybuilding cannot long endure unless there is ample evidence to warrant their survival. And, in this regard, the realm of science has had plenty to say about the nature of the muscle growth process. Not surprisingly, few bodybuilders—and virtually no magazine publishers or supplement salespeople—have bothered to listen, as they've never had a horse in that race.

One of the most dedicated scientists to ever look into the actual nature of muscle growth was the late Dr. Arthur Steinhaus. It was Mike Mentzer who first mentioned the good doctor's name to me, indicating that Steinhaus had amassed considerable data on scores of experiments that dealt with strength production and muscle building. I came to learn through subsequent research that Steinhaus did far more than this; he effectively laid the foundations upon which the entire field of exercise science is now based. In 1954 he began correlating and collocating the entire history of strength science, from studies first done in the 1800s up to the late 1950s. He presented this treatise to The Connecticut Valley Conference (it was subsequently published in part in 1955 in *JAPMR* 9: 147–50). The treatise was fascinating for many reasons; three are particularly worthy of note: (1) he brought attention to the research of Morpurgo, who first established that muscle growth is due to hypertrophy (the enlargement of already existing muscle fibers) rather than hyperplasia (the splitting or increase of existing muscle fibers into new muscle fibers); (2) he brought attention to the pioneering work of physiologists Roux, Lange, Petow, and Siebert, who discovered that muscle growth is due to the intensity of effort rather than the volume of effort; and (3) he revealed the work of two brilliant German physiologists, Erich A. Muller and T. L. Hettinger, who were true pioneers in the study of static or Max Contractions and their effect on stimulating muscle growth.

These three points are of crucial importance in understanding the scientific underpinnings of Max Contraction Training. Some of the material I'm about to touch on may seem rather technical. However, if you keep your attention on the conclusions these gentlemen reached regarding the nature of "muscle growth," your understanding of this entire issue will be very clear indeed. Let's now take a look at what these physiologists reported from the world of science on the nature and expression of muscle growth.

ON HYPERTROPHY

In 1897 Professor B. Morpurgo, of the Pathological Institute of the University of Sienna, reported two major conclusions regarding the actual physical process of muscle growth and the first step in the intensity/duration continuum as it pertained to the muscle growth process. Morpurgo established that two months of running in which one dog ran a total of 3,218 kilometers and another 1,550 kilometers in exercise wheels, resulted in 53 percent and 55 percent increases respectively, in the cross section of the dogs' sartorius muscles, which were taken out after exercise and compared with those taken out before the exercise period. This increase in size was attained with no increase in the number of muscle fibers. The average cross section area of 249 fibers from the muscle taken out before, compared with that of the 252 taken out after exercise in the case of the second dog was 1:1.54. Thus the exercise increase in cross section was fully accounted

for by increases in the cross section of individual fibers.[1]

"INTENSITY" AS THE TRIGGER MECHANISM

As early as 1905, a physiologist by the name of Roux observed that the muscles of various athletes differed and that not all muscles in one athlete were equally large. He postulated that the size and strength of muscles were related not to the total amount of work done but rather to the amount of work done "in a unit of time," that is, to the intensity factor. As Steinhaus would later point out:

> This is well illustrated in the muscles of the miler and sprinter. The miler does more work than the sprinter but, in comparing intensities, the 10-second man runs 30 feet per second and the four-minute miler only 22 feet per second. Therefore the sprinter has larger muscles.[2]

According to Petow and Siebert,[3] a physiologist named Lange, who was a student of Roux, expressed Roux's views on stimulating muscle growth thusly:

> Only when a muscle performs with greatest power, i.e., through the overcoming of a greater resistance in a unit of time than before, would its functional cross section need to increase. . . . If, however, the muscle performance is increased merely by working against the same resistance as before for a longer time, no increase in its contractile substance is necessary. . . . Hypertrophy is seen only in muscles that must perform a great amount of work in a unit of time. The athlete who in a few seconds generates great power in lifting a weight . . . possesses massive musculature. Distance runners, walkers or swimmers lack the same.[4]

Petow and Siebert then went on to restate the Roux/Lange generalizations more precisely as follows:

Hypertrophy results from an increase in the intensity of work done (increase of work in a unit time) whereas the total amount of work done is without significance.[5]

In a second paper Siebert reported having stimulated the gastrocnemius (or calf muscles) of seven frogs. In each instance the leg on one side was tied firmly to the frog board to prevent any leg movement; the opposite leg was permitted free movement. Both legs were then stimulated with identical strengths of tetanizing currents alternating three seconds of stimulus with three seconds of rest for a total of 20 minutes on 14 successive days. The muscles from the tied legs that contracted statically (more intensely) weighed on the average 13 percent heavier than those from the untied side.[6]

Thus Petow and Siebert were able to demonstrate experimentally that skeletal muscles grew in size in direct proportion to the intensity of the work demanded of them. They also showed that the greater the intensity, the greater the muscle growth. Or, as Dr. Steinhaus concluded, "Only when the intensity is increased [overload] does hypertrophy follow."

THE SIGNIFICANCE OF MAXIMUM CONTRACTION

For more than 10 years physiologist Erich A. Muller experimented in Fortmund, Germany, to discover the fastest way to increase muscle strength and size. Success came when, toward the end of this period, he began to work with one of his students, T. H. Hettinger, on static contractions performed with isolation movements in which intensity and duration were easily measured. No less than 71 separate experiments were performed on nine male subjects over a period of 18 months.[7] All training was done in the form of pulling and holding a predetermined amount of tension against a spring scale. Most observations were made on the biceps muscles with the forearms held horizontally at right angles to the upper arm. On Saturdays maximal strength was measured. The

higher reading of two trials was recorded. Sunday was a day of rest. Mondays through Fridays were devoted to training sessions in which the intensity of contractions, the length of time held, and the number of sets performed per day were varied to determine the effects of varying protocols on the development of strength and muscle size.

Muller and Hettinger used static contractions in their now famous experiments because they were easy to measure, and it was also a simple matter to graduate and control this kind of exercise. Their 10 years of work led to the conclusion that one set was better than multiple sets, that 6-second holds were better than holds lasting upwards to 45 seconds, and that a contraction equal to 40 percent of maximum, held for 6 seconds once a day, made muscle strength grow as fast as it can grow. They later learned that a 100 percent maximal contraction held for just about 1 second did the same thing.[8]

MAINTAINING STRENGTH AND MUSCLE MASS

Professor Muller later communicated to Dr. Steinhaus in a letter dated June 6, 1954, that he and Dr. Hettinger had also investigated how much exercise was necessary to maintain strength once it had been developed. Their findings are summarized as follows:

1. Under the training regime already described, the average increase in muscle strength is about 5 percent per week. If training is discontinued after a few weeks, strength recedes at a loss of about 5 percent per week back to the original value.

2. However, a muscle trained to be, for example, 50 percent stronger than its original strength may thereafter be maintained indefinitely at this level by only 1 maximal contraction every two weeks.

3. When a muscle that had been trained to 50 percent greater strength was maintained at this level for 12 weeks by 1 maximal contraction every 2 weeks and then given no further training or testing, the results were astonishing.

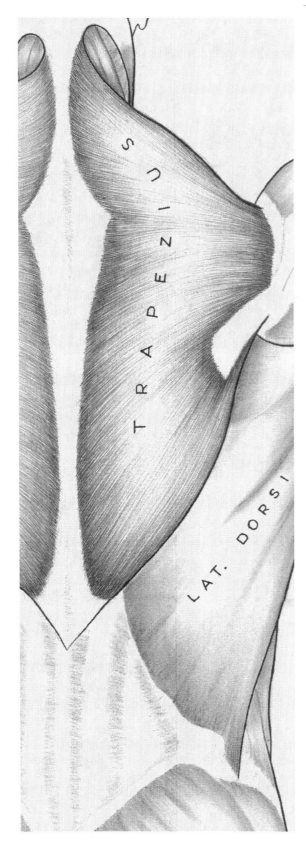

In the first 12 weeks of no strength training, strength was almost completely retained at the high level; in the following 28 weeks, Professor

Muller reported that "strength was still far from having returned to the level it started from at the beginning of the experiment."

From these experiments the following conclusions essential to the understanding of size and strength may be summarized:

1. The extent of hypertrophy of a muscle is determined by two limiting factors as follows:
   • The number of muscle fibers is fixed by heredity and conditions of embryonic development, and cannot be changed by exercise.
   • Small muscle fibers hypertrophy under exercise but only up to a fixed limit.

2. No matter how much a muscle is used, it will not grow larger or stronger until it is *overloaded*. This means that the *intensity* of the work required of it must be increased above that to which it is currently accustomed; that is, it must be required to work against greater resistance than before.

3. If increased strength is maintained for a time, it becomes fixated or anchored in the muscle.

4. There is no magic in the 6-second holding rule. The contraction should be held for a period that is about 10 percent of the maximum time that it can be held. A maximum contraction that usually can be held just under 10 seconds needs be held only 1 second once a day to induce maximum increases in strength. A 0.4 maximum contraction can be held about 60 seconds, hence the emergence of the original 6-second rule (10 percent of 60).

5. One maximum contraction performed only once every 2 weeks is enough to maintain the increases in size and strength due to training.

6. Strength lost in atrophy is gained to normal about three times as fast as it can be increased above normal.[9]

This scientific data reveal some startling results. For one thing, a lot less training is required to stimulate maximum increases in size and strength than the bodybuilders and the muscle magazines have led us to believe. According to the data, if proper training methodology is applied (i.e., Max Contractions), a 1-second hold (or 10 percent of a maximum hold of 10 seconds) is all that is necessary to stimulate maximum muscle growth. As we shall learn in future chapters, this fits perfectly into the anaerobic pathways. And, assuming 10 exercises to cover each of the body's major muscle groups, it makes for a total workout (assuming the whole body is trained in one session) of only 10 seconds in length! If the 6-second protocol is employed, the workout will grow to approximately 1 minute (on the high end). And, the best part, once you've reached the optimal size and strength level as dictated by your genetic potential, you will be able to maintain it in perpetuity with a 1-second Max Contraction per bodypart performed only *once every two weeks*! Let me put a little sharper point on the economics of time in this revolutionary news: you will only need to perform *one 10-second workout* (total in-the-gym training time) *once every two weeks*—or 20 seconds of exercise per month—to maintain your physique and strength in perpetuity! Who doesn't have time for this?

Also revealed by the data was that the intensity of muscular contraction was the key factor in stimulating muscle growth. Mike Mentzer correctly advanced the proposition that "the biochemical changes that result in muscle growth are the same in all individuals and the specific stimulus required to induce those biochemical changes is also the same. And it just so happens that this specific stimulus is high-intensity training." Remember, it wasn't repetitions, it wasn't a "pump," it wasn't long workouts or training one's muscles from a host of different angles that made these test subjects bigger and stronger; it was the intensity of effort. And Max Contraction, as you'll soon see, generates the highest possible intensity—and hence growth stimulation. It does this by meeting Roux/Lange's criteria for hypertrophy by "the overcoming of a greater resistance in a unit of time [i.e., 1 to 6 seconds] than before," and by employing the technique found by Hettinger and Muller to be most effective for stimulating strength and size increases (i.e., maximum contraction)—in short by training the muscles exclusively in a position of maximum contraction, that one position where all of a muscle's fibers are fully activated, thereby creating the greatest contractile force or intensity of muscular contraction.

Max Contraction trainee Irwin Heshka shrugging 1,005 pounds. The heavier the weight, the more muscle fibers are recruited to assist with the task—and stimulated to grow bigger and stronger.

Chapter 5

MAX TACTICS: MAXIMIZING MUSCULAR INVOLVEMENT

Training with Max Contraction is so brief that it's hard for many trainees on the system to justify the hefty membership fees most commercial gymnasiums charge to use their facilities. After all, if you are using their weight room for a 10- to 60-second workout once every 7 to 14 days, that means that you're only going to the gym 2 to 4 times a month, or 24 to 48 times a year; by contrast, trainees on conventional programs are heading to the gym anywhere from 12 to 20 times per month, or 144 to 240 times a year. When put in the balance, it would appear that the heavy membership fees are charged with an eye toward encouraging the trainee to take advantage of daily opportunities to train, thus encouraging high turnover in the gyms, better sales at their supplement or nutrition bars, and very little progress, if any at all.

For this reason I and many others either train at home and make the investment in sturdy and safe home gym equipment, or when we do venture into commercial gymnasiums, do so paying per workout. It was during one such foray into a large commercial gym recently that I was shocked to discover that not one of the trainees I observed training in the gym that day knew the slightest thing about proper exercise performance. Watching them go through their various workouts, I had the distinct impression that their primary goal was merely to move the weights up and down in any manner possible, and usually by the easiest (and often by the most dangerous) manner. As a direct result of such haphazard training, many of these individuals have little or nothing in the way of worthwhile results to show for their efforts, and many others develop painful injuries to tendons and muscles and end up sidelined for months or quitting working out altogether.

This is not limited to merely the casual enthusiast who works out with light to moderate weights. I've also noted that there has been a sharp increase in training-related injuries among professional bodybuilders. Torn biceps, triceps, pecs, quads, and hamstrings; sore shoulder joints; rotator cuff injuries; and

The majority of bodybuilders train in a haphazard fashion, selecting exercises and protocols that don't allow for maximum muscle fiber recruitment.

severely inflamed knee and elbow tendons seem to be besetting bodybuilders with an alarming frequency. For those seeking the most rapid increases possible in muscular size and strength, proper exercise performance is of crucial significance. To ensure that you are actually training with maximum intensity, you must learn to maximize muscular involvement during each repetition you perform. A clear understanding of some of the basic principles of proper exercise performance, along with an understanding of how your muscles actually contract, could make the difference between wasting your training efforts and fulfilling your most cherished bodybuilding goals.

ELIMINATING OUTSIDE FORCES

Research studies were conducted with subjects standing on a force plate that was connected to an oscilloscope measuring device. The studies indicated that repetitions performed quickly produced peaks and drops on the oscilloscope,

revealing that a 100-pound barbell can exert anywhere from 500 pounds of force to zero force. Such an erratic variation of force is extremely dangerous to the joints, muscles, and connective tissues, in addition to providing very little worthwhile stimulation to the muscles. Moreover, these studies also revealed that once the speed of a repetition exceeds a certain rate, momentum takes over almost entirely, thus eliminating muscular involvement. The muscle in such cases actually becomes slack, losing all contractile force.

A contraction that is sustained or motionless, however, results in force produced that is equal to the amount of weight on the barbell or machine and no more. And, if the resistance is heavy enough, this will recruit the maximum number of muscle fibers available in a manner that is not dangerous, as well as being a highly effective method of increasing the intensity of the exercise. Remember that high-intensity muscular contraction is a requirement for developing bigger and stronger muscles.

For best results, you are advised to perform your Max Contractions slowly. Initiate each contraction very deliberately, with no sudden jerks or thrusts. If you are having a training partner lift the weight into the fully contracted position for you, make sure that he does not simply "drop" the weight, which will amplify the force brought to bear on the muscles being trained to such a degree that injury can occur. You should contract against the heaviest weight possible, not impossibly heavy weights. Avoid impact forces at all times; if the weights you will be employing in the Max Contraction position are modest (which they will be initially), you should have no problem contracting your muscles into a position of maximum contraction on your own and simply sustaining this contraction for 1 to 6 seconds. If, however, the weights you are employing have become so heavy that you cannot move them into a position of full contraction, have your partner lift the resistance for you and then slowly contract your muscles into the Max Contraction position. Then have your training partner slowly transfer the weight to your muscles until you are contracting against the full weight by yourself for 1 to 6 seconds.

It is important when training on the Max Contraction system to lift the weight into the fully contracted position slowly and under control—and then keep it there for 1 to 6 seconds.

Beginners to Max Contraction Training should start out by having their muscles contract against their 1-rep maximum weight, that is, the weight with which you can perform only 1 repetition through a full range of motion. After you can contract against this resistance for 6 seconds, you might want to have a training partner assist you in pulling the weight down into the position of full contraction for you to contract against.

PROPER WEIGHT SELECTION

One of the most pervasive problems of both beginning and advanced bodybuilders involves the proper selection of weight for each exercise. How does one determine if the weight is too light or too heavy? Is there any foolproof way to accurately determine the proper weight for each set? A good rule of thumb for beginners is to take as a starting point their one-rep maximum that they are presently capable of using for a full-range set. Simply lift the weight into the fully contracted position utilizing the force of muscular contraction alone. If you can lift the weight into this position easily, it is too light; keep adding weight until maximum effort is required to hold the resistance in the fully contracted position for 1 to 6 seconds.

You may discover that while you can lift 120 pounds with some difficulty, you cannot move 130 pounds at all—that's fine; just reduce the resistance back to 120 pounds and hold this for the recommended Max Contraction time frame. You will also find that your first workouts will be probative in nature, as you will be finding out what your ideal weight is and then building from there. Your first time you might select what you consider to be a heavy weight only to find that you can sustain the contraction easily for well over 6 seconds. If so, then the weight is too light, and you will need to increase it for your next workout so that you are reduced to a 1- to 6-second contraction.

As you become stronger, you will find that leverage factors involved in full-range exercise actually preclude your using weights that you are capable of contracting against in the Max Contraction position. At this point you will need a training partner to assist you in lifting the resistance into the position of Max Contraction and then transferring it until just your muscles are contracting against it. If you cannot pause in the Max Contraction position for one full second, then your muscles aren't really contracting against the weight. You either dropped the weight or lowered it out of the position of Max Contraction. Performing each set as described will help you to achieve maximum results.

TRAINING TO FAILURE

Many bodybuilders fall short of optimal progress due to their reluctance to carry each set to a point of momentary muscular failure. To stimulate increases in muscular size and strength, it's imperative that you regularly attempt the seemingly impossible. For example, if a bodybuilder can sustain a contraction against 100 pounds for 6 seconds, and never attempts to increase the resistance employed, his body has no reason to enlarge upon its existing level of muscle mass. It is only by regularly attempting the seemingly impossible that inroads are made into the body's reserve capacity. Since reserves are limited, the body compensates with increased size and strength so that future workouts won't use up the reserve.

Contrary to the belief of many, the last second of a set carried to failure while using proper form is not the most dangerous. In fact, it should be the safest, since at the end of the set you are at your weakest, barely able to generate enough force to sustain the contraction. It is the first few seconds of a set, when you are strongest and most capable of generating more force than is required to complete the contraction, that tend to be the most dangerous. So, don't stop any of your sets short of failure for fear that they are dangerous. The closer you get to exerting 100 percent intensity of effort at the end of a set, the greater the growth stimulation

you will receive. By training to failure, you will ensure that you have crossed that threshold below which growth won't be stimulated and above which it has to be.

THE NATURE OF MUSCLE FIBER RECRUITMENT

We've seen that a muscle must be in a position of maximum contraction to recruit all of its available muscle fibers—but this is only one half of the equation. The other half is the amount of weight, or the "load," the muscle fibers are made to 45contract against. In fact, it is this second half of the equation that effectively recruits and stimulates the muscle to grow larger.

Human anatomy and physiology studies have revealed four distinct muscle fiber types within our species. If you talk to most would-be experts or personal trainers, you'll hear a very simplified (and scientifically incorrect) synopsis that there exist only "fast-twitch" and "slow-twitch" muscles. However, physiologists have actually identified three types of fast-twitch muscle alone!

Classification of the Four Fiber Types

I	SO (Slow, Oxidative); S (Slow)
IIA	(Fast, Oxidative; FR (Fast, Fatigue Resistant)
IIAB	FOG (Fast, Oxidative-Glycolytic); FI (Fast, Intermediate Fatigueability)
IIB	FG (Fast, Glycolytic); FF (Fast, Fatigueable)

Fast-twitch muscle fibers differ from their slower cousins in many ways, endurance capacity being one of them. In fact, it's in the endurance realm rather than in the velocity or speed department that their differences become most apparent. The fast-oxidative (FO), or Type II A, fibers have relatively good endurance (the term *oxidative* refers solely to the aerobic machinery within the fast-oxidative fiber itself). Another fast-twitch fiber is the fast-glycolytic (FG), or Type II B. FG fibers contract very quickly and are very powerful but have nothing to offer in the way of endurance (the term *glycolytic* refers to the anaerobic machinery within the fast-glycolytic fiber itself). As an example, the huge deltoids and massive arms of Mr. Olympia–caliber body-builders are composed almost entirely of FG fibers.

Intermediate in speed, endurance, and power are the fast-oxidative-glycolytic (FOG), or Type II AB, fibers, which contain both the anaerobic and aerobic machinery within their cellular makeup. On the other side of the coin are slow-muscle fibers (S), or Type I, which are slow in comparison with, say, FG fibers. S fibers are endurance fibers used primarily for long-distance activities. They are very powerful aerobically with lots of aerobic enzymes, blood vessels, and myoglobin (an oxygen-storing endurance compound). On the down side, however, the S fibers aren't capable of creating much force and, consequently, don't possess the inherent mass potential of their quicker cousins.

An individual's fiber type and distribution appear to be genetically predetermined—a product of breeding as opposed to environmental influences. Still, most of us are brought into the world with a more or less even distribution of all types of fibers—both fast and slow twitch. This is not good if you want to be a powerlifter, as obviously a higher complement of FG fibers would be of greater benefit here—but then some of us were born to be marathoners, not sprinters. As a result, premiere powerlifters have a high FG fiber percentage, while distance runners have a greater complement of type-S fibers.

MAX CONTRACTION AND MUSCLE FIBER RECRUITMENT

The mind and body being interrelated, it should come as no surprise that it is our brain that recruits the body's muscle fibers solely as it perceives the need for them. This is accomplished via the brain's motor nerves, which, in keeping with the dictates of the brain, follow a relatively fixed order in the recruitment process. The process involves only the precise amount of electrical current necessary to turn on the required muscle fibers.

The huge deltoids and massive arms of seven-time Mr. Olympia winner Lee Haney are composed almost entirely of FG fibers.

Of the four fiber types, the S (slow) fibers are the easiest to engage owing to the fact that they don't require a lot of current. Slightly more energy is required to engage the FO fibers and more still for the FOGs. The ones that require the highest electrical output to engage are the FGs. It is of the utmost importance to have your muscles contract against the heaviest weights possible if you wish to activate the FGs: the brain is in no hurry to hit the switch for those FG fibers—the ones you want to stimulate for size and strength increases. The brain would rather engage the least amount of muscle fibers necessary to accomplish a given task. After all, the brain is an organ of survival; it knows how to conserve energy, as the conser-

Max Contraction trainee Joe Ostertag performing a one-arm Pec Deck exercise—with 585 pounds of plates, two training partners weighing 190 and 195 pounds, and one of the training partners holding an additional 45-pound plate, for a total of 1,015 pounds! With his left pectoral in the fully contracted position and this much weight, you can be sure he's activating every possible fiber in his chest!

vation of energy has proven over millions of years to be an asset for survival.

The brain will first attempt to contract against a heavy resistance by recruiting only the S fibers, but these will prove inadequate for the task. The brain will then recruit the FOs and shortly thereafter the FOG fibers to assist with the task of contraction. If the weight is light or moderate, then these are the only fibers that will be recruited. However, if the weight is truly heavy enough, that is, so heavy that you can only contract against it for 1 to 6 seconds, the brain will have realized that it needs more fire power than it's been providing and only then will it send out the signal to engage the elusive FG fibers. This process is known in physiology circles as "orderly recruitment," for the brain does not engage in the firing of muscle fibers randomly. When recruiting muscle fibers for the purpose of contraction, the brain doesn't concern itself with issues of speed but of force. It has no concern with how fast you want to lift a weight or how quickly you wish to run; again, it cannot randomly recruit muscle fibers. Instead, the brain ascertains the exact amount of force your muscles require to move a precise resistance and, accordingly, recruits the precise amount of muscle fibers required to do the job.[1]

An interesting aspect of this phenomenon is that when the brain sends sufficient current to activate the FG fibers in a Max Contraction set, we automatically know that the FOs and FOG fibers—that is, *all* of the available muscle fibers—have also been recruited and engaged, thereby ensuring the greatest possible growth stimulation.

AEROBIC AND ANAEROBIC PATHWAYS

There exist only two types of energy systems in the muscles, consisting of two types of processes or pathways that are mapped out by the central nervous system: anaerobic and aerobic. For the purpose of building your muscles to their absolute biggest size (i.e., to the uppermost limits of your genetic potential), your training efforts should always fall within the time frame of the anaerobic pathways.

The aerobic system, as the name implies, burns mainly body fat for fuel and requires the presence of oxygen to do so. Aerobic training is a necessity if your objective is endurance-related activities such as distance running or cross-country skiing. When your objective is building additional muscle mass, however, you will not be burning oxygen, but rather glycogen as your fuel of choice, which is stored within the muscles you are training. The first 1 to 6 seconds of muscular contraction are fueled by ATP (adenosine triphosphate), which is a compound responsible for all bodily functions, from muscular contraction to thought. There is generally enough ATP within each muscle to sustain a contraction for up to 3 seconds. To reach 6 seconds of contraction, additional ATP must be created, which the body does by breaking creatine phospate (CP) down into its constituents of creatine and phosphate; the energy released from this breaking down of CP can take an ADP molecule (adenosine diphosphate) and attach another phosphate, thus creating a new ATP molecule. There is sufficient CP stored in the body to keep one's muscles in ATP for up to 10 seconds of contraction—which is more than enough for Max Contraction exercise.

There is actually an anaerobic window of approximately 60 seconds in which a set can last, theoretically, and still be considered anaerobic. However, anytime an exercise extends beyond 90 to 100 seconds, the aerobic system kicks in and begins to take over. In fact, by the 2-minute mark of a set of exercise, the aerobic system is responsible for 50 percent of your energy output. This means, in effect, that if your set lasts this long you will be splitting your training stimulus for muscle mass in half—50 percent going to the aerobic system and 50 percent to the anaerobic. However, had you kept your set duration within the anaerobic confines, you could have had 100 percent of the training effect fall within the muscle building system. This is why training protocols that have you performing one exercise for up to 2 minutes per set (such as Superslow™) are not as efficient in stimulating maximum muscle growth.

The aerobic pathways work wonders for your endurance, but do precious little of anything in the way of promoting muscle growth. This is where most bodybuilders make a serious tactical error that, in some respects, accounts for all of their other bodybuilding errors: they equate the idea of more training with muscle building training. As they get stronger, they realize (correctly) that something about their workouts must progressively increase if their muscles are to grow progressively larger and stronger. However, perhaps not being familiar with the pertinent scientific data, they don't know that what must increase is the intensity of their workouts and that with every increase in intensity there must be a corresponding decrease in duration. Thus, as they gain size and strength, they mistakenly believe that they need to subject their muscles to more exercises, more sets, more repetitions, and they end up converting their anaerobic muscle building workouts to aerobic endurance building workouts. The result is that their muscle building progress eventually comes to a complete halt.

If it were true that as one progressed toward the upper limit of one's size and strength potential one would have to increase both the amount of exercises performed and the length of the workouts, then one would ultimately end up training 10, 12, 20 hours a day. This would be impossible, as the body only has a limited ability to compensate for the effects of stress. In order to make your muscles grow progressively bigger and stronger, it is not the duration but the intensity of your training that must increase. If you are not progressing in your bodybuilding training, it is either because you have begun training longer (a step toward aerobic conditioning) or because your muscles have adapted to a particular level of training intensity. Further progress will not come until you increase the intensity level and thereby decrease the duration of your training.

Part III

TRAINING CONSIDERATIONS

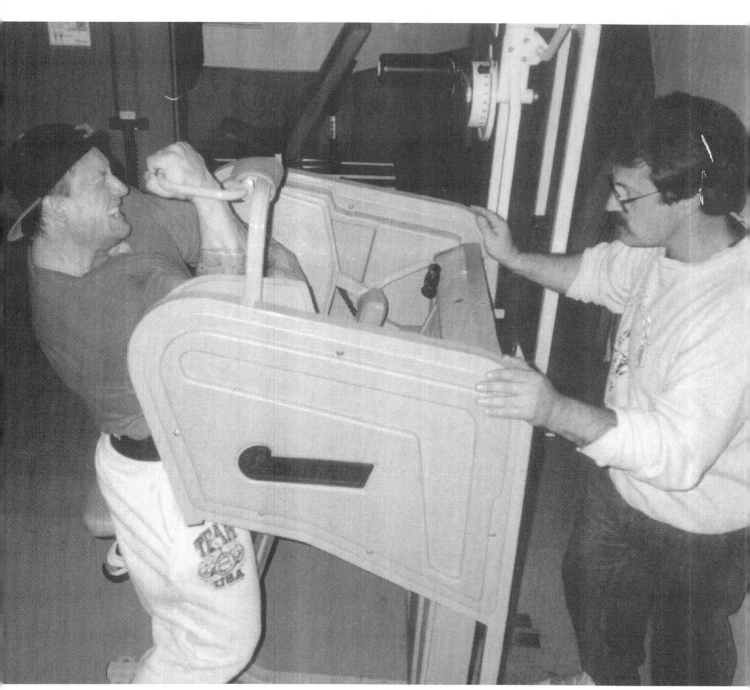

Multi–Mr. Olympia winner Dorian Yates (left) knows the meaning of maximum intensity. He's shown here fighting to sustain a position of full contraction under the watchful eye of high-intensity training pioneer Mike Mentzer (right).

Chapter 6

THE ROLE OF INTENSITY

In previous chapters I have touched on the fact that the key to bodybuilding success is high-intensity muscular contraction, and that the greater the intensity of contraction, the greater the muscle growth stimulation. Of all the training systems presently in existence, only Max Contraction Training offers maximum intensity of contraction owing to the fact that both the weights and the contraction of the muscles are maximum. Such an unprecedented degree of intensity directly translates into more muscle fiber stimulation per set.

However, for every increase in intensity, there must be a corresponding decrease in both the time of contraction and the total amount of training in a given workout. Since Max Contraction provides a quantum leap in intensity, the volume of the workout itself must be scaled back considerably. Bodybuilding pioneers such as Arthur Jones and Mike Mentzer have pointed out that muscle growth is a defensive reaction of the body to the stress of exercise in much the same way that the production of melanin is a defensive reaction of the body to the stress of ultraviolet light.

An organism's response to high-intensity stress is usually immediate; when you go out into the hot July sun for the purpose of getting a suntan, for example, you don't have to wait days to see the body's response to the stress of the ultraviolet light. You will see it soon after you are exposed to it via a reddening or tanning of your skin. If this response were not immediate, you would not be able to tolerate exposure to the sun without severe burning and, perhaps, death. You have probably noted from experience that the degree of your tan will vary depending upon the intensity of the sun's rays. The reason why you are unable to acquire much of a tan during the months of October or November is because when the sun is no longer overhead, its ultraviolet rays are not as intense. You could tolerate hours and hours of such low-intensity ultraviolet exposure, but doing so would provide little or no stimulation of a suntan.

This likewise explains why your skin requires only a short exposure to the intense rays of a midsummer sun. So intense and concentrated are the ultraviolet rays in the sum-

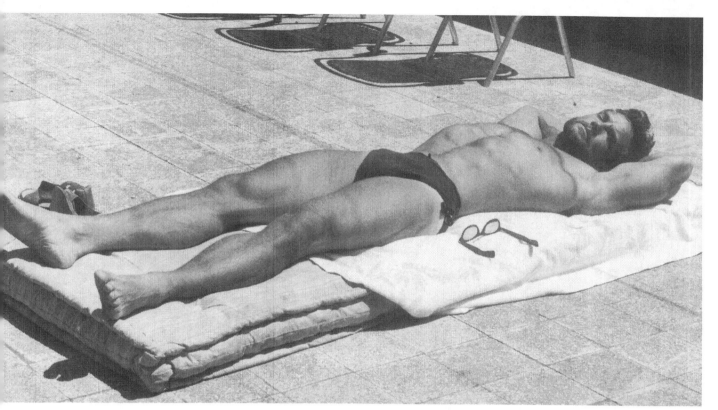

The body's buildup of muscles is a defense mechanism that allows the body to cope more successfully with intense muscular contraction in much the same way that a suntan is a defense mechanism that allows the body to cope more successfully with intense ultraviolet light. Here the great Steve Reeves is putting this latter defensive mechanism of the body into action during a break from filming *Hercules* in sunny Italy.

mertime that your body can only successfully cope with brief exposure to them; however, the effect is immediate and dramatic. The reason why you need so little exposure to the sun's rays in July is that its intensity is high, which means the duration of the exposure must be very low in order for the body to successfully defend against or adapt to it. Even at this, the sun's rays in July are still of modest enough intensity (while substantially greater than in October, admittedly) that you can usually endure several minutes to an hour of direct exposure without risking a major sunburn. If, however, it were physically possible to bring the sun a little bit closer to the earth (without burning the earth to a crisp!), your body would theoretically only be able to endure microseconds of such exposure to the stress of the ultraviolet rays. It would quickly (almost instantly) begin its defensive reaction of stimulating more melanin production, forming a suntan as a protective barrier to the ultra-high-

intensity ultraviolet light it had just been exposed to.

With resistance training, we have the luxury of being able to "bring the sun a little closer to the earth" by being able to vary the intensity of the training stress applied to our muscles almost at will. We can raise the intensity to such high levels that we can tolerate only 1 second of direct stimulation, but that 1 second will, like the suntan example, stimulate an immediate adaptive response from the body in the form of developing a bigger muscle as a protective barrier against future assaults of like severity. In fact, a maximum 1-second contraction will stimulate a far more dramatic adaptive response from the body in terms of muscle growth than would longer exposure to any training stress of lesser intensity.

If we stay at the low-intensity end of the spectrum, we can, of course, extend the length of our sets and/or perform many sets of an exercise (or exercises), as our muscles can

During the photo shoot for this book, fitness model and personal trainer Leslie Cockwell performed the one-arm Pec Deck exercise against 100 pounds of resistance with little difficulty, indicating that minimum muscle fiber recruitment and stimulation were taking place.

endure hours of low-intensity training stress with little problem. However, training in such a fashion will see us net out with little or nothing to show for our efforts except an enhanced capacity to tolerate longer periods of exercise. By contrast, at the high-intensity end of the spectrum, we cannot tolerate anything but the briefest possible exposure to a training stress that has been dialed in to maximum intensity, and yet our adaptive response will be immediate and pronounced.

TRAINING FOR A SPECIFIC PURPOSE

Since each of us has a genetic limit to the size our muscles can become, it follows that the

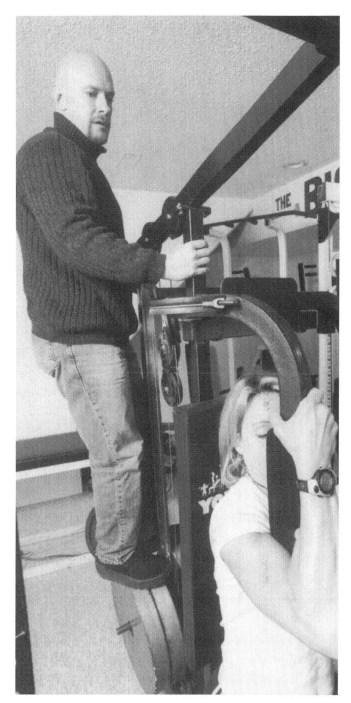

As an experiment during the same shoot, the author loaded up the Pec Deck machine with 400 pounds and then stood on the weight stack, adding another 195 pounds of resistance. Leslie found that she was able to contract her pec muscles against 595 pounds of resistance—with one arm! If her chest muscles had the capacity to contract against 595 pounds, of what benefit for bodybuilding purposes would it have been for her to limit herself to working out with 100 pounds? Both men and women are much, much stronger than they allow themselves to believe and are capable of much greater progress—when they train with Max Contraction.

human body likewise possesses a finite or limited adaptive response to build these muscles. Understanding this, if your goal is to build maximum increases in size and strength, your training efforts are best directed by training 100 percent specifically for size and strength. And this is possible, by definition, only when the intensity of your muscular contraction is absolutely 100 percent and the duration of your workout is therefore very, very brief. You will recall that intensity and duration exist in an inverse ratio to each other, and while you can tolerate low-intensity exercise for long periods, you cannot tolerate high-intensity exercise to the same extent.

Bodybuilders training with multiple sets and repetitions are dividing the training stimulus between strength and endurance, which means that they are training inefficiently. If there are 100 units of adaptation energy available and half of it goes toward increasing your muscle mass and the other half goes to increasing your endurance, you have effectively divided the impulse. This results in only 50 percent of the gains in muscle mass that you could be obtaining.

If you picture intensity as being expressed across a broad continuum, you will note that there are varying degrees of intensity. The lower the intensity of contraction (or IOC), the longer the time of contraction (or TOC) can be. If the intensity is raised to the moderate level, you will be able to workout for a moderate period of time (say, 45 minutes to an hour); but if the intensity is maximal, you will not be able to train for anymore than 1 to 6 seconds. Simply defined, duration is the amount of time you spend training or the length of any given training session, whereas intensity is an indication of the degree of effort put forth during the exercise or training session. Intensity can be either low or high; distance running and common everyday activities such as walking are on the low end of the spectrum, and sprinting and Max Contraction exercise are on the high end.

As an increase in muscle mass is the body's defensive response to the stress of high-intensity muscular contraction, it should be obvious that you must give your body a reason—a powerful reason—to trigger this defen-

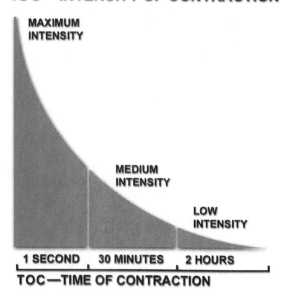

If your IOC is high, your TOC will be low, and vice versa. Productive bodybuilding exercise must be intense and brief; the higher the IOC, the better.

sive response. Your body, in other words, must detect that its homeostasis is being threatened. Mild, low-intensity effort will not be perceived as such a threat and will do next to nothing to stimulate maximum gains in muscle mass. As we've seen in the scientific literature, only a maximum intensity of effort, a maximal muscular contraction, results in an increase in size and strength. This is where the integration of mind and body becomes a factor again; cultivating a strong will to succeed will be essential to your continued progress.

There is a natural psychological disinclination for most bodybuilders to increase the intensity of their exercises, which is why they prefer the easier, less threatening route of adding sets and exercises, and otherwise reducing the intensity of their workouts by increasing their duration. As Mike Mentzer once pointed out:

> There is a strong mental barrier to inducing greater and greater muscular contractions. A very large and strong muscle contracting with maximum intensity places much greater demands on the body's recuperative sub-systems than does a smaller, weaker one. Because these demands upon the

It takes a strong will to sustain a maximum-intensity muscular contraction, even for as little as a 1-second TOC. Here Mike Mentzer demonstrates mind over muscle in the Max Contraction position on a Nautilus Lateral Raise machine.

body's resources are [perceived as] potentially life-threatening, your mind as well as your body will do everything possible to prevent such taxing high intensity exertion. Lassitude, anxiety and even a preference for low intensity workouts are manifestations of the mind's disinclination to engage the body in such maximum efforts. Therefore, as your muscles get stronger and stronger, you must exercise your will to get stronger apace.

Bodybuilders who choose not to exercise their will rationalize their reduction in intensity by convincing themselves that longer workouts equate to more work, which they equate with being a progression of sorts. However, their actual goal as bodybuilders is not to see how much exercise they can tolerate, but rather to perform the precise type of exercise required to trigger the growth mechanism of the body into motion. That type of exercise, as we've established, is high-intensity muscular contraction. Whenever one increases the dura-

tion of an exercise session by adding either sets or reps to the routine, one can only do so by reducing the intensity of muscular contraction. This is the only way that the duration of the workout can be extended.

This antipodal relationship between intensity and duration is both immutable and universal and, consequently, one of the more fundamental laws of exercise science. It applies to all activities, from concentrating for an exam, to splitting wood, to swimming, to running, to bodybuilding—the more intensely you do *anything*, the duration of that activity must be decreased. And, as pertains to the purposes of this book, if you want to build big muscles as fast as possible, then you must train with the highest possible intensity of effort. In other words, if you want to build muscular mass, then you've got to train for short periods of time so that you'll be able to train intensely. That, in essence, is the nature of the relationship.

For example, no one can engage in an all-out sprint for a distance of a mile. Why?

Because an all-out sprint is a high-intensity activity and, thus, cannot be engaged in for more than 400 meters. Consequently, anyone who tells you that they are training "intensely" in a workout that stretches beyond an hour (and some bodybuilders will train in the gym for up to three hours) is displaying a profound ignorance of the definition of this term.

Intensity can be gauged within Max Contraction Training quite objectively and on a double progressive basis. If the IOC of your max contraction is such that you can only manage a 1-second TOC, then shoot for a 6-second TOC during your next workout. If you find that you have adapted to the intensity of the workout (IOW) and your IOC is now such that your TOC lasts 6 seconds, increase the resistance you are using to make for an increased IOC and aim for a 1-second TOC again. You don't need to take computer printouts, graph paper, or a calculator to the gym with you; you simply need to make your mus-

The key to successful muscle building is to make every effort to raise the IOC.

cles contract against more weight within a 1- to 6-second time span on a progressive basis. Nor do you have to increase the number of sets in your workouts. All you have to do is train as hard as you possibly can each and every set and try to improve upon the amount of weight your muscles are contracting against (the IOC) or the TOC—or both—each time you head to the gym. Each workout—and each set of each workout—is something to be surpassed and should be viewed as a hitching post along the path to greater bodybuilding progress.

Nobody has yet successfully challenged the fact that muscle growth does not come easily. You have to force growth to occur. And you cannot force growth by having your muscles contract against light weights or by performing tasks that are already well within their existing capacity. Your objective in bodybuilding is to maximize muscular involvement, not to diminish it. Therefore, anything you do to make your exercises more intense (by increasing the IOC) will increase muscle fiber involvement and, hence, the productivity of the exercise. A high intensity of effort is the only way to build bigger muscles.

Mike Mentzer used to be attacked in certain muscle magazines (usually after he left their employ) by people and scribes who would claim that "high-intensity training only works for a select few. It only works if you have the genetic makeup of a superman and take steroids." Such statements only served to reveal their ignorance of Mentzer's postulates and, indeed, the nature of productive bodybuilding exercise, in addition to exposing their own unwillingness to seriously and objectively look into training methodology and the science that underpins it. If a method works, it works. Period. It can't work only during the month of August but not in October, or work for one human being and no one else (given the same conditions and context); after all, it's human muscle physiology we're dealing with. Max Contraction Training has the backing of exercise science to support it and it also can be presented in a logical fashion (i.e., its conclusions follow of necessity from its premises). Unfortunately, the same cannot be said for most traditional training methods.

The point of the matter is that we as a species are, physiologically speaking, all essentially the same; we all need calories, we all require sleep, we all burn carbohydrates at the rate of four calories per gram, and we all need intense exercise to stimulate muscle growth beyond normal levels. In fact, Mike Mentzer might have waxed his most philosophical (he was not only a former Mr. Universe, but a dedicated objectivist philosopher) when he said:

> We're all unique as individuals but when a young man or woman goes to medical school to study muscle physiology, whose physiology do you think they're studying? Everybody's! We all have the same muscle physiology. The biochemical changes that lead to growth in Mike Mentzer are the same as those in yourself, your training partner and your neighbor. It follows from this that the specific stimulus required to induce those biochemical changes leading to muscle growth in Mike Mentzer, yourself, your training partner and your neighbor is the same—high-intensity muscular contraction!

If there exists any confusion over this, it lies in the fact that we as individuals all adapt to high-intensity training at varying levels of speed. Whereas some of us gain muscle at a very quick rate, others may grow at a much slower pace. However, each of us grows muscle faster when we train more intensely. If you personally are not gaining much at the moment, you will gain more quickly as soon as you increase your training intensity. Adaptation to the stress of high-intensity exercise varies on an individual basis owing to such factors as age, sex, existing physical condition, motivation, and so on, but the underlying muscle physiology is the same.

Therefore people who say that we have different training requirements are entirely misinformed. We have the same training requirements; however, the confusion enters because we each possess varying levels of innate adaptability to the stress of exercise. Some are able to adapt quite quickly, while others require many weeks to adapt. What is indisputable is that our physiology—human physiology—increases its store of muscle mass in direct proportion to the intensity of the exercise our muscles are exposed to. Again, to quote Mentzer:

> If we all had different physiologies, medical science could not exist. A doctor would have to study each individual as a separate physiological entity and learn all of the intricacies of his physiology. Then he would have to devise medicine around this one individual. The fact that they can take the basic principles of physiology and are able to successfully apply them to the whole human race is what makes medical science a viable discipline.

It is also what makes Max Contraction a viable discipline.

Since all human beings are essentially the same physiologically, it follows that both men and women respond similarly to the same stress of Max Contraction exercise—by getting stronger and more muscular.

Downtime is crucially important to the bodybuilding process, allowing your muscles to both recover and grow.

Chapter 7

RECOVERY ABILITY

In November 1992 two individuals were preparing books that would represent radically new approaches to bodybuilding training. One was Mike Mentzer, the first bodybuilder to acquire a perfect score in competition, who was then in the midst of completing a revised edition of a training book he had first published in the late 1970s titled *Heavy Duty*. This revised book would reveal the fundamental principles of bodybuilding science and become the touchstone of modern high-intensity theorists who universally believe that exercise, to be productive, must be intense, brief, and infrequent.

Arthur Jones had postulated what were considered to be the three cardinal tenets of high-intensity training six to seven years prior to Mentzer's arrival on the scene. However, Mentzer validated these postulates, building, as did his younger brother, Ray, a championship physique utilizing these principles. Moreover, Mike began to see a new application with regard to recovery ability that, apparently, Jones had missed. Whereas Jones had through-

out the 1970s advocated three weekly workouts of roughly 20 sets (total), Mentzer saw 20 sets as being excessive for building muscle and three days per week as a purely arbitrary time frame. What, after all, was magical about training three days out of every seven? Why was it better than, say, training twice every seven days or three or four times out of every 30?

By 1992 Mentzer had assumed a career as a personal trainer, and, in an attempt to answer these questions, he dramatically cut back on the amount of sets he assigned to his training clients and began to have his clients train much less frequently. People began talking about his new approach, as his clients' results were far superior to those of other personal trainers who had their charges training with more sets and greater frequency.

I was the other individual preparing a book in 1992 and, together with my co-author Peter Sisco, was in the midst of finalizing some research materials prior to its publication. The book, *Power Factor Training*, made the case that a full range of motion (another cardinal

Mike Mentzer (right) puts one of his personal training clients through his paces at Gold's Gym in Venice, California. It was from training such clients that Mentzer made many of his most innovative insights into bodybuilding science.

tenet of Jones's original high-intensity theory) actually had an importance of somewhere between "zero" and "very little" with regard to stimulating muscle growth. I had learned through studying the research of the men cited in Chapter 4 that it was "the amount of work performed in a given unit of time" that had, more than any other factor, been responsible for muscle growth. Once "work per unit of time" was firmly isolated as the sole stimulus for stimulating muscle growth, it struck me that heavier weights would allow for far greater "work" (i.e., overload). After speaking with several world champion powerlifters, bodybuilders, and strength athletes, I came away convinced that the greatest weights and, thus, the greatest overload to the muscles, could be provided by lifting weights solely in one's strongest range of motion. A full range of motion actually made it impossible—owing to leverage disadvantages—to lift heavy weights, thus limiting the effective overload that the muscles were capable of contracting against.

Peter and I had also come to the same conclusions as Mentzer about the drawbacks of training three or more days per week (as advocated by many bodybuilding champions and, indeed, the bodybuilding orthodoxy). Moreover, we also discovered a supposition that had passed for fact in both physiology circles and among certain high-intensity training theorists, namely, that muscle tissue will somehow decompensate or atrophy if it isn't trained within 96 hours. At one point, both Peter and I took an eight-week layoff from our bodybuilding workouts only to discover upon our return to the gym that we were both *stronger*.

I had known Mike at this point for 13 years. We would frequently call each other to compare notes on recovery time and what impact (if any) this had on the muscle growth process. As we were both in the midst of writing books on our respective training approaches, we would on occasion read aloud to each other certain chapters of our books as we completed them. Mike loved to report on the progress his clients were

The author, supervising the Power Factor protocol of bodybuilding champion Paul DeMayo during a photo session for the book *Power Factor Training*.

making and I was quite keen to share with him some of the results that I had experienced. Mike, apart from being a brilliant teacher, was also a good listener (I've subsequently learned that the two go together). He would listen to what I reported with great interest and then offer his own comments and speculations as to why a particular training protocol worked, how it could be made to work more efficiently, and what its potential drawbacks were. As he had over 30 years of experience at the highest level of bodybuilding, his insights were particularly meaningful to me.

I recall one of these conversations with particular vividness. I was just preparing to leave for Graz, Austria, to cover an amateur bodybuilding contest for *Flex* magazine. Prior to leaving, I had wanted to touch base with Mike to record his comments on training with heavy partial repetitions during his competitive days in the late 1970s. My plan had been to record Mike's recollections and then, once in Austria, transcribe his comments and insert

The author (left) discusses a point of bodybuilding with Mike Mentzer (right) during a conversation in 1981. The men remained close friends and colleagues until Mentzer's death in 2001.

them into the relevant chapter of my book. One thing quickly led to another, and a conversation that was supposed to be about the merits of partial repetitions quickly turned into a dissertation from Mike on his new views on recovery ability.

When I arrived in Graz and played back the tape recording of our dialogue, I was so impressed with Mentzer's insights that I probably replayed the conversation six times, taking notes each time I did so. Mike had touched on the astounding results his trainees (including then newly crowned Mr. Olympia, Dorian Yates) had obtained by taking protracted recovery periods—in some instances lasting several weeks—in between workouts. His words were full of illumination and would forever alter and add to my understanding of the factors that influence successful bodybuilding. Perhaps the most significant insights he

revealed to me that day (and which represent, in my estimation, Mentzer's greatest contribution to the science of bodybuilding) concern the reasons why one set of an exercise is potent enough to stimulate maximum growth and the fact that growth stimulation and growth production are two distinct processes; the former takes place via the workout, and the latter requires sufficient time to elapse in order to occur. Here is an excerpt from our conversation that touches on these particularly salient points:

Mentzer: You know, John, you've got to be real careful with this heavy high-intensity stuff. I may have mentioned it to you before, but what I'm beginning to see a lot more clearly is just how *demanding* this stuff is. Arthur Jones said some years ago that for every slight increase in intensity there has to be a dispro-

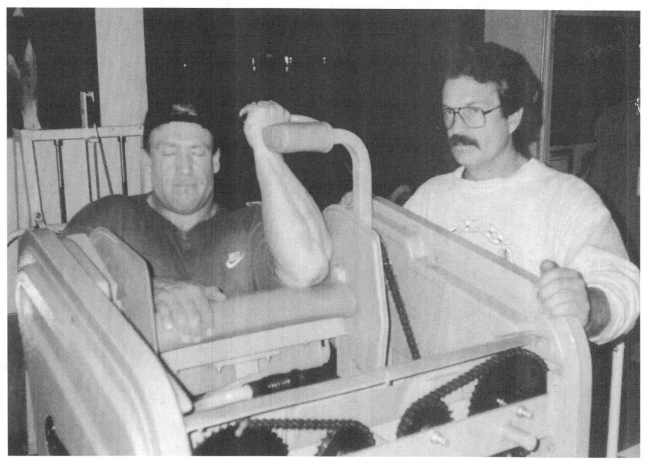

Mike Mentzer (right) and multi–Mr. Olympia winner Dorian Yates (left) during their famous Gold's Gym workout sessions in 1993.

portionate decrease in volume—and he was not joking. This high-intensity stuff places a demand on the body of an order that is *phenomenal*. If you were to draw a horizontal line from left to right across a page of paper with that line representing zero effort and then off of that line graph your daily effort output— that is, you get up in the morning, you take a shower, you scrub yourself down, you dry yourself, you walk to the car, climb some steps to get into a building, you push a pencil, et cetera—the graph representing that kind of effort output would barely leave the flat line; it would be a little squiggly sine wave. Then all of a sudden you go into the gym and you perform a heavy set of partial bench presses or a set of heavy Nautilus laterals, whatever, all of a sudden that little squiggly line starts to take off in a straight vertical line off the paper, out the door, down the street, and around the block! Now within that space is how much more biochemical resources are used up. Do you see how dramatic that is?

Little: Absolutely.

Mentzer: I used to occasionally have, and still do occasionally have, people do a second set, for instance, of Nautilus laterals. And I realize that that kind of an increase is wrong [i.e., the second set], it's way too much. Rather than have someone do a second set, what they should do is maybe do an extra rep. . . . You have to start out very, very small because, again, the demands from even that one set are of an enormous magnitude. And I'm beginning to understand much more clearly how precise all this has to be. Science is a precise discipline, and there's no way of accurately measuring all these things, but there are accurate and precise ways of increasing volume, resistance, intensity, and all that. What I've come to understand more clearly is something else Jones said, and that is that from the time you start training you should be able to reach the absolute upper limit dictated by your genetic endowment within two years—and he was right. If you are imposing a sufficiently intense training stress upon your musculature, and you are neither training too long nor too frequently, then you

should be witnessing progress not on an irregular, haphazard, occasional basis, but every single workout. Now here comes the difficult part for most people: the general theory advanced by Jones over 20 years ago—train hard, train brief and infrequent—was valid [but] there is a wide-range of variation among individuals I'm seeing with regards to recovery ability; that is, the ability to tolerate intense exercise. Everybody needs intense contractions to stimulate growth, but what the individual has to work with is just how much volume and frequency he can tolerate. I have asked at least a dozen individuals over the last couple of weeks if they have not always noticed that even after a two- to three-week layoff they come back and they're stronger. I have noted with all of my clients—I have had clients that were either forced to take layoffs or just took layoffs for whatever reason—almost all of them expressed an anxiety that "Geez, I'm afraid I'm going to lose something." I've had people take up to three weeks off, and they almost in every single case come back stronger. I asked Dorian Yates the same thing the other week, and he said, "You know, Mike, that's true." This is not just a minor point to be glossed over, John. I'm beginning to suspect this thing with frequency has a hell of a lot to do with it.

Little: Are you suggesting that, perhaps, in the future people could train intensely and then back off for two to three weeks before training again?

Mentzer: Maybe train each bodypart once every two weeks—why not? Progress should not be an unpredictable, irregular phenomenon if you are training intensely enough to stimulate growth. Growth is only stimulated during the workout, but if you're working out too long and too frequently, you will short-circuit both the recovery and the growth process.

Little: So your thoughts now are that the higher the intensity—even if your workout is comparatively brief—might still be too much to recover from in only seven days? So even a workout as low as three sets could prove too much for the system to recover from—assum-

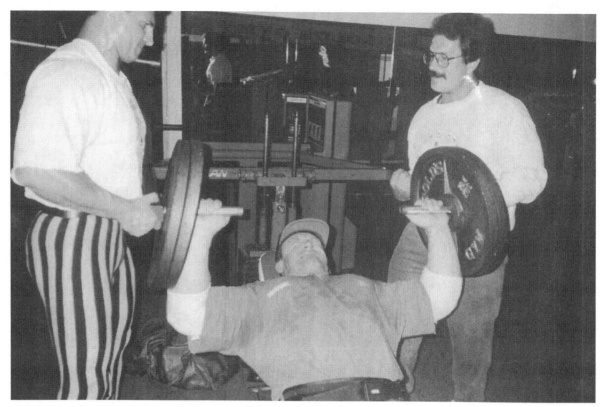

Mike Mentzer (right) recognized that someone as strong as Dorian Yates (center) generated such high intensity during his workouts that additional rest days would be required simply to recover from his workouts.

ing the intensity was sufficiently high—over the course of a week then?

Mentzer: Three sets could prove too much. I have no doubt this is the direction this has to go in. This high-intensity stuff places a demand on the body that is unreal. There obviously is something used up, and I see now that there is more used up than I realized. I don't know what the biochemicals are—I know some of them—but there's a lot that probably nobody knows. This high-intensity stuff is really quite fascinating. If I had the money, I'd like to fund my own research. I had a talk with Dorian [Yates] about this the other day; we've been staying in closer contact. I got him real psyched up. I said, "Listen, Dorian, there has never been a single bodybuilder, including myself, that has ever reached the upper limit dictated by his genetic potential. Why can I say that with absolute certainty? Because in order to do so you'd literally have to train *perfectly*— and no one has ever done that, including me." Even though I understood the general theory

advanced by Jones—and it is valid—what I didn't understand when I was training for competition was the practical application. I took that thing as an arbitrary prescription and plugged it in and stayed with it, not striving to regulate the volume and frequency over a period of time. I said, "Look, Dorian, you pride yourself on being radical, why don't you become the first already super-advanced bodybuilder to take a Mr. Olympia physique to the absolute zenith?" He started getting really excited—you know how these guys [hardcore bodybuilders] are. [Laughs.] He said, "You're right. I *am* radical." [Laughs.] I told him, "All right, Dorian, you're my kind of guy."

Little: That's got to be a nice feather in your cap to advise the fellow who goes on to win the Olympia in '92.

Mentzer: You better believe it—and he's even more receptive now.

Little: How could he not be? Every time I interviewed him, I always asked him about going back to that day with you in the gym and he starts raving about it.

Mentzer: You know it's curious because he is kind of a low-key guy. He never said that much about that. Even when he left here that many months ago, I talked to him until I was blue in the face—almost like I'm doing now—but he's the kind of guy who doesn't really respond much. You don't really know if it's clicking or not. Then, the next thing I hear, the guy wins Mr. Olympia, and he's telling all the interviewers that he did take my advice and he did cut back to one set per exercise and it really did work. I was delighted.

Mentzer had, in fact, been exploring this phenomenon of protracted recovery periods since the late 1970s. During a conversation that we shared in 1990, he had revealed the following:

Mentzer: The formula is brief training, intense training, infrequent training. Young bodybuilders reading this should be cautioned against doing too many sets on too many days for all bodyparts. Their enthusiasm is often a hindrance; they're so willing and able to train marathon-style to acquire a muscular physique that they often overtrain. I train in Gold's—when I do train—and I see this as probably the most pervasive mistake of all bodybuilders, including advanced bodybuilders. They grossly overtrain.

Little: I was speaking with your former idol—when you were growing up—Bill Pearl, the other day, and I was completely shocked by his training approach, which is, like, two and a half hours a day, seven days a week. And I thought, *This is the guy who was dispensing advice to Mentzer when you were growing up?*

Mentzer: Yeah.

Little: Was it the same sort of thing that he was telling you? And did you make any progress on it?

Mentzer: [Reflects] Well, no I didn't. Earlier in my career, in the earlier 70s, I was training on the typical marathon type of training routine: 20 sets or more per bodypart for six days a week, and I hit a plateau in my progress which

Dorian Yates displays the phenomenal muscle mass that results from properly balancing high-intensity training workouts with adequate periods of rest and recovery.

I couldn't overcome doing the 20 sets per bodypart. So I used the reasoning that "more is better," and I figured, "Well, if 20 sets wasn't doing it, I need 30 sets." At one point, I even got up to 40 sets for my chest! I couldn't even get a pump after a while! And after months and months and months of no progress, I was about to abandon my training altogether, thinking it wasn't worth it. And that's when I had the good opportunity to meet Casey Viator at the 1971 Mr. America and was shocked to learn that he was only training 45 minutes, three days a week. And then in subsequent phone conversations with Casey and his mentor, Arthur Jones, I learned the theoretical framework and embraced it intellectually, and that made it easier to do in the gym, and, of course, I went on to become a strong advocate and proponent of high-intensity training, which is what we've been talking about.

Little: Yeah. You've also single-handedly led bodybuilders away from their aberrant dietary and training practices. How did you first hit

Mike Mentzer (right) was on hand to witness Dorian Yates's (left) second straight Mr. Olympia victory and to offer his congratulations. Mentzer took great pride in bodybuilders such as Yates who employed a reasoned and logical approach to their bodybuilding training.

upon the discovery of prolonged recovery periods and breaking out of viewing training within the seven-day confines of the Gregorian calendar?

Mentzer: Well, it was back in '79 or '80. My brother and I were training for contests together. We were training extremely intensely with heavy weights, training to failure with forced reps and negatives. And I remember it was on a Tuesday morning after a very heavy Monday workout. Ray and I met in the gym, as usual, and we were still hell-bent on making maximum progress. I was thinking about the workouts and analyzing them and analyzing their effects on my body from day to day, and I said to my brother, "Ray, how do you feel today?" And he—like me—was exhausted, having still not fully recovered from the Monday workout. And I reasoned—I said, "Ray, if we haven't even recovered from our workout yesterday, we're not going to be able to invest our workout today with the intensity that is required to stimulate maximum muscle growth. And if we did, in fact, stimulate growth on Monday—which we probably did— we're not going to grow anyway because, again, recovery has to come first." Recovery and growth are two distinct physiological processes, both requiring time to fulfill or complete. And, again, "If we hadn't completed the recovery process, we're not going to produce any growth that we have stimulated." Growth stimulation and growth production are two distinct physiological processes, too; you have to stimulate growth in the gym, and then allow growth to produce itself or manifest itself. Again, growth stimulation and growth production are two distinct processes, and the growth production has to be preceded by the recovery process. So, what happens when you train again before you recover is that you short-circuit the growth process. And I explained this to Ray, and he agreed that he wasn't feeling recovered, that it was ridiculous to try and train again, let alone be concerned about growth. We would have been spinning our wheels, in effect, so we decided to take another day off, and that helped a lot and we recovered. And we found

sometimes we even needed 2 days off in between workouts, so we started doing a 4 day out of every 9 or 10 day split—not allowing tradition and convenience and compulsion, at some points, to supersede logic and reason.

Little: That's good—and also you made probably the best progress of your life when you did that.

Mentzer: Yes, we did make the best. We had hit a plateau there for a while. Our gains had slowed down, as is often the case with advanced bodybuilders, but when we adopted that program our gains skyrocketed again— even for advanced bodybuilders! At one point there I had gained 10 pounds of muscle in three weeks and lost 4 pounds of fat at the same time.

Little: So a 14-pound lean mass gain?

Mentzer: That's right.

In a study that was published a mere six months after our conversation, a team of exercise physiologists verified Mike's hypothesis (as evidenced in our first exchange) that substantial periods of time are required to simply recover from intense exercise. In May 1993 the *Journal of Physiology* reported that a group of men and women aged 22 to 32 took part in an exercise experiment in which they trained their biceps muscles in a negative-only fashion to a point of muscular failure. Negative contractions are considered by some exercise physiologists to be more intense than positive or concentric contractions because more weight can be employed, and, thus, the intensity of the exercise can be increased.

In the experiment, the subjects sat on a preacher bench and performed three negative-only sets of preacher curls in which the resistance was raised for them and they had to concentrate on lowering the resistance (determined to be 90 percent of their maximum isometric force capability) in a time span of 5 to 9 seconds. Typically, each set consisted of 5 to 15 such repetitions. After a 2-minute rest period, a second set was performed in this fashion with a resistance that had been reduced

Mike Mentzer in peak condition at the 1980 Mr. Olympia contest. By 1979 Mentzer had only been training 4 days out of every 10—and came into the contest 14 pounds of muscle heavier than when he'd been training more frequently.

by 10 percent. After another 2-minute rest, a third and final set was performed with another 10 percent reduction in weight. All of the test subjects were found to be most sore two days after exercising (a common occurrence), but the soreness in their biceps was gone by the ninth day. However, what was even more telling was not the highly subjective report of soreness in the muscles, but the far more tangible report of the impact of the workout on their recovery ability. The day after the exercise, the subjects exhibited what the experimenters termed "a dramatic 35 percent loss of strength. . . . Even on the tenth post-exercise day the muscles had recovered only to about 70 percent of their control strength."

The experimenters, John N. Howell, Gary Chleboun, and Robert Conaster (from the Somatic Dysfunction Research Laboratory of the College of Osteopathic Medicine and the Department of Biological Sciences, at Ohio University, Athens), concluded in their summary, "Muscle strength declined by almost 40 percent after the exercise, and recovery was only slight 10 days later; the half-time of recovery appeared to be as long as 5 to 6 weeks."

It is also interesting to note that the iconic runner Roger Bannister revealed in the December 1996 edition of *Runner's World* magazine that he in fact *rested*—for five full days—prior to breaking the 4-minute mile barrier. Bannister believed that not running during those days allowed him to take his mind off the race; his days of rest undoubtedly also allowed his body's recuperative subsystems to replenish themselves and grow stronger, thus allowing him to run the first-ever sub-4-minute mile.

In seriously considering this data cited, we are forced to conclude that the recovery process can take not 1 to 2 weeks—but up to 10 to 12 weeks! That is to say, up to three months off might be required in order to simply recover from a high-intensity workout. Additional research, conducted on marathon runners some 12 years earlier by Michael Sherman at Ball State University in Indiana, also indicated that the recovery period required after training can extend to a period running into

months. In the January 1985 issue of *American Health* magazine, Stephen Kiesling reported the following on Sherman's research:

> Sherman found that even after a full week of rest, marathon runners had not regained pre-race strength and power. Returning to [even] moderate running after the marathon delayed recovery. And some races may take months to recover from.

The conclusion to draw from the research cited is simply that training creates far greater demands on the body's recuperative subsystems than was previously thought. The intensity of the workout (IOW) determines how many days off training (DOT) you require, with the greater the energy expended, the longer the recovery process needing to be. If the IOW is moderate, you might well be ready to head back to the gym in a day or two, but if the IOW is maximum, you may require twelve or more DOT. In fact, the recovery process, which always precedes the growth process, can in some instances actually take in excess of several months to complete. This is important to remember, particularly in light of the workout routines advocated by champion bodybuilders in the pages of the various muscle magazines that would have the trainee working out with up to 40 sets per bodypart and training up to six days per week.

The problem with such an approach is that every set of bodybuilding training has a negative effect on the body in that it makes a further inroad into the body's limited reserve of recovery ability. And the longer you train, the more of this reserve you use up and the less is available to serve the growth mechanism of the body. Like the distance runner, if you engage in this activity for prolonged periods of time and do not allow your recuperative subsystems time to recover, not only will you feel overtrained, you'll never recover from your workouts. With these facts in mind, it is recommended that you make a conscious effort to do the following three things if you desire unbreached progress from your bodybuilding training:

IOW—INTENSITY OF WORKOUT

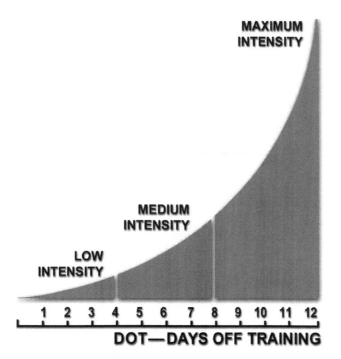

The greater the Intensity of the Workout (IOW), the more Days Off Training (DOT) you require. Depending on the IOW, you may need upwards of two weeks to recover and grow.

1. Increase the intensity of your workouts.
2. Allow adequate time for recovery to take place.
3. Allow another period of time to elapse to allow for manifestation of the growth you have stimulated.

As Mentzer indicated, the growth process never precedes the recovery process—recovery always precedes growth. It can't be otherwise. If you weren't able to recover from your workouts, you would eventually run out of energy and die. Growth must be stimulated first through high-intensity training, then you must allow yourself enough time to recover from the workout—and then you must allow an additional block of time to elapse in order for the growth that you stimulated to take place. If you train again before recovery has occurred, you will have interrupted the growth process, preventing it from taking place. In fact, if you worked out again before the recovery and growth processes have taken place, all you will have succeeded in doing is prolonging the recovery process, as you would then have to recover from your most recent training session

Train as intensely as you can in your Max Contraction workout, then go home, relax, rest, and recover.

in addition to the one prior to that. And, if you allow enough time for recovery to take place but not enough time for growth to occur, you still won't grow! It takes time for the growth process to complete itself, and no one is exempt from this basic law of biology—not you, me, or Mr. Olympia.

Muscle growth is a biological process, and therefore is not mediated by the Gregorian calendar or seven-day week. It's not unlike the process of nail or hair growth—both of which are processes that operate biologically—not mathematically—and cannot be rushed. You could go into a hair salon every day and have your hair professionally washed, styled, blow-dried, or cut—but that won't hasten the hair growing process, which, being biological in nature, cannot be affected by anything other than your DNA. Unlike the hair, however, muscle growth beyond normal levels can be influenced by outside factors such as the amount of tension or stress you subject your muscles to during a given training session. After that, it's up to your own metabolism to produce the growth you've stimulated and that will occur according to your own biology.

When I refer to this process, I am of course referring to the recovery of the physical system as a whole. Localized muscle recovery, as touched upon earlier, can take place quite rapidly in certain individuals, but that still doesn't alter the fact that complete systemic recovery always precedes the final growth process. This last block of time is the most important requisite in the muscle growth process apart from the stimulation provided by training. To better illustrate this point, perform a high-intensity leg workout on Monday and then attempt to perform a high-intensity back training session on Tuesday. You won't feel the inclination. The reason is that your whole system was called upon for the purpose of adapta-tion and overcompensation the day before when you performed the leg workout; demands were made upon all of your body's recuperative subsystems in addition to your legs. This is an important point to bear in mind.

Of course, if you train with low intensity, you might well be able to recover sufficiently to train again the next day, but your progress in terms of muscle gains will be nil. Your objective in bodybuilding should never be to see how much exercise you can tolerate, nor how many different exercises you can perform, but rather to see just how little exercise is required to accomplish the desired effect. Once you have determined this, perform the necessary exercise and then get out of the gym.

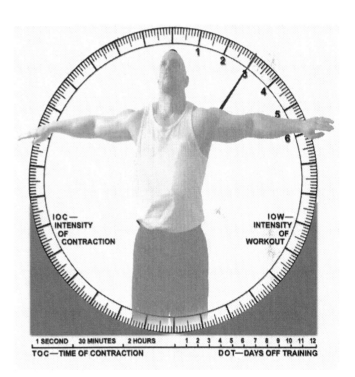

By carefully regulating your IOW and DOT, Max Contraction takes into account all the variables necessary to determine the precise amount of exercise required to strengthen your body.

A bodybuilder looking to build muscle might have to hit the gym only once every two weeks.

Chapter 8

TRAINING FREQUENCY

If, as indicated in the scientific literature presented in Chapter 4, maximum muscle growth can be maintained by single workouts spaced two weeks apart, could it be possible that a bodybuilder would *gain* muscle on such an abbreviated training schedule—provided that the intensity of the workouts is *increased*, rather than merely *sustained* at a maintenance level? Just what is the optimal training frequency?

These are tantalizing questions, to be sure. Moreover, they are questions that most exercise physiologists have never even thought to ask. They have been so busy attempting to determine the *cause* of muscle growth, that is, the training stimulus, that they have for the most part lost sight of another equally important consideration: how and when muscle growth is produced. I believe that these questions would probably have remained unanswered had it not been for the pioneering efforts of a select few exercise physiologists along with Mike Mentzer's philosophical mindset and focused research into recovery ability, which I shared with you in Chapter 7.

To date, I have noted that the vast majority of my training clients are making their best gains by training once every six to seven days. I should think that beginners to Max Contraction Training—and beginners to any other type of bodybuilding training—would be fine training three days per week to start. However, they would have to reduce their training frequency to once a week once they had increased their strength substantially, say, by 30 or more pounds in their leg, back, and chest exercises.

As individual recovery ability varies along a broad continuum, some among us will be able to tolerate Max Contraction Training two or three times a week and grow muscle. Others—the great majority of us—will not be able to tolerate training any more than once a week at a high-intensity pace if we expect to grow. This does not mean that we would grow better on a less intense training program, however, for it is the high-intensity nature of Max Contraction Training that makes it so productive. Any step toward diminishing the intensity of one's workouts will be, as the physiologists have revealed, a step in the wrong direction. While

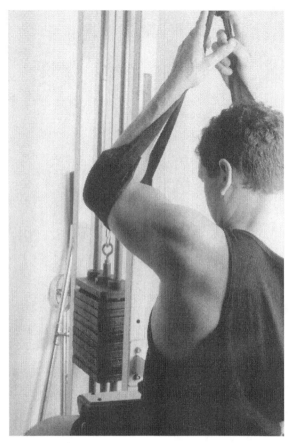

The author's personal training clients are presently making their best gains by training only once every six or seven days.

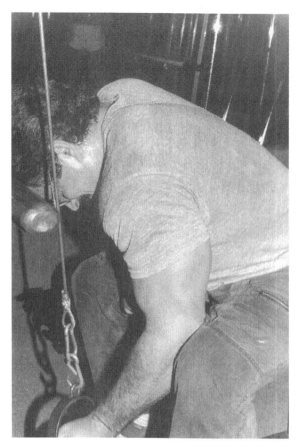

Even though Mike Mentzer was the foremost advocate of intense and infrequent workouts, he would later conclude that he would have made even better progress had he trained even *less* frequently.

each of us can tolerate only so much high intensity in terms of frequency, we all require a high intensity of effort to build muscle.

Those who train three or more days per week are the genetic thoroughbreds of our species and have a tremendous capacity to tolerate the stress of muscle building exercise. This doesn't mean that they necessarily grow muscle faster, but they can endure more frequent sessions and recover from them quicker. Mike Mentzer, for example, switched to a four-day split routine from a three-day-per-week whole-body routine in 1977. He had been doing three to five sets per bodypart (performed far more intensely than most high-intensity theorists today would advocate, as Mike performed forced reps and negatives on each set in each workout) in a whole-body workout that he repeated three times a week.

This had left him too drained to effectively train the smaller bodyparts at the end of his workout and too drained to recover fully in between workouts.

He was probably correct in his reasoning; however, gauging from what we know now regarding training frequency and recovery ability, he could have continued with great success on his three-day-per-week routine (which by all reports seemed to have worked wonders for him, in fact allowing him to win the Mr. America title in 1976) if he had not then been locked in to the notion that he *had* to train three days per week or had to perform three to five sets per bodypart. If he had cut his whole-body workouts down to once a week or even once every two weeks, he probably would have recovered sufficiently in between workouts to continue making progress.

Also, if he had cut his sets back to just one performed (in fact, he came to recommend the one-set protocol to his own training clients some twenty years later), the overtraining or exhaustive effects of the workout would more than likely never have been an issue. I'm not speaking out of school, here, as this was something that Mike himself conceded during his final years: "The one major training mistake I made was that, despite having been the arch-advocate of lesser training, I was still over-training, that is, training too long and too frequently."

To some intermediate and advanced body-builders, particularly those who are accus-tomed to daily training, even the idea of reducing one's training to once every five days or once a week will be met with cries of pro-test. And were it not for the scientific facts supporting it, such a proposition would be considered to be so far off center from how the vast majority of bodybuilders presently think on such matters as to be incompre-hensible to them. But then, being one of the crowd—particularly when the crowd doesn't know what it's doing—shouldn't be something any rational individual would want to be a part of. As Mike Mentzer once said, "If you want to lead the orchestra, you first have to turn your back on the crowd."

Bodybuilding champion Berry DeMey hits the Max Contraction position during a set of triceps pushdowns at Gold's Gym in Venice, California. Each set that you perform in a given workout makes an inroad into your recovery ability, which can quickly lead to overtraining.

HOW MANY SETS SHOULD ONE PERFORM?

The question as to the ideal number of sets an individual should perform in order to stimulate maximum muscle growth has been fraught with controversy for many years. A quick overview of bodybuilding's history reveals that protocols advocating 3 to 5 sets have built muscle, protocols advocating 20 sets have built muscle, and protocols advocating 1 set have built muscle.

In terms of the scientific literature on this matter, Dr. Ralph N. Carpinelli, who teaches the neuromuscular aspects of strength training in the Department of Health, Physical Education and Human Performance at Adelphi University, indicated after an extensive review of the scientific literature (along with his colleague R. M. Otto), "24 out of 25 strength training studies reported that there was no significant difference in the magnitude of muscular strength or hypertrophy between training with single versus multiple sets."[1] Carpinelli concluded, "There is no evidence that a greater volume of exercise will elicit a greater response."[2] Carpinelli further revealed that a study comparing muscle fiber enlarge-

ment in bodybuilders, who typically perform higher sets with shorter rest periods, and competitive weight lifters, who typically perform higher-intensity/lower-volume training with longer rest periods, indicated that no significant difference in the size of muscle fibers in the two groups was found.[3]

In speaking recently with Dr. Richard Winnett, the publisher of the *Master Trainer* newsletter and a man who (not unlike the author) has enjoyed an enduring fascination with the role of science in bodybuilding, I discovered that there was much of value to be found in the studies conducted by physiologist Dr. R. A. Berger. Dr. Berger conducted these studies more than 40 years ago in which various training protocols were tested to determine superiority and maximum efficacy in stimulating size and strength increases.[4] Berger experimented with untrained male students whom he taught at college. After a three-week break-in period, in which the subjects were taught the mechanics of the squat exercise and to allow for neuromuscular or motor learning, several classes (rather than individual students) were randomly assigned to seven experimental groups, each training with a variant of the one-rep max (1-RM) protocol. Each group performed *one repetition* of the squat across the six weeks of this phase of the study. The first group did 66 percent of their 1-RM twice per week; group two did 80 percent of their 1-RM twice per week; group three used 90 percent of their 1-RM twice per week; group four used 100 percent of their 1-RM twice per week; group five used 66 percent of their 1-RM three times per week; group six only trained once per week and did a 1-RM; group seven was a control group and did not train at all. Berger's conclusion was that: ". . . training once weekly with a 1-RM was considered as effective for increasing strength as either training twice weekly with various proportions of the 1-RM, and once weekly with the 1-RM, or three times weekly with the 1-RM."

The interesting bit of news regarding this study is that it revealed, again, that a lot less training was required to stimulate increases in size and strength. The protocol of 1-RM training requires the heaviest weights you can lift through a full range of motion. As a full range of motion actually requires a reduction in the amount of weight your muscles are capable of contracting against (in order to move them through a full or exaggerated range of motion), a "one-rep max" is actually a "one-rep submax." It was the heavier weights that the muscles were made to contract against in the protocol that resulted in a more intense muscular contraction and thus its success. A true Max Contraction is, of course, far more intense, because there is no artificial range of motion requirement to fulfill; it is maximal contraction with weights that are truly maximum in the muscle's strongest position—which is why the stimulation imparted by Max Contraction is that much greater. Nevertheless, Berger's study established that one maximum contraction (even if only near maximum) performed but once a week was all that was required to stimulate a size and strength increase. Additional sets and increased frequency of training yielded no additional benefits.

Require still more scientific validation in support of one-set training for size and strength? In 1997, physiologists K. J. Ostrowski, G. J. Wilson, R. Weatherby, P. W. Murphy, and A. D. Lyttle, in an article titled "The Effect of Weight Training Volume on Hormonal Output and Muscular Size and Function" and published in the *Journal of Strength and Conditioning Research*, conducted a 10-week total body training study in recreational weight lifters in which various set schemes were tested.[5] Their conclusion? That one set per exercise was as effective as two sets and four sets for improving muscular size, strength, and upper-body power.

We must observe that any amount of training over the precise amount required to accomplish the desired effect is, by definition, overtraining. In addition, any type of bodybuilding training, no matter what the duration, depletes the body of its energy and biochemical reserves, which will have to be replenished before the growth process can commence. High-set training in particular leaves the body very depleted, in addition to not stimulating much in the way of growth. (The more sets you perform, the less intense the workout becomes, splitting the training stimulus between strength and endurance.)

As you will recall, physiologists have placed intensity (anaerobic exercise) at the opposite end of the spectrum from endurance (aerobic exercise), with intensity isolated as the sole factor influencing the rate of skeletal muscle growth. Therefore, even if both the low-volume and high-volume approaches stimulated an equal amount of muscle growth, it is doubtful that there would be sufficient resources left over for such growth to occur after a high-volume workout (remember Mentzer's words about the metabolic cost of a single set as well as the study conducted on the marathon runners) to allow such growth to manifest.

It is also interesting to take a closer look at what really transpires during a high-set workout. The "20-sets advocates" typically perform 4 sets of 5 exercises in reaching their target number of 20 sets per bodypart, which

Bodybuilding champion Mike Matarazzo (left) digs in to get the most from each rep of every set he performs.

consist of 3 progressively heavier warm-up sets until they reach their top weight. The 3 warm-up sets are usually stopped at a point well before muscular failure, and only the last (heaviest) set is taken to a point of muscular failure; thus, it might well be argued that only their last working sets are sufficiently intense enough to stimulate muscle growth. If this is true, then one might question the need for so many "warm-up" sets, as once the temperature of the body has been warmed by even one degree, the "warm-up" has already taken place. So if we discount these warm-up sets, we find that even the 20-sets advocates are only performing a total of 3 to 5 working sets for the purpose of stimulating muscle growth.

This is the way that bodybuilding champions Arnold Schwarzenegger, Frank Zane, and Lee Haney trained, as well as scores of other bodybuilders, professional and amateur alike. Mike Mentzer, discarding the superfluous warm-up sets from his own training, also built

most of his mass by training with only 3 to 5 working sets per bodypart. In fact, when Mentzer first started his bodybuilding training at the age of 12, he performed only 3 sets per bodypart, training his whole body three times a week on alternate days. The formula proved so successful that Mentzer went from a bodyweight of 95 pounds with 9-inch arms to a bodyweight of 165 pounds and 15½-inch arms in three years—a gain of 70 pounds of muscle, or an average of 23.33 pounds per year. Moreover, once he decided to become a professional bodybuilder, Mentzer recognized that the energy demands of his training were systemic rather than localized, and he took care to limit the frequency of his training to two to three workouts per week and seldom performed more than two to four sets per bodypart.

By contrast, his chief competitors on the professional bodybuilding scene, Schwarzenegger, Zane, et al., were slavishly working in the gym six days a week, and sometimes twice a

Multi–Mr. Olympia title winner Lee Haney typically performed 12 to 16 sets per bodypart.

Mike Mentzer always made his best gains in muscle mass when he trained more intensely, which resulted in his performing no more than 2 to 5 sets per body-part. Later, he would advise that only 1 or 2 sets per bodypart were necessary to build muscle size.

day. Mentzer's first interview in a hardcore bodybuilding magazine was conducted in 1976 by a longtime bodybuilding scribe named Gene Mozee, who expressed astonishment that Mentzer performed so few sets. Later, Mentzer reflected that even though he had performed only two to four sets per bodypart, he had been overtrained during his competitive days, and then recommended that one set was all that was required to "hit the growth switch" of the muscle building mechanism of the body.

The research that I have conducted with Max Contraction Training supports both Mentzer's eventual conclusion (born of trial and error) and the research of Drs. Muller, Hettinger, Berger, Ostrowski, Wilson, Weatherby, Murphy, Lyttle, and Carpinelli, that is, that one set is all that is required. And if one set can be proven to stimulate muscle growth (which it has), then four or five sets—or even two sets, for that matter—represent gross overkill. Many of those who have applied the principles of Max Contraction to their training have gained upwards of 30 pounds of muscle performing no more than one set per bodypart.

One subject whom I trained personally in 2001 trained only one day a week on the Max Contraction method performing one 1- to 6-second set of 9 different exercises for his whole body. His workouts lasted from 22 to 34 seconds of actual training time for an average monthly total training time of 1 minute 22 seconds to 2 minutes 16 seconds. At the end of five weeks on this system (and only five workouts), the subject's strength had improved 65 percent over his starting levels in all exercises, and, more importantly, his muscle mass had increased by a total of 16 pounds. Considering how difficult it is to gain even 10 pounds of pure muscle in one year's time while training with conventional multi-set methods, you can well appreciate the effectiveness of this one-set protocol (performed in Max Contraction fashion).

Similar results have been recorded on hundreds of other subjects over the 17 years since the system's inception. The lowest muscle mass increase reported was 8 pounds, but that was on a highly advanced bodybuilder who was already very close to the upper limits of his genetic potential. Moreover, he hadn't gained a pound of muscle in over 4 years of training on his previous system of bodybuilding exercise.

With each passing decade, the scientific literature supports the conclusion that one set of one maximal contraction is all that is required to stimulate gains in size and strength and that performing more sets is simply a waste of your time. I know from having trained hundreds of clients that one set is all that is required to stimulate the growth mechanism of the body into motion. Thus, additional sets (which require lighter weights and thus diminish fiber recruitment) have no place in a workout engineered solely for size and strength increases.

With Max Contraction Training, only one set lasting a mere 1 to 6 seconds per bodypart is required to stimulate significant muscle growth.

Chapter 10

THE CASE FOR FULL BODY TRAINING

There is some evidence from exercise physiology that when muscle growth is stimulated, it is stimulated systemically, rather than just locally. When you train your legs with high-intensity exercise, for example, you are, of course, stimulating growth in your legs—but you are also stimulating overall growth in the body as well. Arthur Jones wrote about this phenomenon over thirty years ago and called this the "indirect effect" of exercise—and it is consistent with what we know today to be the case regarding muscle growth.

The "growth switch" within the muscle is hit when you contract your muscles maximally, that is, with the highest possible intensity—when even one more second of contraction is impossible. But this growth switch—which is simply a metaphor, as there is no such mechanism to be found on an anatomy chart or in a textbook on human physiology—is tied into the central nervous system (CNS). The CNS does not just supply a particular muscle group, it supplies the entire body. When the growth switch is hit, the CNS would, according to its

nature, have to respond centrally, or generally, allowing growth to spread out over the whole body with a larger percentage presumably going to the area that it detected required it most (i.e., the muscle group or groups that were trained). As Ray Mentzer once told me:

> You know, bodybuilders do this system, "two days on, one day off" or "three days on, one day off"—I always ask them what that *means*. They have no idea what that means! They say, "Well, you've got to get your other bodyparts in!" Well when it comes to energy cycles, [such as] the Krebs Cycle, your body works as a unit; your body can't distinguish between whether you're working the thighs or the pecs. As far as the hormones that have got to be produced and the energy cycles that have got to be produced, it's all the same. So, you've got to let those things recover. . . . If you don't, you're going backwards; you're spinning your wheels. So it should be the other way round; it shouldn't be "three days

on/one day off," it should be "one day on/two or three days off"—just the opposite!

This being the case, why not train your body as the one system that it is? You don't rest individual bodyparts on separate days; you don't nourish individual bodyparts on separate days. So why would you train individual bodyparts on separate days? The body works as a unit; if you don't believe this, try to perform a set of heavy barbell curls for your biceps after you've pulled an abdominal or lumbar muscle. The body is a completely integrated—not isolated—biological system that burns calories, processes nutrients and delivers them to the energy systems, and releases the energy to working muscles. All of its many facets work together in concert when it comes to lifting weights and stimulating muscle to grow.

As the body works as a unit, it makes sense to take this into account when you train it— and to train the whole body, every time you train. When you run, for example, it isn't just your calves that are involved; it's your heart, your lungs, your kidneys, your bloodstream, and many additional muscle groups. When you train your pecs with the bench press, for example, your glutes and legs are involved statically for stabilization, as are your lats and abs. Of course, your arms and shoulders also contribute to the performance of this renowned "chest" exercise.

Arthur Jones once trained Ray Mentzer on such a whole-body routine, in which Jones wisely reduced the sets performed per exercise

Regarding the energy cycles, your body works as a unit. It can't differentiate between training with your chest or your thighs—or training with free weights or exercise machines. It concerns itself solely with producing sufficient energy to supply the demand your muscles have made.

to one, the sets per bodypart to one or two (maximum), and the total sets of the whole-body workout to eight. Moreover, he had Mentzer back off on the frequency of his whole-body workouts to only twice a week. Mentzer's routine consisted of the following exercises:

1. Nautilus Duo Squat
2. Nautilus Lower Back
3. Chin-up
4. Dip
5. Nautilus Pullover
6. Pulldown
7. Nautilus Arm Cross (Pec Deck)
8. Decline Press

The results of Mentzer's twice-per-week workouts were reported by Ellington Darden in *The Nautilus Advanced Bodybuilding Book*:

Ray Mentzer, on his first visit to Nautilus Sports/Medical Industries, weighed 253 pounds. He was in fair condition, with an upper arm measuring 19¼ inches. During his brief visit, he requested a supervised workout from Arthur Jones. The date was January 5, 1983. . . . Ray flew back to California, continued his workout as he had been instructed to do, and returned to Florida on February 21, 1983. He looked—well, incredible. He had gained 7 pounds, but he was far leaner than the last time we had seen him. . . . Arthur studied him carefully, "You stick with that program?" . . . Ray nodded. "Like clockwork. Just like you told me," he said. "Twice a week every week for six weeks." His face brightened. "You know what? I've had to alter my pants twice. The thighs had to be made larger and the waist smaller. I can hardly believe it." Jones showed only a poker face. . . . Ray rolled up his sleeve and contracted his biceps. Arthur made the measurements, and we saw the first indication of pleasure. "Now, pay attention," he commanded Ray and the others. "This is what serious, no-nonsense training can produce. It's 20⅛ inches. That's ⅜ inch more than it was previously."[1]

Ray Mentzer performed 1 set to failure of 8 exercises—a whole-body workout repeated only twice a week for six weeks—and he put on 7 pounds of muscle, and his arm grew to a massive 20⅛ inches! This is an absolutely mind-boggling accomplishment—given that Ray was already a massive (253 pounds worth!) and highly advanced bodybuilder who was putting on *new* muscle mass.

In fact, this accomplishment was so mind-boggling, I recall taking Ray's older brother Mike aside during a visit in 1986 and asking him whether or not the report in Darden's book was true. Mike replied:

Yes. As a matter of fact, it was astonishing to me. Ray, when he won the Mr. America contest at about a bodyweight of 230 pounds, was enormous. But in subsequent years, especially the last two years, the second year of which included DeLand, Florida [where Nautilus Sports/Medicine Industries was located], Ray had reduced his training to two days a week, sometimes as low as 10 sets a workout for his entire body and he was enormous! He was up to almost 260 pounds in bodyweight, not ripped but very hard; he had abs, serratus, and his arm at that point was the biggest ever measured by Arthur Jones—over 20 inches cold, and measured accurately. No benefit of the doubt—it was a tight tape; it was not a reduced or shrunken tape, it was not flip-flopped or tossed to an oblique angle. It was a very, very solid measurement. The only other legitimate 20-inch arm that Arthur has measured—and he has measured most of the top bodybuilders, including Arnold and Sergio—was Sergio Oliva's. Arnold's was never 20 inches cold, neither was Casey Viator's. . . . To the best of my knowledge . . . Ray still trains two days a week, and he's enormous. At one point last year, at about a bodyweight of 270 pounds, he squatted almost 900 pounds and 800 pounds for 4 reps!

Both Mike and Ray Mentzer experienced tremendous success with whole-body routines infrequently performed, Mike winning the

Mr. America title and Ray building an absolutely staggering amount of muscle mass and strength. But whole-body workouts don't work only for the Mentzer brothers; most bodybuilders started their training careers on a whole-body workout schedule. Arnold Schwarzenegger, Larry Scott, and John Grimek (to name some of the better-known champions) all began their muscle building programs utilizing a whole-body workout performed three times per week. Other champions such as Steve Reeves stayed with a whole-body workout performed three days per week for their entire careers.

Three-days-per-week training is an arbitrary frequency, admittedly, but given that newcomers to bodybuilding are weak, that is, they start out training at a submaximal capacity, they do not expend sufficient energy to create a condition of overtraining on a three-day-per-week program. It is only months later, as they begin to raise the intensity of their workouts with heavier weights and greater effort, that overtraining becomes a real concern. It is also at this point that they should back off on the frequency of their training to once a week.

Another professional bodybuilder who made dramatic gains while training on a whole-body workout program performed only three times per week was multiple Mr. Universe winner Boyer Coe, who happened to be in Florida with the Mentzers when Ray was performing those now legendary workouts. Coe decided to train in a similar fashion and had similarly impressive results. Mike Mentzer often supervised Coe's workouts during this period, so his recollection of Coe's progress while on the 1-set, whole-body workout is particularly meaningful and accurate in relation to the potency of this training protocol. Here is what Mike told me:

> Back in 1983, Boyer Coe and I worked for Arthur Jones at Nautilus and, during the six months that I was there, Boyer did do 1 set per bodypart, three days a week, and his daily average workout lasted 17 minutes. When I arrived in Florida to work for

Steve Reeves trained his entire career on a whole-body routine performed only three days per week.

> Arthur Jones and I saw Boyer Coe, I was surprised because he'd uncharacteristically let himself get out of condition. He had very little muscle mass in the upper body and very little definition. Six months later, following this program religiously, he transformed himself and became very large and muscular again—without steroids, by the way. So, perhaps you can't make a general statement and say that it's going to work for everybody as it did for Boyer, but I think that the fact that an "advanced" bodybuilder was able to make that kind of improvement on a 1 set per bodypart program three times per week at least *suggests* that there is some merit to it.

Remember, of course, that bodybuilding champions such as Steve Reeves, Boyer Coe, and the Mentzer brothers were not only "advanced" bodybuilders but also possessed an abundance of genetic advantages. Consequently, they were all capable of tolerating more frequent bouts of exercise without suffering the ill effects of overtraining. With these points in mind, a three-times-per-week training protocol would be fine for beginners (people with no bodybuilding training), but probably too much for intermediates and advanced trainees.

After one month on the Max Contraction method, the beginning bodybuilder should reduce his training frequency from three workouts per week to once every five days (say, on Mondays and Saturdays), and when he has increased his strength again, he should cut back the frequency of his workouts to once every seven days. As you grow stronger, you will have to back off the frequency again in order to compensate for the increased expenditure of effort and to allow time for manifestation of the growth you have stimulated. Again, the higher the intensity, the briefer and more infrequent the workouts must be.

Max Contraction Training advocates a whole-body workout (even when specializing on particular bodyparts), which allows the trainee to take advantage of the indirect effect cited earlier. It specifically advocates only one set per muscle group, which allows the muscles to be worked at the highest possible intensity (and makes for the briefest and most productive muscle building workouts), and it spaces the workouts sufficiently apart to allow for full recovery and growth to take place. Eventually, when the trainee is ready to switch over to a maintenance routine, his workouts will be reduced to one whole-body routine lasting only

10 seconds that is performed only once every two to three weeks. There is no other training method that can deliver the size and strength gains that Max Contraction Training does, particularly with such a minimal time investment.

Max Contraction Training advocates a whole-body workout—even when specializing on particular bodyparts such as the legs.

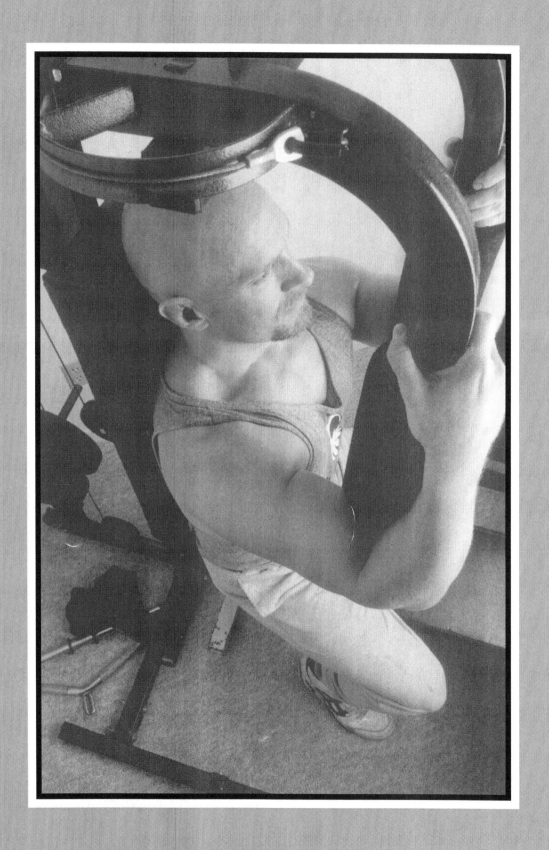

Part IV

A NEW APPLICATION

Chapter 11

AN OVERVIEW OF MAX CONTRACTION TRAINING

When using Max Contraction Training, you must throw out all preconceived notions of training methodology. You will no longer be using repetitions by which to gauge your progress; from now on you will be counting the time of contraction (TOC). You will no longer be looking for a variety of exercises to tax the various aspects of a muscle; instead you will be using only one exercise per bodypart. Yes, this training system is different from any other method you might have seen before, but don't be alarmed by its novelty. Ever since its conception (way back in that Greek history class in 1984), I have refined its application, and through discussions with bodybuilding champions and trailblazers, in addition to testing and experimenting with hundreds of clients, the system has evolved to the point where it has put more muscle on more trainees than any other training system I've encountered. Given the fact that I've been in this business for over 20 years, that's saying something.

THE THEORY

The Max Contraction system of bodybuilding exercise can be grasped by anyone successfully if they comprehend the basic principles underlying it. It is based upon empirically validated data that has been amassed over the past 120 years, as well as common sense (as opposed to commercial interests). What has worked in the physiology labs can be repeated with equal, if not better, success with you—if you make a diligent application of these principles. If you do, you will make muscular progress in the space of one month that would have otherwise have taken you several years to achieve. It is essential when embarking upon a system such as Max Contraction to understand some of the basic physiological principles such as the "all or none" principle of muscle fiber contraction and the nature of muscle fiber recruitment in order to reap the full benefits of this training method.

"ALL OR NONE"

In his textbook, *The Physiology of Exercise*, Herbert A. DeVries of the University of Southern California, states:

> If a muscle fiber (or motor unit) is stimulated by a single impulse at or above threshold value, it responds by a contraction, or twitch, that is maximal for any given set of conditions of nutrition, temperature, etc. In other words, stimulation by impulses much larger than threshold value will result in no increase in either the shortening or the force of contraction. The muscle fiber contracts maximally, or it does not contract at all, and this fact is referred to as the *all-or-none* law of muscle contraction.[1]

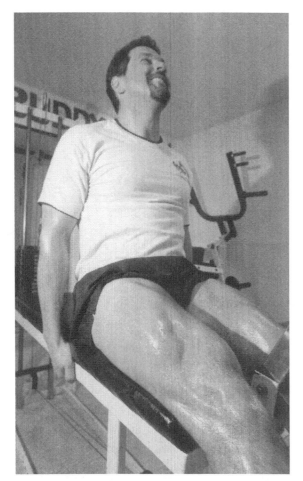

Muscle fiber contracts maximally, or it does not contract at all. This is referred to as the "all-or-none" law of muscle contraction.

Professor DeVries goes on to say, "This law applies to the motor unit, since all its component fibers are innervated by the same nerve fiber and impulse—it does not, of course, apply to whole muscles." This principle, or physiologic law, refers to the fact that when a given muscle fiber is stimulated to contract, it will contract maximally while the rest of its fibers do not contract at all—this as opposed to an entire muscle's fibers contracting all at once but to a lesser degree.

THE PROBLEM WITH REPETITIONS

In conventional training methods, one performs repetitions, or a series of contractions. A typical set of repetitions sees one initiate a given movement in a position of literally zero resistance. Then, as the weight is moved, the muscle shortens or contracts until it finally ascends to the position of full or maximal contraction. In this final position the greatest number of muscle fibers are brought into play and stimulated to grow bigger and stronger. And yet with conventional training protocols, this position of Max Contraction is seldom, if ever, emphasized, with the result that maximal growth stimulation is seldom, if ever, achieved.

A perfect example of this is the leg extension exercise performed in the conventional manner (i.e., up and down). Looked at physiologically, this exercise will see the trainee initiate the movement using only the barest amount of muscle fibers required to do the job. At the halfway point, a few more muscle fibers will have been called into play and then, at the position of full muscular contraction or where the legs are fully extended, as many fibers as can possibly be recruited will be activated to keep the resistance in this fully contracted position. However, long before the fibers have been stressed maximally, the resistance is typically lowered (often dropped), giving the momentarily stressed quadriceps muscles a chance to disengage (and recover to a certain extent), which is the very opposite effect of what you should be trying to accomplish.

This means, in effect, that in a given 10-rep set which lasts about 60 seconds, maximum muscular involvement takes place for a total of only 10 seconds—only 1 second after every 5. So out of a possible 60 seconds' worth of maximum muscle stimulation, the trainee is obtaining only $\frac{1}{10}$ of the results he is capable of deriving from the movement. Viewed in this light, it becomes painfully obvious that the trainee is wasting the other $\frac{9}{10}$ of the time he's been employing on the exercise. Conversely, when a given muscle group is brought into a fully contracted position and made to contract maximally against a heavy resistance for a full 60 seconds, the maximum amount of muscle fibers that can be activated to assist in the task will be called into play and thoroughly stimulated until they are incapable of supporting the full contraction. As soon as the trainee can no longer hold the contraction, he will have effectively exhausted all of the muscle fibers involved in that contraction, that is, all of them.

The 60-second time frame indicated is purely for purposes of illustrating the difference in efficiency between conventional (or

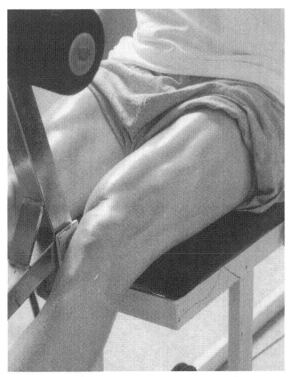

Max Contraction takes the muscle into a position of full contraction and keeps it there throughout the duration of the set, thereby stimulating greater fiber recruitment.

full-range) training protocols and Max Contraction—or $\frac{1}{10}$ efficiency versus $\frac{10}{10}$, or 100 percent, efficiency. As we've seen, research has indicated that only 1 to 6 seconds of maximal intensity stimulation is necessary—*if* the muscle is in the fully contracted position. Training closer to one minute requires activating the body's aerobic system to some degree, thus compromising the pure anaerobic element, which is the element most responsible for size and strength gains. As I've discussed this in great detail elsewhere in the book, I will not belabor the point here, except to say that since the system's inception, various contraction times and set protocols have been tested: without question, the most productive time frame for the vast majority of bodybuilders has been a maximum contraction lasting between 1 and 6 seconds and a set protocol of one set per bodypart.

In contrast to the conventional, full-range protocol, with Max Contraction a given muscle group is made to spend the entire duration of a set in the fully contracted position, in which all of the fibers that can be activated are activated, and subsequently fatigued, until the resistance can no longer be supported and the contraction must be released. Remember that with Max Contraction Training you are performing your set in the position of *full* muscular contraction and against the heaviest load your muscles are capable of contracting maximally against, thereby subjecting your muscles to 100 percent of the stimulation they are capable of receiving. It is this methodology that makes this system so effective and that separates it from all other training systems.

Max Contraction Training doesn't rely on such arbitrary and subjective indices as "pump" or "feel"; it utilizes maximum muscular contraction against quantifiable resistance, which allows one to objectively gauge the productivity of one's workouts. And as the resistance can be varied, the system allows for far more growth-inducing methods to be employed. With advanced trainees, the method of "strip-offs," or "drop sets," can be employed. For example, in exercises such as the close-grip pulldown or barbell wrist curls, when it becomes impossible for the muscles in

The technique of "strip-offs" can be employed on Max Contraction exercises such as barbell wrist curls, allowing the trainee to hit deeper and deeper layers of muscle fibers.

your upper back or forearms (respectively) to sustain the position of Max Contraction, the resistance can be effectively "stripped-off." This will enable you to resume a second Max Contraction hold in the fully contracted position for an additional bout of 1 to 6 seconds until the contraction can again no longer be sustained, thereby stimulating the fibers to an even greater degree, resulting in even greater growth stimulation. This can be carried on until contraction against even a very light weight becomes impossible, thereby stimulating every available muscle fiber and drilling your reserves for all their worth. (I wouldn't recommend this technique to beginners or intermediates; it is best suited for specialization training or for very advanced trainees who will be working out only once every two to three weeks. This type of training would be so intense that you would require a minimum of

two weeks' rest to allow for full systemic recovery to take place and for growth to occur.)

MAX CONTRACTION VERSUS FULL-RANGE TRAINING

Muscle is an amazingly simple tissue. Quite simply, muscle tissue does one of two things: it contracts (shortens) or relaxes (extends). If the muscle is made to contract against progressively heavier resistance, it will grow bigger and stronger. If it is made to contract against the same resistance, it stays the same. If it is not made to contract at all, it gets smaller and weaker. We've seen that muscle contracts by getting shorter and that only when all its fibers have contracted maximally (when the muscle is in its shortest position) can all of its fibers be stimulated. We've also seen that repetitions (either concentric or eccentric) simply move the muscle fibers into (concentric) or out of (eccentric) a position of full muscular contraction. Therefore, any training protocol that involves movement takes the muscle fibers out of a position of full muscular contraction and therefore in the wrong direction, by virtue of the fact that it is diminishing muscle fiber involvement. By contrast, the most productive position in a muscle's given range of motion is the Max Contraction position; everything else is less than maximal by definition and therefore less efficient for stimulating maximum muscle growth.

The main problem with full-range or conventional training methodologies is that they require you to train with submaximal weights in order to be able to lift them through a full range of motion. So even when you enter a position of full contraction (albeit intermittently) throughout the course of a set, the weight is too light to stimulate all of the fibers into growth. How can this be construed as an efficient way to train for the purpose of stimulating maximum muscle growth? Nowhere has the scientific literature ever indicated that a full range of motion is the sine qua non of maximum muscle growth stimulation.

Conventional full-range training restricts you to using lighter weights than your muscles are capable of contracting maximally against, thereby reducing growth stimulation.

Maximum contraction of a given muscle has, by contrast, been determined to be the best way to stimulate maximum size and strength increases. All the academics aside, it all boils down simply to very, very hard work. And the harder the work you do, the less work you are capable of doing. It's not even a debatable point. Intensity and duration are inversely related: if you train hard, you can't train long, and it takes hard training to build big muscles.

MAX CONTRACTION VERSUS NEGATIVE-ONLY TRAINING

Exercises performed in a negative-only fashion, which have been highly touted by researchers such as Arthur Jones, share common ground with Max Contraction. The sole benefit to negative-only training is that heavier weights are employed in their execution (usually about 40 percent more than the trainee would normally lift positively or concentrically) and that

Negative-only training requires you to lower under control a resistance that is typically 40 percent heavier than you would be able to lift in a regular concentric contraction.

the negative repetition is originated in a position of full muscular contraction (i.e., a Max Contraction) and held there for at least one second prior to the trainee making a concentrated effort to lower it slowly to a fully stretched position. As we've learned that maximum size and strength can be stimulated with as little as a 1-second maximal contraction performed in the muscle's fully contracted position, I would venture to say that all of the benefit derived from eccentric or negative training occurs in the first 1 second of contraction—when the muscle is in the fully contracted position and contracting against a heavier load than would normally be employed in a conventional (i.e., positive or full-range) set. Everything else is simply a diminishing of fiber involvement as the muscle moves out of full muscular contraction and into full extension. Considering these points, the Max Contraction position is the most productive protocol the trainee can employ.

TIME

With Max Contraction Training your sets should be of the briefest possible duration. This does not mean that you arbitrarily terminate a set at 1 to 6 seconds, but that the set must terminate itself at this point. In other words, despite your greatest efforts, you will not be able to sustain the contraction any longer than 1 second (briefest) to 6 seconds (longest)—and you should be doing everything in your power to increase the resistance to the point that 1 second is all you can endure. Another plus from this training protocol is motivation; since the set is so brief in duration, it is relatively easy to psyche yourself up for it and there is no need to hold back for additional sets or additional repetitions.

WHY MAX CONTRACTION IS SO EFFECTIVE

The reason for the dramatic success of Max Contraction Training is simple: any time movement is involved in a bodybuilding exercise, you're simply doing one thing—not stimulating maximum muscle growth. Whenever you move your muscles out of or toward a position of full contraction, you are (obviously) not *in* a position of full muscular contraction, which is the only position in a muscle's range of motion in which maximum fiber stimulation can take place. Therefore, anything involving either positive or negative movement, that is, toward or away from this one position, has diminishing levels of intensity. In a Max Contraction exercise, all of a given muscle group's fibers are under a stress/intensity of the highest possible order from the moment the contraction (the effective "set" in this system) is initiated until its completion 1 to 6 seconds later.

CASE STUDIES

One of the more widely read articles published on a preliminary version of this training system (which advocated longer hold times) was penned by renowned bodybuilding science writer and research author James E. Wright, Ph.D., in a 1992 edition of *Muscle & Fitness* magazine:

> The Static Contraction System [the original name of the system] was developed by Canadian bodybuilder/journalist John Little, based on 15 years of personal research on training and muscle growth. Most of the fundamentals of the system were based upon empirically validated data, going back over 100 years in some instances, as well as on common sense. Little's feelings were that what has worked in physiology labs can be repeated with equal if not better success if people apply themselves diligently. His intent was to provide a system in which each set could be taken to 100 percent of your momentary ability—what Mr. Universe Mike Mentzer refers to as the "break-over" point. That point in a set below which growth is impossible but above which it is stimulated. Once you transcend this break-over point in terms of momentary effort generated, your results will increase geometrically.

> Only one set of one exercise per bodypart is used. . . . My own experiences using this program for a month were amazing.[2]

I recently trained a young man named Irwin Heshka. Irwin is naturally big; he has good genetics, strong bone structure, and so on. For the past several years, Irwin had been training conventionally, that is, three to four days per week, 10 to 12 sets per bodypart, with every exercise performed through a full range of motion. I put him on the Max Contraction method, employing squats as the sole leg exercise (I have since discarded this exercise in favor of leg extensions, as squats are too hard on the spine when the weights mount up). In a little over a month and a half—training only once a week for a total of six workouts—Irwin's squat went from three reps full-range with 315 pounds to 1,005 pounds for a 10-second Maximum Contraction.

You read that correctly—his muscles were able to lift an additional 690 pounds after only six workouts in which his average leg training workout lasted between 1 and 10 seconds for 36 seconds of total training time for his legs! And for those of you who were wondering what effect training without motion has on one's full-range strength, after doing his 1,005-pound squat, Irwin decided to try his old squatting weight for full-range repetitions and banged off 10 reps—a new personal record—after not having trained full-range in a month and a half!

Another trainee named Joe Ostertag, who worked out with Irwin occasionally, became interested in the protocol and asked me to put him through a Max Contraction workout. Joe was initially very skeptical about getting stronger from performing a mere 1-second contraction. All the scientific research notwithstanding, he just could not wrap his mind around the brevity of the workout. He had been training previously on a four-day-per-week program, performing up to 16 sets per bodypart. To increase his comfort level intellectually and emotionally with the system, as well as to prepare his muscles for the high-intensity stress of Max Contraction training, I broke him into the system gradually.

Irwin Heshka pulls 1,005 pounds off the power rack for a Max Contraction shrug. He later went on to shrug 1,035 pounds!

Over a period of eight weeks, I gradually reduced his workouts to once a week, his sets per bodypart to one, and his hold times from 60 seconds down to 1 second. After his first 1-second hold—on a plate-loading Pec Deck machine—he hit failure with an impressive 630 poundage after 1 second. He looked at me as if to say, "Did I do enough?" He felt every fiber in his chest contract maximally, and his chest muscles were pumped—but was it really enough to stimulate an increase in strength? I told him to take a week off (as he had been accustomed to by this point) and that we would have our answer in seven days.

One week later he came back. When it came time to do the Pec Deck exercise, we loaded up the 630 pounds again. He could now sustain the maximum contraction for 7 seconds! He was able to sustain the contraction seven times longer as a result of 1 second's worth of stimulation performed seven days before. The next week we increased the weight to 700 pounds—which he then proceeded to sustain in the fully contracted position for 2 seconds! The next week, that weight went up to 750 pounds for 1 second. Two weeks later, he passed the 1,000-pound mark—with one arm! His shrug weight showed a similar improvement, going in one week from a respectable

535 pounds for a 4-second Max Contraction set to 625 pounds for 1 second.

Similarly impressive results were obtained by Joe's workout partner on the program, Irwin Heshka (whose squat results I cited previously). He went from a 605-pound shrug for 6 seconds on October 18, 2001, to 625 pounds for 6 seconds on October 23 to 715 pounds for 6 seconds on October 28 to 825 pounds for 5 seconds on November 11 to 1,005 pounds for 4 seconds on November 25 to an absolutely staggering 1,035 pounds for 2 seconds on December 2!

I actually had a hard time getting Irwin down to just a mere 1-second hold time, because his substantial jumps in weight saw an attendant increase in his holding times. All of this progress was the result of the barest amount of training stimulation possible—in most instances 2 to 4 seconds of direct stimulation. In fact, the average total workout time for Joe and Irwin (for a whole-body workout!) was 25 seconds and 37 seconds, respectively, per workout. These gains are not that uncommon when one engineers one's workouts specifically for size and strength increases.

"All right," you ask, "how does one engineer his workouts specifically for size and strength increases?" A good question. And one I intend to address fully in the next chapter.

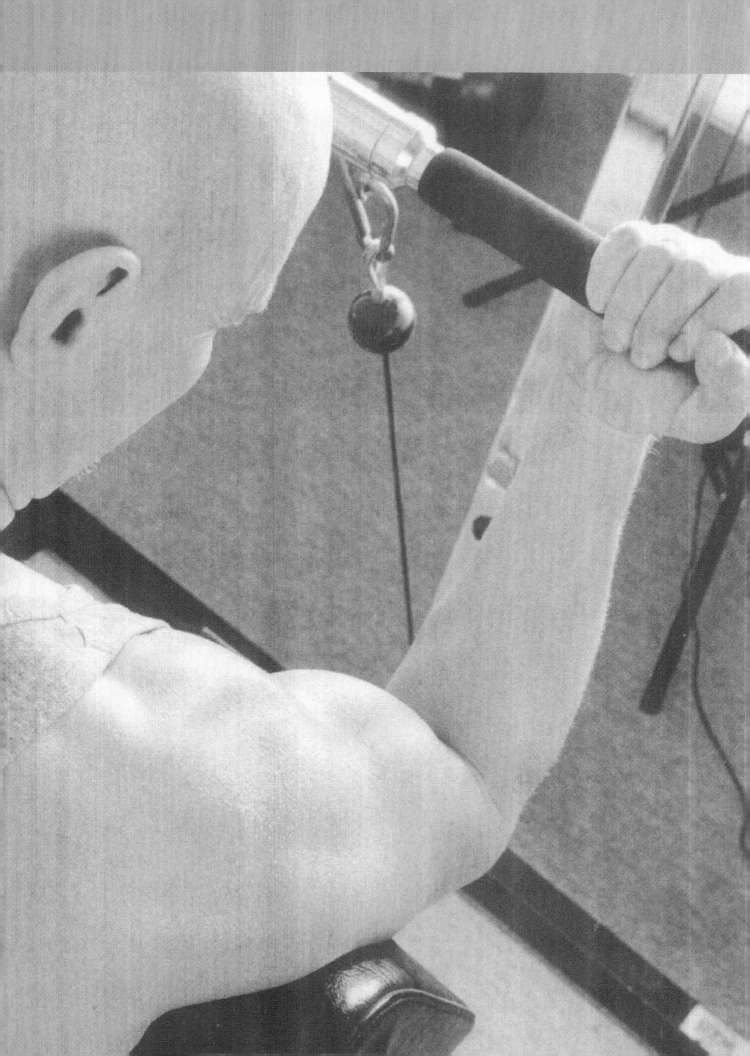

Chapter 12

THE IDEAL WORKOUT PROGRAM

Now that you have a handle on the theoretical principles and history of Max Contraction Training, there's still one more thing you need to know about the system in order to reap the greatest possible results from your efforts in the gym: proper exercise selection.

It's vitally important to select exercises that allow you to activate the maximum number of a given muscle's fibers while in the fully contracted position. Certain exercises performed with conventional equipment don't incorporate the proper physics to provide maximum resistance in the fully contracted position. I'm thinking here of movements such as squats, standing barbell curls, and most types of pressing movements wherein the resistance falls off once you're past the halfway point of the movement.

It is this lack of direct resistance in the fully contracted position that makes these exercises inefficient for Max Contraction Training. Exercises must be selected that enable a targeted muscle group to be moved into a position of full muscular contraction against resistance and held there for 1 to 6 seconds. Experience has revealed the following exercises to be perfect for

Max Contraction Training, as they fulfill the criteria just described and, thus, allow for maximum muscle growth stimulation:

Exercise	Muscle Group
1. Leg Extensions	Quadriceps
2. Leg Curls	Hamstrings
3. Standing Calf Raises	Gastrocnemius
4. Max Straps Pulldowns	Latissimus Dorsi
5. Shrugs	Trapezius
6. Pec Deck	Pectorals
7. Lateral Raises— Side and Rear	Deltoids
8. Bent-Over Laterals	Rear Deltoids
9. Max Straps Kickbacks	Triceps
10. Palms-Under, Close-Grip Chins or Steep-Angle Preacher Curls	Biceps
11. Max Straps Crunches	Abdominals

These exercises place a high-intensity training stress on the targeted muscle groups from the beginning to the end of the set and are, therefore, the most productive exercises one can perform. Remember, there are no repetitions involved in this program; you will be determining your progress in terms of seconds. In a conventional set of 10 repetitions, for example, the intensity of such a set would vary dramatically, starting off very low and ending moderately high, resulting in an inconsistent training stimulus to the muscles. By contrast, in Max Contraction Training the intensity is always of the highest order throughout, thus allowing for greater growth stimulation to actually take place.

THE ROUTINE EXPLAINED

1. Leg Extensions

Emphasis: Quadriceps

Sit on a leg extension machine and place your feet behind the roller pads so that your knees are snug against the seat. Keeping your head and shoulders straight, slowly straighten both legs until you reach the fully contracted position. Hold for 1 to 6 seconds, until you can no longer contract against the weight.

2. Leg Curls

Emphasis: Hamstrings

Lie facedown on the leg-curl machine and place your feet under the roller pads with your knees just over the edge of the bench. Slowly curl your lower legs up until they are almost touching your buttocks. Hold this maximum contraction for 1 to 6 seconds.

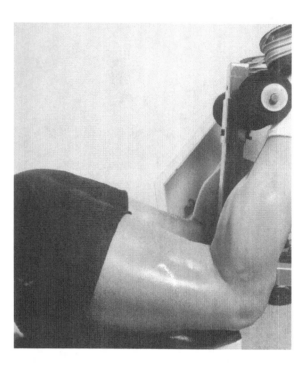

3. Standing Calf Raises

Emphasis: Gastrocnemius (calves)

Place your shoulders under the pads on a standing calf-raise machine. With the balls of your feet firmly on the platform, slowly rise on your toes until your calves are in a fully contracted position. Sustain the contraction for 1 to 6 seconds.

4. Max Straps Pulldowns

Emphasis: Lower lats, upper back, chest, upper abdominals (1 set)

Position yourself in a lat pulldown machine and insert your arms through the Max Straps so that the bottom padded part of the strap is

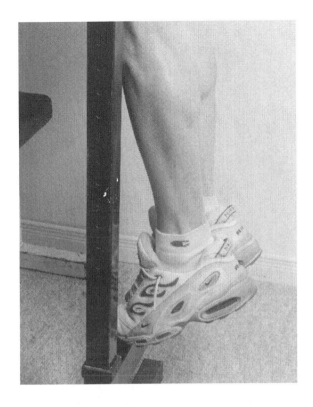

over the end of your upper arm (nearest the elbow joint) and your hands are resting against the side straps. Don't close your hands on the straps, as this will unnecessarily involve and fatigue the forearm muscles and (to a lesser extent) the biceps. Using only the strength of your latissimus dorsi muscles, draw your elbows down and back until they are just to the sides of your lower ribs. Sustain this full contraction for 1 to 6 seconds.

5. Shrugs

Emphasis: Trapezius, shoulders, forearms

This exercise is best performed on the bench press station on a Universal Gym machine, as the handles are situated at approximately midthigh, negating the need for you to lift a heavy barbell up to your waist. If you do not have access to a Universal Gym machine or a Hammer Strength Shrug machine (which allows you to sit or stand for the exercise and similarly does not require you to deadlift the resistance to the starting position), use a barbell in a power rack and set the pins that will be supporting the barbell at midthigh height. Grasping hold of either the handles of the appropriate machine or the barbell, stand up straight—with your back flat—and make sure to keep your arms fully extended. Now, using only the strength of your trapezius muscles, shrug your shoulders upward. Hold this fully contracted position for 1 to 6 seconds.

6. Pec Deck

Emphasis: Pectorals

Adjust the height of the seat so that when you sit down and place your upper arms on the pads they are more or less parallel to the floor. With your arms on the pads attached to the lever arms, slowly—with the strength of your pec muscles alone—draw your elbows together in front of your torso. When you've reached the fully contracted position, hold it for 1 to 6 seconds, or until you can't keep your elbows together.

7. Lateral Raises—Side and Rear

Emphasis: Deltoids

This exercise can likewise be performed on either a shoulder raise machine or with free weights. If you use free weights, use dumbbells. Bend over and pick up a pair of dumbbells and stand up straight. Slowly raise the dumbbells out to the sides (keeping a slight bend in your

elbows to relieve pressure on your elbow joint), until the dumbbells are perfectly parallel to the ground. Hold this position for 1 to 6 seconds.

8. Bent-Over Laterals

Emphasis: Rear deltoids

Taking hold of a pair of dumbbells, bend forward at the waist until your torso is at a 90-degree angle to your legs. Slowly raise the dumbbells into a position slightly above and behind your shoulders. Sustain this full contraction for 1 to 6 seconds.

9. Max Straps Kickbacks

Emphasis: Triceps

With the ring of the Max Straps attached to the hook at the end of a floor pulley, bend over at the waist so that your torso is at a 90-degree angle to your legs. Place your hands through the Max Straps so that the pads are across your wrists. Maintaining the bent-over position, draw your arms behind you until they are as far behind your torso as you can move them and your arms are fully locked out. Sustain this maximum contraction for 1 to 6 seconds.

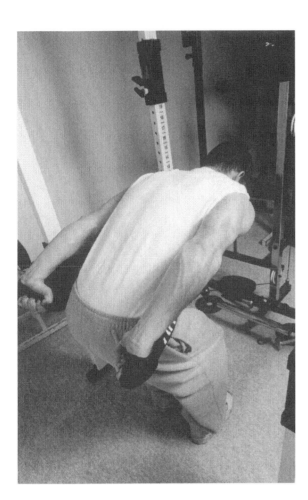

10. Palms-Under, Close-Grip Chins or Steep-Angle Preacher Curls

Emphasis: Biceps

If you choose to perform palms-under, close-grip chins, begin by standing on a chair and placing your hands on the chinning bar with an underhand palms-up grip. Assume a position where your eyes are level with the bar and your biceps are fully contracted. Now, easily, step off the chair until your biceps contract fully, thus holding you up. Hold for between 1 and 6 seconds, depending on your personal bodyweight and existing strength levels. Then slowly lower your body down to the fully extended position.

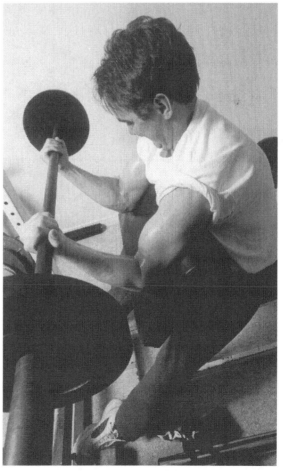

To perform the steep-angle preacher curls, pick up a barbell or have a training partner hand you the bar once you've placed your arms over the top of a 90-degree angled preacher bench. Contract your biceps maximally and sustain this contraction from 1 to 6 seconds.

11. Max Straps Crunches

Emphasis: Abdominals

Attach the Max Straps to an overhead pulley (ideally on a lat pulldown machine that has a seat and knee pad). Sit down on the seat and place your arms through the Max Straps so that the pads are over the bends in your elbows. Lower your elbows down to a point and out to the sides so that the base of the Max Straps is touching the back of your neck. Now slowly bend your torso over while drawing your elbows downward until your elbows are almost touching your knees. Once you've hit the fully contracted position, sustain it for 1 to 6 seconds.

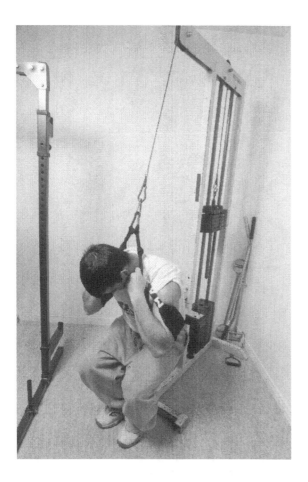

Points to Keep in Mind

• *Longer hold times for beginners.* If you are a beginner to bodybuilding training or, indeed, if you are an experienced trainee who is a beginner to Max Contraction Training, you will be well served if, during your first four to six workouts, you hold each contraction for 60 seconds. The longer hold time will help to develop greater neuromuscular efficiency and to better acclimate you to the new training protocol. After your first four to six workouts, however, you should increase the intensity by increasing the resistance and reducing your time of contraction (TOC) to 1 to 6 seconds.

• *Keep a training logbook.* Learning and advancement are almost always reached through trial and error. By making a trial and missing the mark and then noting the error, you can make proper adjustments and move on toward the goal. A training logbook will prove invaluable in this regard. Keeping a record of every proper turn (as well as every mistake—such as training too frequently) can help you avoid the pitfalls that will slow you down. A logbook serves as a record of workouts and should include daily caloric intake (including the types of foods), the weights used in each exercises, the TOC of each exercise, and the total weight lifted (TWL), that is, the total weight, taken as an aggregate, of all the exercises you performed in a given workout. These figures (particularly the TWL) will allow you to know at a glance whether or not you are progressing in your efforts, plateauing, or even regressing—sure indices of progress, inadequate recovery, and overtraining, respectively. By also recording your daily food consumption, you can calculate your nutritional requirements for future weight gain and loss as well as observe the effects of certain diets on moods, training drive, and progress. Experimenting with different weights, contraction times, and specialization routines and charting your progress can yield invaluable training data. Eventually you'll have enough information in your journal to make precise determinations.

• *Exercise caution.* If you do not have a training partner, you must use extreme caution when commencing any exercise using Max

Contraction. For example, lift the resistance slowly (to avoid damaging any ligaments or muscle tissue) into the position of full muscular contraction, just as you would if you were performing a regular set. However, instead of lowering the resistance, you will hold this fully contracted position for 1 to 6 seconds. If you can hold the resistance longer than 6 seconds, it's too light to be maximally effective and you should heavy it up by 5 percent or so for your next workout. If you can't hold the resistance for 1 full second, then it's too heavy and you should reduce the resistance by 5 percent until you can contract the muscle against the resistance for 1 full second.

• *Training partners.* If you do train with a partner or two who can lift the weight into the fully contracted position for you, make sure he or they don't simply drop the weight into your control once you're in the fully contracted position; the sudden shock to the joint of articulation could prove traumatic. Every movement must be performed slowly, particularly when settling into the fully contracted position.

• *The nature of high-intensity exercise.* You may notice that your target muscle group might begin to shake rather violently at the 1- to 6-second mark, but that's fine. It's simply an indicator that your muscles are firing more and more fibers to maintain the contraction, and the more they use, the greater the growth stimulation will be. After a Max Contraction workout, you will feel like your limbs are made of Jell-O owing to the high volume of muscle fibers you will have activated. At this point you will be entering the stage of recovery and growth, requiring you to rest completely (i.e., take part in no other form of strenuous exercise) until your next workout a minimum of 48 hours later.

• *Workout frequency.* Beginners to Max Contraction Training should structure their workouts 48 hours apart, such as Monday, Wednesday, and Friday, with Tuesday, Thursday, Saturday, and Sunday off for recovery and growth. Intermediates should structure their workouts 96 hours apart, or once every four days (such as Mondays and Fridays). Advanced trainees should train no more than once a week.

• *Strive to increase intensity.* Always strive for increased intensity via additional seconds of contraction until a full 6 seconds have been obtained. At this point you can increase the resistance imposed on the muscle group and aim for 1 second again. If you continue to do this, you will be rewarded for your efforts with the best gains of your bodybuilding career.

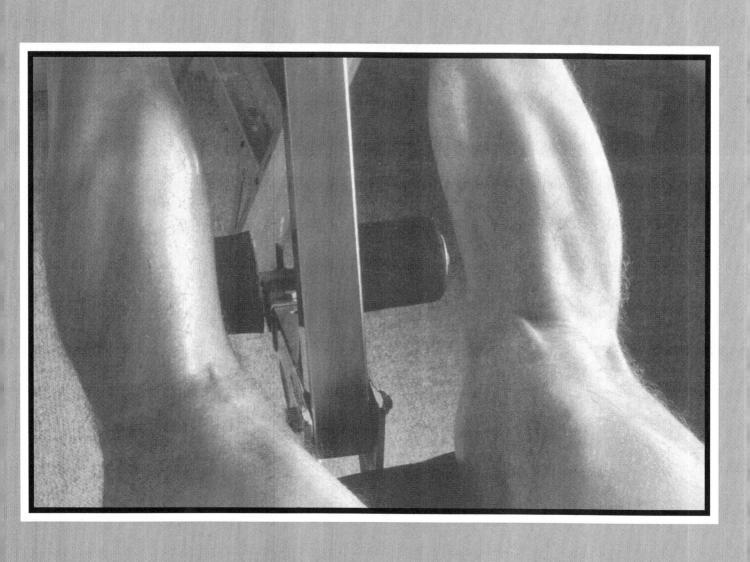

Part V

BODYPART SPECIALIZATION

Specialization will keep your enthusiasm for training primed, allowing you to look forward to every training session.

Chapter 13

A GUIDE TO YEAR-ROUND TRAINING

One of the biggest obstacles to bodybuilding success is a lack of motivation. While the human race is productive, creative, and, at times, even heroic, our bodies over the millennia have learned, as a matter of survival, to conserve energy whenever and however possible. We are a problem-solving species, and one of the problems we find ourselves most inclined to solve is that of the expenditure of labor. We've gone to great lengths to conserve our own energy in this regard; virtually every invention we've ever embraced have been ones that make our lives a little easier. While such an attitude is almost in our blood, we will need to toughen our resolve and train our intellect against this inclination—at least while we're in the gym.

I recognize that it's tough to psyche ourselves up for an all-out effort every time we workout. And, as the growth of muscle beyond normal levels is a cosmetic—rather than a practical—concern of most people, it often requires a supreme act of will to engage in the type of training required to make our bodies stronger (see Chapter 6). We create plenty of excuses as to why we should miss the odd workout or, perhaps, alter our training program to something a little less taxing. However, doing so only compromises our muscular results.

Fortunately, there is a method that will not only keep our enthusiasm up for our quest to build bigger and stronger muscles, but also help to ensure that each bodypart is receiving thorough stimulation to develop maximally. This method, called "specialization," is accomplished by simply altering our routine a little from month to month. Nothing major, mind you, just subtle variations on the same Max Contraction theme. How does one perform these subtle variations? Simply by selecting one bodypart to be specialized on each month and making sure to specialize on all bodyparts at some point during any given 12-month period.

It is important to keep your sets for the targeted bodypart to a maximum of five if you're a beginner, and three if you're an intermediate or advanced trainee. This is necessary to maintain an adequate degree of intensity to stimulate growth (as any more sets than this will require you to substantially reduce your intensity levels in order to complete them—a step in the wrong direction if your object is a muscle mass increase). Also, perform a *maximum* of only one set for the remainder of your bodyparts. This will ensure a degree of intensity sufficient to induce overall growth of the body's muscular systems, while remaining sufficiently brief enough to prevent overtraining. It will also keep your training sufficiently diverse to prevent you from becoming too accustomed (or intimidated) by any one routine.

Key Points to Remember

• Beginners should work out no more than three times per week; intermediates should train only twice a week; and advanced trainees should limit their training to only once a week.

• Beginners may sustain their Max Contractions for up to 60 seconds; intermediates and advanced trainees should increase their resistance and aim for 1 to 6 seconds.

• Train your whole body each session.

• Never perform more than 12 sets in any given workout. (Intermediates should perform only 10 total sets in any given workout.)

• When specializing, beginners should perform only 5 sets for the bodypart being specialized on, with each set being a legitimate all-out effort. Intermediates should reduce their sets for the targeted muscle group to a maximum of 3.

• Work the specialized bodypart first in the workout (when your energy levels are highest) and then your other bodyparts in descending order (i.e., from the largest to the smallest).

• Take one full week off from weight training every 10 weeks.

• When not specializing, use the basic Max Contraction routine for balanced muscular development.

• When specializing, select a different bodypart every month. This ensures balanced development and prevents overtraining of any one muscle group.

A SAMPLE YEAR-ROUND SPECIALIZATION SCHEDULE

The following list is a sample of how one might set up a year-round specialization schedule. It is not etched in stone. You are free to be creative in formulating your own schedule, arranging bodypart specialization workouts as you deem necessary to your own development and goals.

1. February: general workout (total body).
2. March: deltoid specialization.
3. April: leg specialization (i.e., quadriceps, hamstrings, calves). Note: In mid-April take one week off from weight training and engage in only mild exercise (e.g., aerobics, jogging).
4. May: arm specialization.
5. June: back specialization (including the trapezius muscle).
6. July: chest specialization. Take the week of July l to July 8 off from weight training and engage in only mild exercise (e.g., swimming, biking, running).
7. August: return to the general workout (total body).
8. September: deltoid specialization. During the third week of September, abstain from all forms of weight training and perform only aerobic activities.
9. October: leg specialization.
10. November: arm specialization.
11. December: back specialization. Take the first week in December off from weight training and perform whatever form of mild aerobic exercise that you prefer.
12. January: chest specialization.

The above list should serve you well as a guide to setting up your own training schedule for the following year (and every year thereafter). Take 1 full week off after every 10 weeks of Max Contraction Training. This will both help keep your enthusiasm primed to a high degree and help keep your energy reserves fully replenished. Also keep in mind that during your week off you should be performing some form of aerobic activity in order to prevent the expansion of your body's fat cells. The activity (or activities) should be of a very low-intensity nature and somewhat enjoyable (such as jogging, distance walking, badminton, swimming, dancing, martial arts, yoga, bicycling). The low intensity of these activities will not make major inroads into your body's recuperative subsystems, thereby leaving them ample time to build

up in anticipation of your return to bodybuilding training, in addition to burning up calories that might otherwise be stored as fat. In other words, your schedule might be 10 weeks of all-out training to build size followed by 1 week of endurance or aerobic training to prime your metabolism, work an alternate energy system, burn calories, and "rip up."

If you couple this program with a balanced calorie-reduced diet, you will look and feel better than ever. In the next chapter, let's take a look at those specialization routines.

It is advisable to take 1 full week off from Max Contraction Training every 10 weeks to allow your energy systems to fully replenish. During such breaks, you may wish to try something new that will help to burn calories, such as martial arts.

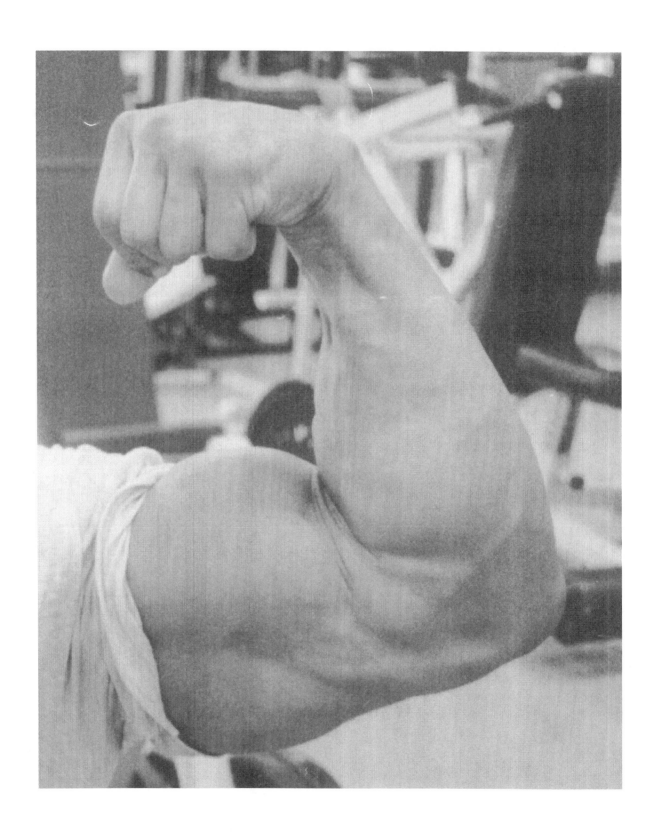

Chapter 14

FOCUS ON ARMS

It is important to specialize on different body-parts from time to time. The reasoning behind this is twofold: First, specialization allows you to really stimulate a bodypart that has acclimated to the rigors of high-intensity training, allowing you to focus more effort, attention, and intensity on it without running the risk of overtraining. Second, after 30 days on the same routine, your mind will begin to crave a respite from the monotony of performing a predictable routine that your body's muscles have already become accustomed to.

The problem actually lies not so much in the workout no longer being able to stimulate growth in the muscles so much as in the mind's inability to sustain enthusiasm for an activity that is no longer new and exciting. Once the excitement of something new has worn off, your mind is left with the prospect of having to engage your muscles in the extremely arduous task of increasing the difficulty or intensity of your training sessions. Only rare individuals are willing to persevere and summon the

strength of will required to see this task through to the end.

Many bodybuilders crave variety and find motivation easier when they approach their objective from slightly different (not essentially different) perspectives from time to time. You will find it much easier, on both your psyche and your body, to alter the content of your routine from month to month in order to ensure that your training remains interesting and fresh, while still providing a means of productive stimulation to both your muscles and your cognitive faculties.

ANATOMY AND KINESIOLOGY

To properly design a specialization program for your arms, you must first know how the muscles in your arms function. Once you understand this, it becomes relatively simple to select exercises that will accommodate the Max Contraction protocol.

The Biceps

The biceps muscle, as its name indicates, is a two- (bi-) headed muscle group that has its point of origin under your deltoid or shoulder muscle and its point of insertion below your elbow. The function of the biceps is also twofold, to supinate (turn from a palms-down to a palms-up position) the wrist and to raise the forearm up towards the shoulder. Any exercise, therefore, that fulfills these two functions and provides resistance in the fully contracted position will serve our purposes of growth stimulation perfectly. Three exercises come to mind right away: palms-up chins, steep-angle preacher curls performed with Blaster Straps, and dumbbell concentration curls. These three exercises will form our entire biceps specialization routine.

The Triceps

The triceps muscle is a three- (tri-) headed muscle group, which works in direct opposition to the biceps. The triceps attaches itself— like the biceps—just under your deltoid and just below your elbow. The function of the triceps is also twofold in nature: to extend the forearm away from the shoulder and to draw the humerus, or upper arm bone, behind the body. The problem when selecting exercises to train the triceps muscles using conventional equipment such as barbells is that most traditional triceps movements involve a "locking out" of some sort, in which the resistance is transferred in large degree from the triceps to the bones and ligaments. This is completely contrary to the philosophy of Max Contraction Training.

Exercises such as the close-grip bench press, cable pressdowns, and French presses all involve a locking out of the elbows; consequently, they provide no direct resistance to the triceps in the fully contracted position. Such movements (if employed at all) are best employed as the finishing movement where two exercises are performed one after the other with no rest in between (what is commonly referred to as a "superset"). In this instance, you would hit your triceps hard with a pure

isolation exercise, and, after you have prefatigued the triceps muscle doing that, you might follow up immediately with an exercise such as weighted dips.

Apart from using machines such as Nautilus, Cybex, Hammer Strength, and the like— which are both expensive and not always readily available (particularly if you train at home)—the triceps exercises that fit the bill for providing the highest intensity of muscular contraction and also engage both functions of the triceps in their execution are Max Straps kickbacks and dumbbell kickbacks (a barbell kickback can also be employed). To supplement this solitary movement in order to specialize on triceps, we will also add reverse-grip, single-arm cable extensions.

THE ARM ROUTINE

As noted earlier, while using Max Contraction Training specialization programs, beginners will still be training on a three-day-a-week routine; they will train on alternate days during the week (e.g., Monday, Wednesday, and Friday) and then take the weekend off for additional recovery and growth. Intermediates will only be training twice a week and advanced bodybuilders only once a week. No matter what your level of training experience, however, you will continue to train your entire body in each session, and you will perform only three to four sets for each specialized bodypart, and only one for each of the remaining muscle groups. Here is the Max Contraction arm specialization program.

Biceps: Close-Grip Chins (1 Set)

Pull yourself up to the top of a chinning bar into a position where your biceps are fully contracted, with the chinning bar right under your chin. Hold this fully contracted position for 1 to 6 seconds. Upon completion, move on to your next exercise. (Note: If you find that you can hold the fully contracted position of the chin-up for more than 6 seconds, then you should add weight around your waist via a

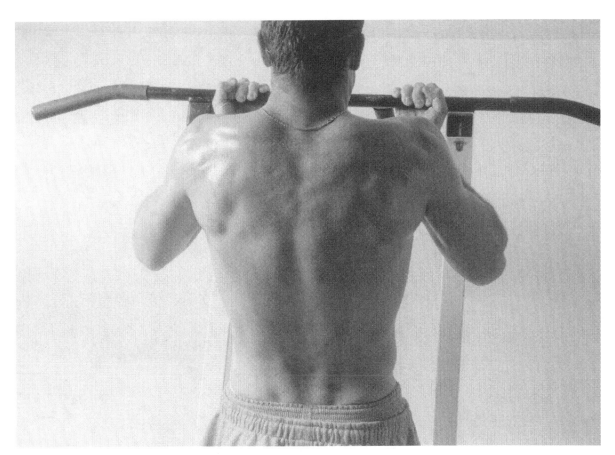

Close-grip chins.

weight belt so that you are limited to the 1- to 2-second time frame.)

Biceps: Steep-Angle Preacher Curls (Incorporating Max Straps: 1 Set)

Sit down on a preacher bench that has a padded arm surface that is at a 90-degree angle to the floor. Attach the ring on the Max Straps to the floor pulley so that the pads are situated just above your wrists (this will bypass the weak link of the forearm muscles in this exercise, thus placing the training stress directly on the biceps muscles). Slowly raise your forearms until your biceps are in the fully contracted position. Fight the tendency to let your hands come together and try instead to keep them at shoulder width with your palms facing up. Once you are in the fully contracted position, sustain the contraction for 1 to 6 seconds or until the contraction is broken. Then move on to your final biceps exercise.

Steep-angle preacher curls.

Biceps: Concentration Curls (1 Set)

Pick up a dumbbell in your right hand and bend over at the waist with your left hand braced upon your left knee. With the elbow of your right (or curling) arm braced against the inside of your right knee, slowly curl the weight up until your biceps muscle is fully contracted. Hold this position for a full 1 to 6 seconds or until you can no longer maintain the full contraction. Now switch the dumbbell to your left hand and repeat the exercise with that arm. Your biceps should be absolutely rubbery at this point of the routine, and, although you have performed only three sets, you will have stimulated phenomenal growth!

Triceps: Dumbbell Kickbacks (1 Set)

Grasp a dumbbell in your right hand and, bending over at the waist so that your torso is at a 90-degree angle to your legs, place your left hand upon a flat bench for support. Draw your right elbow up and back until your upper arm is also at a 90-degree angle to your legs. Next, extend your right forearm until the dumbbell is behind your hips, all the while making a focused effort to keep the right arm that is holding the dumbbell completely locked straight. Hold this fully contracted position for a full 1 to 6 seconds or until you can no longer

Concentration curls.

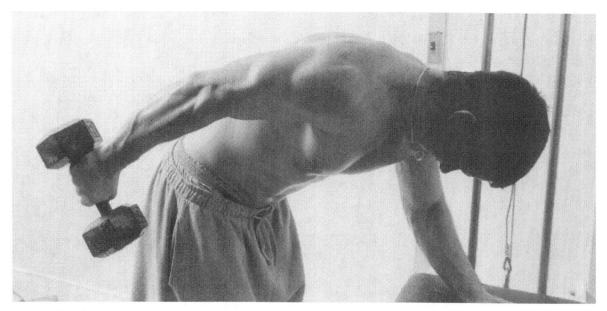

Dumbbell kickbacks.

sustain the contraction (whichever comes first). Then slowly lower the dumbbell back to your hip. Transfer the dumbbell to your left hand and repeat the exercise. Upon completing this, move to the one-arm cable pulldown machine for the next exercise.

Triceps: Reverse-Grip One-Arm Pressdowns (1 Set)

With your palm facing upwards, grasp the handle on a triceps pressdown unit. Step close to the machine and slowly extend your forearm while maintaining this grip. Continue to extend your forearm until your arm is completely locked out behind you and your triceps muscle is fully contracted. Hold this fully contracted position for a full 1 to 6 seconds or until the full contraction can no longer be maintained. Repeat the movement with the opposite arm. Upon completion, proceed to the next (and final) triceps exercise.

Max Straps Kickbacks (1 Set)

With the ring of the Max Straps attached to the hook at the end of a floor pulley, bend over at the waist so that your torso is at a 90-degree angle to your legs. Place your hands through the Max Straps so that the pads are across your wrists. Maintaining the bent-over position, draw your arms behind you until they are as far behind your torso as you can move them and your arms are fully locked out. Sustain this maximum contraction for 1 to 6 seconds. This concludes your workout arm specialization routine.

Max Straps kickbacks.

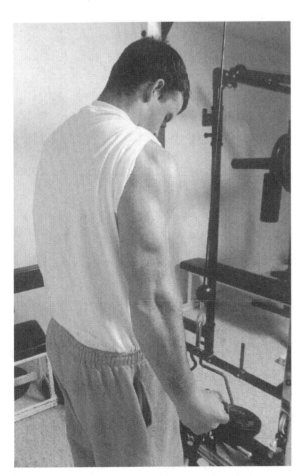

Reverse-grip one-arm pressdowns.

The remainder of your exercises are for the rest of your physique.

Strongest-Range Hack Squats (1 Set)

Place a barbell within a power rack across the uprights, which should be preset so that the barbell is just above the backs of your knees. Facing forward with the barbell behind you, grasp the barbell with a shoulder-width grip. Using leg strength alone, straighten your legs to the point where they are two inches shy of locking out. Support this contraction for 1 to 6 seconds.

Strongest-range hack squats.

Leg Curls (1 Set)

Sustain in the fully contracted position for 1 to 6 seconds.

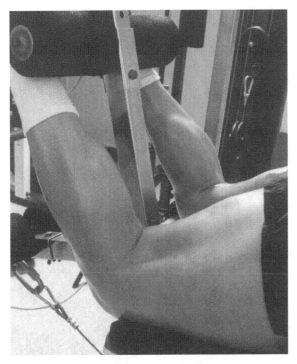

Leg curls.

Bent-Over Barbell Rows (1 Set)

Bend over at the waist, taking a shoulder-width grip on a barbell. With a slight bend in your knees to eliminate lower back strain, draw the barbell up and into your upper abdomen. sustain this fully contracted position for 1 to 6 seconds.

Cable Crossovers (1 Set)

Taking hold of two crossover pulley handles, draw them down and across the midline of your torso. Hold this fully contracted position for a full 1 to 6 seconds.

Within a month of starting this program, your arms will be considerably bigger than they are now (two trainees whose workouts I supervised gained over two inches on their arms following this program), and it will be time to move on to specialization on another body-part—the shoulders!

Bent-over barbell rows.

Cable crossovers.

Chapter 15

FOCUS ON SHOULDERS

The objective of this chapter is to provide you with specific exercises to develop your shoulder muscles. These muscles are important in physique training, as they alone create a sense of "broadness" in the upper body and also serve to foster the illusion of a smaller waist. Our objective is to select exercises that involve the largest percentage of shoulder muscle fibers possible. Thus, it behooves us to take a minute to study the anatomy and function of this complex muscle group to assist us in our exercise selection process.

ANATOMY AND KINESIOLOGY

The deltoid, or shoulder, muscle is actually a three-headed muscle, triangular in shape, which starts at your shoulder blade and the scapula at the back of your shoulder and extends down to an insertion point in the upper arm. The function of each deltoid head is to move the arm in a certain direction. The anterior, or front, deltoid lifts the arm to the front; the lateral, or side, deltoid lifts the arm to the side; the posterior, or rear, deltoid head draws the arm behind the torso. When all three heads are activated, it allows you to not only lift your arm but also to rotate it in a full circle.

The trapezius muscle is generally considered a part of the shoulder structure, and, consequently, we must study its function as well in order to select an exercise that will best stimulate this muscle group. The function of the trapezius, or "traps," as they are more popularly referred to, is to lift the entire shoulder girdle, but they are also involved whenever you turn your head and also assist in the action of drawing your shoulder blades, or scapula, to either side or up and down. The best exercise for this is the shrug (with a barbell, dumbbells, Hammer machine, or Universal machine), which, incidentally, will be the exercise that we will be using to specialize on this muscle group.

The function of the deltoids is a little more complex than the traps, owing to the separate functions of each of the three heads. Since your arm is capable of rotating in a 360-degree circumference, there exist many angles at which the individual deltoid muscles can be trained in order to maximally stimulate them into full growth and development. For example, for the anterior deltoid there are at least nine different exercises that can be performed. However, if we attempted to do nine sets utilizing the Max Contraction protocol, we would soon be overtrained and would start noticing muscle decompensation, or loss, instead of gains. Our objective, then, will be to select the best possible exercise for each deltoid head that will provide the maximum resistance in each of the respective head's fully contracted position in order to allow for maximum muscle fiber stimulation.

For the anterior deltoid, the exercise that best accomplishes this is the front raise (performed with a barbell or dumbbells or on a cable machine). For the lateral head of the deltoid, the best movement is without question the side raise with either dumbbells or on a cable machine (a Nautilus machine is also excellent for this movement). The best rear deltoid movement is the bent-over rear lateral raise with either cables or dumbbells, but for practical purposes, since not everyone has access to a cable machine, we'll stick with dumbbells. These exercises place a constant stress/tension upon the target muscle group from the moment you initiate the exercise until the moment you break the contraction at the end of your set. They are, therefore, the most productive exercises possible owing to their extremely high-intensity threshold.

Remember when utilizing the Max Contraction method to lift the resistance slowly (so as not to damage any ligaments or connective tissues) at the beginning of the movement until you have ascended to the position of full muscular contraction. But then, instead of lowering the weight, hold this fully contracted position for a minimum of 1 second (shoot for 6 seconds) or until the contraction can no longer be sustained. If you can hold the resistance for more than 6 seconds, then it's too light and you should heavy it up by 5 percent for your next workout. If you can't hold the contraction for 1 second, then it's too heavy and you should

reduce the resistance by 5 percent until you can contract the muscle for 1 full second.

Some of you may require a spotter (or two spotters if you're really strong) to lift the weight up into the fully contracted position for you. In this case, make sure that your spotters don't just "drop" the weight into your hands when you reach the fully contracted position, as the sudden, violent contraction your muscles will have to make could well lead to a torn muscle. Always exercise caution.

As with the arm specialization routine, after specializing on the shoulders in this workout, we will also need to train the remaining bodyparts to keep your body in proper proportion. And as with the arm routine, we must still train all the muscle groups in the body, but we will only devote one set each to them. We will specialize on the shoulders with three exercises and then perform an additional exercise (barbell shrugs) to specialize on the traps. And now, let's get on with the routine.

THE SHOULDER SPECIALIZATION ROUTINE

Front Raises (1 Set)

Grasp a barbell and, keeping your elbows locked, slowly raise it from a position in front of your thighs to one directly out in front of your chest. Sustain this fully contracted position for a full 1 to 6 seconds or until the contraction can no longer be sustained. Slowly lower the resistance and immediately pick up two dumbbells and move on to your next exercise.

Side Lateral Raises (1 Set)

Keeping your elbows locked, slowly raise the dumbbells out to your sides until the dumbbells are perfectly parallel to your shoulders. Hold this position of full muscular contraction for 1 to 6 seconds or until you break the contraction. Then lower the dumbbells slowly the rest of the way down to your outer thighs. Move immediately to your final deltoid exercise in the routine.

Front raises.

Side lateral raises.

Bent-Over Rear Deltoid Raises (1 Set)

Bending over at the waist, slowly raise the dumbbells up and back until they are parallel in a plane slightly above and behind your shoulders. Try to keep a slight bend in your arms so as not to strain the elbow joint, drawing upwards with the elbows rather than with the hands. Sustain this fully contracted position for a full 1 to 6 seconds or until you can no longer hold the contraction. Slowly lower the dumbbells and move immediately to your traps training.

Barbell Shrugs (2 Sets)

Take hold of a barbell (preferably utilizing straps or lifting hooks to reinforce your grip) and, standing erect, slowly raise your shoulders until they are almost touching your ears. Hold this position for a full 1 to 6 seconds or until

Bent-over rear deltoid raises.

you can no longer hold the contraction. When you reach the "failure" point, which is the point when you are unable to hold the contraction with the amount of weight you've selected (after 1 to 6 seconds), quickly put down the barbell and pick up a preloaded barbell that has a resistance 20 percent lighter than the barbell you just used and repeat the movement.

Barbell shrugs.

This concludes your Max Contraction shoulder specialization routine. While using this specialization routine, the following exercises are required to train the rest of your physique.

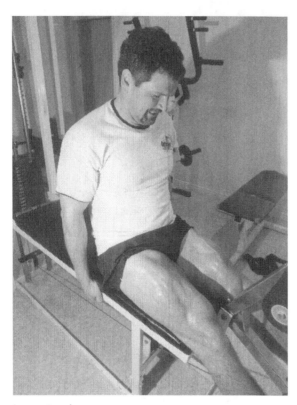

Leg extensions.

Leg Extensions (1 Set)

Sustain in the fully contracted position for 1 to 6 seconds.

Leg Curls (1 Set)

Sustain in the fully contracted position for 1 to 6 seconds.

Chin-Ups (1 Set)

Sustain in the fully contracted position for 1 to 6 seconds.

Pec Deck (1 Set)

Sustain in the fully contracted position for 1 to 6 seconds.

Dumbbell Kickbacks (1 Set)

Sustain in the fully contracted position for 1 to 6 seconds.

Remember that while using the Max Contraction method you will still (if you're a beginner) be training on a three-day-per-week routine, wherein you train on alternate days during the week (i.e., Monday, Wednesday, and

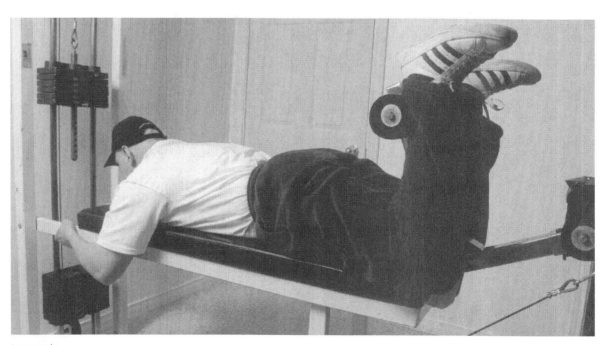

Leg curls.

Friday) and then take weekends off for recovery and growth. Intermediates should only be training on Mondays and Fridays and advanced trainees only one day per week. You should continue to train your entire body in each session; however, unless instructed otherwise in a specialization workout, you should never perform more than one set of any exercise.

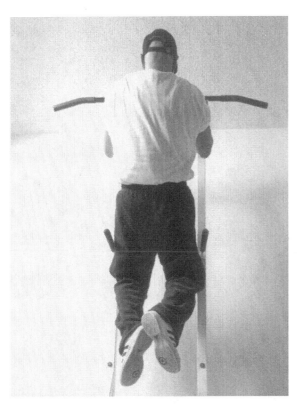

Chin-ups.

Pec Deck.

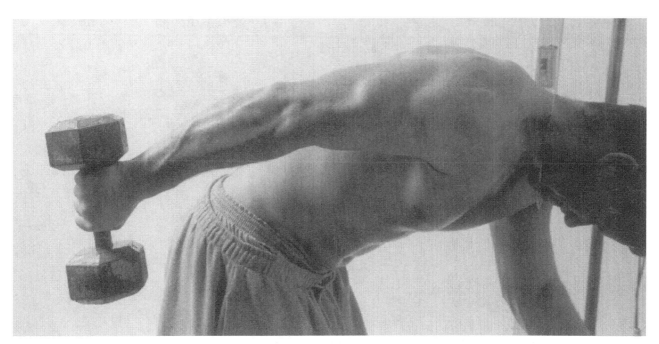

Dumbbell kickbacks.

Chapter 16

FOCUS ON THE CHEST

Developing a thick, muscular chest is one of the earliest goals most bodybuilders set for themselves. Thick, squared-off pecs impart a look of rugged masculinity to the male torso and indicate power and conditioning. As chest training is so popular, it's not at all uncommon to see bodybuilders investing hour after hour in the gym doing rep after rep and set after set of bench presses, flyes (incline and decline), cable crossovers, push-ups, and at least one set on some kind of "pec machine." The tragedy of this type of labor expenditure is that the very enthusiasm that fires their workouts is the very thing that results in their lack of progress and often results in their becoming frustrated with training altogether. Enthusiasm for training is one thing, but when left unchecked, it leads to overtraining, which, as we should know by now, is not at all compatible with our training objective of building a stronger, more muscular body.

When selecting exercises to use in training a specific bodypart, you must know the func-tion of the muscular structure you wish to train. It obviously would do a bodybuilder little good to do a set of bench presses with the mistaken notion that he was in some way pro-viding growth stimulation to his biceps mus-cles. Less obviously, it would be of little benefit to the same bodybuilder to do wide-grip bench presses if his objective was to work the pectoral muscles. This is because the wider the hand spacing on the barbell, the less stress is actually focused upon the pectorals, as the arms are moved away from the midline of the torso (an absolute requirement for maximum contrac-tion—hence, maximum stimulation—of the pectoral muscles). If your goals are indeed those of increased size, shape, and strength in the pectoral region, logic would clearly dictate that you should first learn the function of this muscle group. Next, you should select an exer-cise (or exercises) that will allow you to pro-vide resistance to this bodypart in a manner that will activate the greatest number of its possible muscle fibers in order to stimulate each and every one of them into the greatest muscle growth possible. A bit of good news is that this month's Max Contraction specialization routine consists of a minimum of only nine seconds of actual training. But don't let its brevity fool you; this is a very intense routine.

ANATOMY AND KINESIOLOGY

The chest is a more complex group than most of us would imagine in that there are three different muscles that comprise what we simply refer to as the chest: the pectoralis major, the pectoralis minor, and the serratus anterior. To develop your chest fully, all three of these muscles must be stimulated to grow larger. This can only be accomplished through high-intensity training and best accomplished via Max Contraction Training.

The pectoralis major arises from the anterior surface of the sternal half of the clavicle, or shoulder blade, and the anterior surface of the sternum, the aponeurosis of the external oblique and the cartilage of the true ribs, that is, the anterior extremities of each of the first seven pairs of ribs that are connected with the sternum in front by means of the costal cartilage. The fibers of the pectoralis major converge to form a thick mass, which is inserted by a flat tendon into the crest of the greater tubercle of the humerus, or upper arm bone. The action of the pectoralis major is as follows: if your arm has been raised, the pectoralis major acts along with the latissimus dorsi (the V-shaped muscles of the upper back) and teres major to draw your arm down to the side of your body. Acting alone, it adducts and draws the arm across the chest, which also rotates the arm inwards.

The pectoralis minor is located underneath the pectoralis major—in fact, it's completely covered by it. It arises from the upper margins and outer surfaces of the third, fourth, and fifth ribs near their cartilage and is inserted into the ecoracoid process of the scapula (that little bump of bone on the top of your shoulder). The action of the pectoralis minor is to depress that point of the shoulder and to rotate

the scapula (or shoulder blades) downwards. Additionally, in times of forced respiration, the pectoralis muscles—in total—help in drawing the ribs upwards and expanding the chest.

The serratus anterior, or serratus magnus, arise from the outer surfaces and superior borders of the upper eight or nine ribs and from the intercostals between them. The fibers pass upward and backward and are inserted in various portions of the ventral surface of the scapula. The action of the serratus is to carry the scapula forward and to raise the vertebral border of the bones, as when pushing an object away from you. It also assists the trapezius in raising the acromion process and in supporting weights on the shoulders. Additionally, it serves to assist the deltoids in raising the arms.

As the action of the pectoralis major is to draw the arm down and across the chest, we need an exercise for our Max Contraction Training that will fulfill both of these functions. The one that best provides both of these requisites is the fully contracted position of cable crossovers. As the primary action of the pectoralis minor is to lower the shoulders, the fully contracted position of decline cable flyes (performed, again, on a cable-crossover machine) will best fit the bill for the Max Contraction method of activating the fibers of this muscle. The serratus anterior's function being to carry the scapula forward, we will be making use of the Pec Deck exercise.

THE CHEST SPECIALIZATION ROUTINE

Cable Crossovers (Kneeling: 1 Set)

Grab hold of two crossover pulley handles and kneel down in the middle of the two overhead pulleys. From a position of full extension—with your arms completely outstretched above your head—slowly begin to draw your arms downward and slightly forward until your hands have just crossed over each other in front of your thighs. Hold this fully contracted position for a full 1 to 6 seconds and then rush to your next chest exercise.

Cable crossovers.

Decline cable crossovers.

Decline Cable Crossovers (1 Set)

Taking hold of a pair of floor pulley handles, have a training partner slide a decline bench over to the exact spot where you were kneeling

for the last exercise. Lay down on the decline bench so that your head is at the bottom and your feet are hooked under the roller pads at the top. From this position and with your arms fully outstretched, slowly begin to draw your arms upwards and inwards until, once again, your hands cross in front of your lower abdomen. Hold this fully contracted position for a full 1 to 6 seconds. Then proceed to your next (and final) chest exercise.

Pec Deck (1 Set)

Sit down in a Pec Deck machine and place your forearms on the padded movement arms of the machine. Contract your pectoral muscles by drawing the pads forward until they touch in front of your chest. Hold this position for 1 to 6 seconds.

Now you can rest—briefly—before continuing with the remaining exercises.

Leg Extensions (1 Set)

As you are probably aware, the leg extension is unparalleled for effectively isolating the quadriceps muscles on the tops of the thighs. Other exercises can work the quadriceps thoroughly, but none as efficiently nor as directly as leg extensions. The reason is that there are no weak links in this movement; it is powered

Pec Deck.

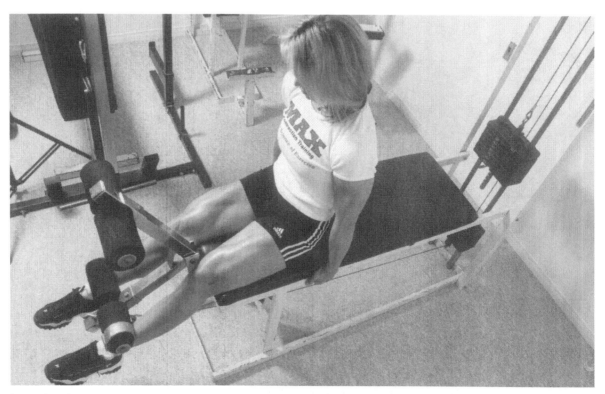

Leg extensions.

solely by the strength of your quadriceps. Sit down on a leg extension unit and place your feet under the roller pads. Slowly begin to contract your thigh muscles until they are fully contracted. Sustain this fully contracted position for a full 1 to 6 seconds before advancing to your next exercise.

Seated Calf Raises (1 Set)

Sit down on the seat of a seated calf raise machine. Place the padded bar over your knees

and position the balls of your feet across the foot bar. Release the safety catch and slowly contract your calves so that the resistance rises and your calves are in the fully contracted position. Sustain this fully contracted position for 1 to 6 seconds before lowering the resistance.

Max Straps Pulldowns (1 Set)

Position yourself in a lat pulldown machine and insert your arms through the Max Straps

Seated calf raises.

Max Straps pulldowns.

so that the bottom padded part of the strap is over the end of your upper arm (nearest the elbow joint) and your hands are resting against the side straps. Don't close your hands on the straps, as this will unnecessarily involve and fatigue the forearm muscles and (to a lesser extent) the biceps. Using only the strength of your latissimus dorsi muscles, draw your elbows down and back until they are just to the sides of your ribs. Sustain this full contraction for 1 to 6 seconds.

Strongest-Range Deadlifts (1 Set)

This is an excellent exercise for developing the erector spinae muscles of the lumbar, or lower back, region. Its muscle building abilities do not stop at the lower back, however. Deadlifts work almost every muscle in the body and stimulate phenomenal overall muscle growth. This movement is best performed—for safety and efficiency reasons—in a power rack. Bend over at the waist and, with an over-and-under grip (one hand grasping the bar from over the

Strongest-range deadlifts.

top, while the other hand grasps it from underneath), grab hold of a barbell that should be resting on pins or supports at upper-thigh height. Your hands should be approximately 14 inches apart. With your hands tightly clenched, lift your torso to an upright position using only your lower back muscles. Lift up until you've ascended to the fully contracted position and sustain this contraction for 1 to 6 seconds.

Standing Dumbbell Curls (1 Set)

Pick up two dumbbells and hold them at your sides. Slowly curl both of them up toward your shoulders until they reach the fully contracted position. Hold this position for a full 1 to 6 seconds. Then slowly return the dumbbells back to their starting position and immediately move on to your next exercise.

Standing dumbbell curls.

Bench Dips (1 Set)

This is an excellent upper-body developer (some call it the upper-body squat), but the main focus is on the triceps muscles on the back of the upper arm. You will need two benches for this movement, one to place your feet on and one to put your hands on. The bench for your arms should be just slightly behind your back so that the secondary function of the triceps (to draw the arm behind the torso) is fulfilled. Place your feet on the bench in front of you (ideally, the bench should be elevated to a position where your feet are higher than your hips) and extend your arms to a locked-out position with your hands on the bench behind you. If possible, have a training partner place a couple of barbell plates on your lap for added resistance. Bend your elbows slightly and hold this position for 1 to 6 seconds or until you can no longer sustain the contraction.

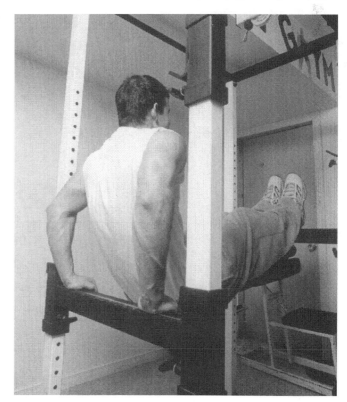

Bench dips.

At this point you can rest. The chest specialization routine is over, and you've definitely earned a break.

Remember that the stronger you become, the greater your ability to make inroads into your capacity for recovery and, consequently, the easier it will be to overtrain. This is why

intermediates should not work out with only 48 hours between sessions (i.e., the standard Monday, Wednesday, and Friday routine). Rather they should allow at least 96 hours between workouts.

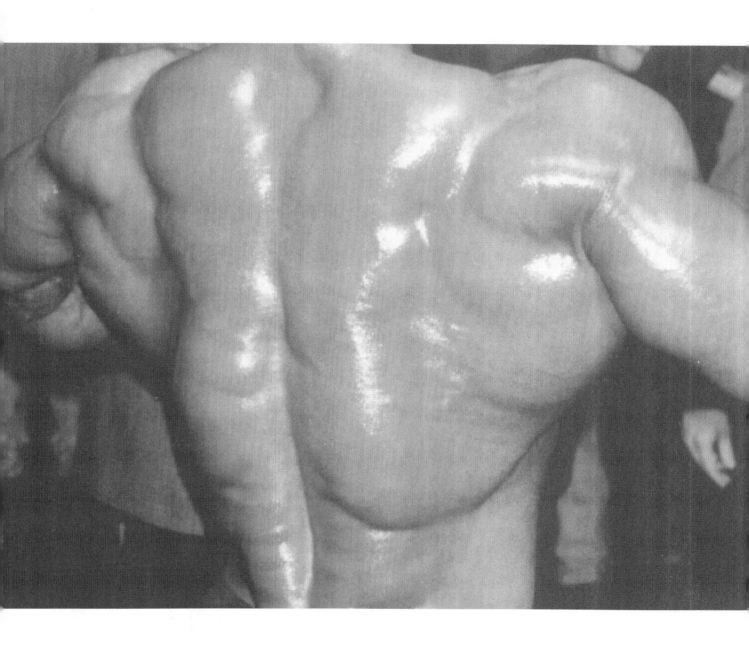

Chapter 17

FOCUS ON THE BACK

When most people think about their back muscles, they invariably envision the "lats," or the latissimus dorsi muscles—the ones most responsible for that highly sought-after V shape. Nevertheless, while certainly impressive, the lats are just one muscle in the total back picture. Other muscles, such as the infraspinatus, the trapezius, teres minor and major, rhomboideus, and erector spinae, all—when fully developed—impart an aura of total development to the bodybuilder's physique. If neglected, they result in perpetual low placings in contests by judges who make it a point not to overlook underdeveloped bodyparts.

Before we launch into the specialization routine for the back, we need to understand the function of this complex muscle group in order to assist us in selecting those exercises that will best provide the required growth stimulation.

ANATOMY AND KINESIOLOGY

The back comprises many diverse muscles, and yet some, like the teres major and the latissimus dorsi, actually have parallel functions. This is a significant point, as the proper performance of one exercise will therefore involve several related muscle groups and, hence, save us much training time. We will start with the trapezius muscle, which we last specialized on in our shoulder specialization workout. However, as it is also prominent in a properly developed back, we are giving some additional attention to it in our back specialization workout as well. To review: the trapezius muscle arises from the base of the neck, extends outward toward the shoulder blades and then down into the middle of the back. Its function is to elevate the shoulders and to abduct the scapula, or shoulder blades. The traps are also activated whenever you draw your head backward and to either side. The best exercise for this muscle would be one that precisely duplicates the trapezius's major function. The rhomboids share a similar function to at least one aspect of the traps, that is, to pull the scapula up and inward. Thus, they will also receive direct stimulation whenever the traps are properly trained with an exercise such as shrugs. Bang! We've hit two birds with one stone right off the bat!

The latissimus dorsi muscle is truly a showpiece muscle for bodybuilders. As its name implies, it's the broadest (latissimus) muscle of the back (dorsi). Its origin extends from the sixth thoracic vertebrae downward; its lowest fibers are attached to the upper edge of the illium (hip bone). The latissimus has its insertion point along the front of the humerus (the upper arm bone) close to its head.

You might recall that whereas the deltoid serves to raise the arm and draw it forward, the latissimus dorsi does just the opposite; it pulls the arm downward and backward. Again to our advantage—in terms of economy of time and motion—we find that the teres major's function is also activated whenever you draw your arm downward, backward, or inward. Consequently, I have selected those lat exercises that also serve to train our teres major muscles. Knowing this, the exercises that best correspond to the primary function of the latissimus dorsi are any type of rowing motion (e.g., Nautilus pullovers, Lat Blaster pulldowns, bent-over barbell rows, T-bar rowing).

With Max Contraction Training, an exercise must be selected that provides resistance in the fully contracted position. Another plus, where possible, is to select an exercise that provides resistance to the targeted muscle group without involving any "weak-link" muscles. When training the back, these exercises would include those involving the smaller and weaker biceps muscles, such as rows or conventional pulldowns on a lat machine. The only exercises that provide direct resistance to the lats would be lat pulldowns incorporating the Max Straps or pullovers performed on an exercise machine such as Nautilus. This routine will make use of the pulldown machine, used in conjunction with the Max Straps, as not all gyms have Nautilus equipment, but all have a pulldown machine to which the Max Straps can be easily attached to convert the movement from a compound into an isolation (i.e., direct resistance) exercise.

The infraspinatus and teres minor are both activated whenever the upper arms are abducted or rotated. "Abduction," in kinesiology parlance, refers to when a muscle group has been activated in such a way as to move it away and out from the midline of the body. If direct resistance is a priority—and it should be—pulldowns incorporating the Max Straps and Nautilus or Hammer Strength Pullover machines are the only ones that incorporate direct resistance to the lats in isolation. Other exercises such as parallel-grip pulldowns on the lat machine or any exercise that keeps your elbows out from the midline of the body will also activate these muscles reasonably well, so make do with what is available to you.

The erector spinae muscles are activated whenever extension of the trunk takes place, as in the performance of hyperextensions, deadlifts, goodmornings, side bends, and the Nautilus Hip & Back machine and Lower Back machine. So much for anatomy and physiology. Now let's get on with the workout.

THE BACK SPECIALIZATION ROUTINE

Straight-Arm Pulldowns on Lat Machine (1 Set)

To begin this exercise, grasp a lat machine pulldown bar from overhead and then kneel down on the floor. Keeping your arms perfectly straight, slowly press the bar downward until it is at chest level (anything beyond this level will transfer the stress more to your abs, pecs, and triceps). Sustain this position for 1 to 6 seconds, then rush to your next back exercise.

Max Straps Pulldowns (1 Set)

Position yourself in a lat pulldown machine and insert your arms through the Max Straps so that the bottom padded part of the strap is over the end of your upper arm (nearest the elbow joint) and your hands are resting against the side straps. Using only the strength of your latissimus dorsi muscles, draw your elbows down until your lats are fully contracted. Sus-

Straight-arm pulldowns.

Max Straps pulldowns.

tain this contraction for 1 to 6 seconds, then rush to your next back exercise.

Close-Grip or Parallel-Grip Pulldowns (1 Set)

This exercise will hit the teres minor and infraspinatus muscles of the upper back in addition to the latissimus dorsi. If you have a choice between a bar that allows you to have a parallel grip and one that allows simply a wide grip, choose the parallel grip bar. The reason is that a parallel grip puts your biceps in a fully supinated position (which is the biceps' strongest pulling position), and, therefore, they are not as much of a weak link to your back training as when you use a pronated grip (which puts the biceps in their weakest pulling position).

To begin this exercise, grab hold of a lat pulldown bar with a close, palms-up grip. Sit down on the bench in front of the lat machine

Close-grip pulldowns.

with your arms fully extended above your head. Begin to slowly pull the bar down toward your chest; however only take the resistance to the halfway point in this exercise as it's not a direct lat movement and will, if carried through to complete contraction, cause the weak-link biceps muscles to give out first. Once you've hit the halfway point, sustain the maximum contraction for a full 1 to 6 seconds, then rush to your next back exercise.

Barbell Shrugs (1 Set)

Do not make the mistake of allowing your ego to dictate your poundage in this exercise. Keep in mind that form should always take precedence over weight for the simple fact that if your muscles aren't responsible for moving the weight, they will not be adequately stimulated. It will, however, be possible to handle some fairly heavy weight in this exercise, as your trapezius muscles are among the strongest in the body. To perform this exercise, grab hold of a barbell and stand erect so that the barbell is directly in front of your thighs. Slowly begin to contract your traps so that your shoulders ascend toward the ceiling. When the weight has been raised as high as it can go, sustain this contraction for a full 1 to 6 seconds. When you can no longer maintain the contraction, slowly lower the weight and go to your next traps exercise.

Upright Rows (1 Set)

Grasp a barbell with a palms-over grip so that your hands are no more than six inches apart. Either position the bar with a slight hitch up to chin level, or have a training partner help you lift it up to this position. The weight should be as heavy as you can possibly use. Keeping the bar at chin level, and keeping your elbows pointed outwards, sustain this position of full muscular contraction for a minimum of 1 second and a maximum of 6. When you can no longer maintain the contraction, slowly lower the resistance and rush to your final back exercise.

Hyper-Extensions (1 Set)

Lie down crossways over a bench so that your torso is hanging over the edge of it. Have your partner hold, sit on, or in some way place resistance on your legs to counterbalance the weight of your torso. Place a weight (a modest one to begin) behind your neck and bend over at the waist. Slowly raise your torso (with your partner's assistance, if necessary) using only your erector spinae (or lower back) muscles until you have ascended as high as possible. At this point you will have activated the greatest percentage of muscle fibers and should try to sustain this fully contracted position for 1 to 6 seconds.

Now you can briefly rest before continuing with the remaining exercises.

Leg Extensions (1 Set)

Sustain the fully contracted position for 1 to 6 seconds, and then move on to your next exercise.

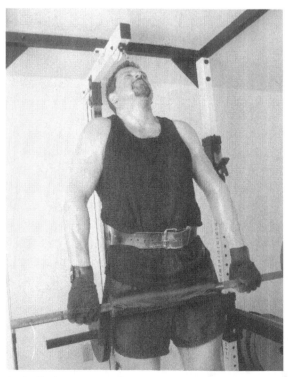

Barbell shrugs.

Hyper-extensions.

Upright rows.

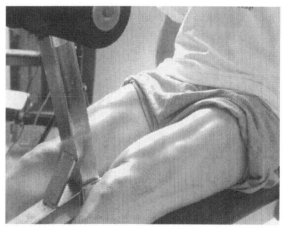

Leg extensions.

Leg Curls (1 Set)

Sustain the fully contracted position for 1 to 6 seconds, and then move on to your next exercise.

Seated Calf Raises (1 Set)

Sustain the fully contracted position for 1 to 6 seconds, and then move on to your next exercise.

Pec Deck (1 Set)

Sustain the fully contracted position for 1 to 6 seconds, and then move on to your next exercise.

Dumbbell Kickbacks (1 Set)

Sustain the fully contracted position for 1 to 6 seconds, then switch hands and repeat the movement.

When you can hold the contraction in any of these exercises for more than 6 seconds, it will be time to increase the resistance and shoot for a minimum of 1 second again. You'll note that there is no direct biceps work in this month's routine owing to the fact that the biceps are stressed quite thoroughly through the parallel-grip pulldowns and upright row movements performed in this workout. This is a positive omission for several reasons: (1) There will be no reason to hold back during

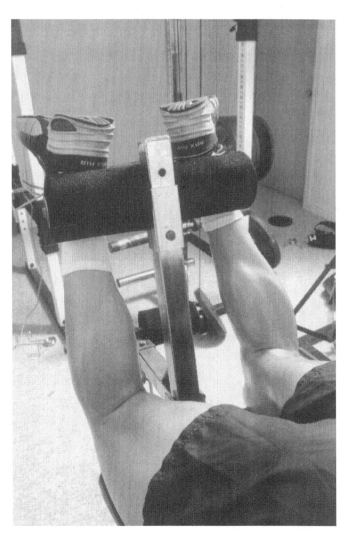

Leg curls.

Seated calf raises.

any of the back exercises, as this will be the only stimulation your biceps will receive this month. (2) Any direct exercise attempted after the all-out Max Contraction sets in which the biceps are involved would constitute overtraining. (3) Physiologists have recently found that muscles that are not worked directly sometimes (albeit briefly) can hypertrophy due to the indirect effect of strenuous exercise (discussed in Chapter 10) and the extra time allotted them for recovery and growth.

You may also have noticed that there is no direct abdominal work in this specialization routine. The reason is that the abdominals receive a tremendous workout during all of the pulldown movements, as they work to assist the lats in pulling down and also to stabilize the torso during most movements. More importantly for our specialization purposes, this workout hits *all* of the back muscles and has been tried and proven effective. In fact, this routine has served to pack the most muscle on trainees engaged in Max Contraction Training.

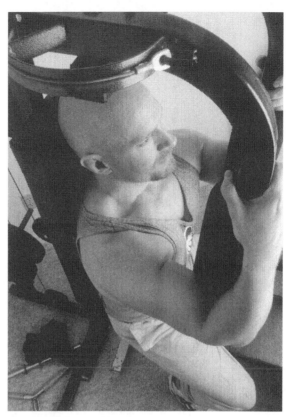

Pec Deck.

Dumbbell kickbacks.

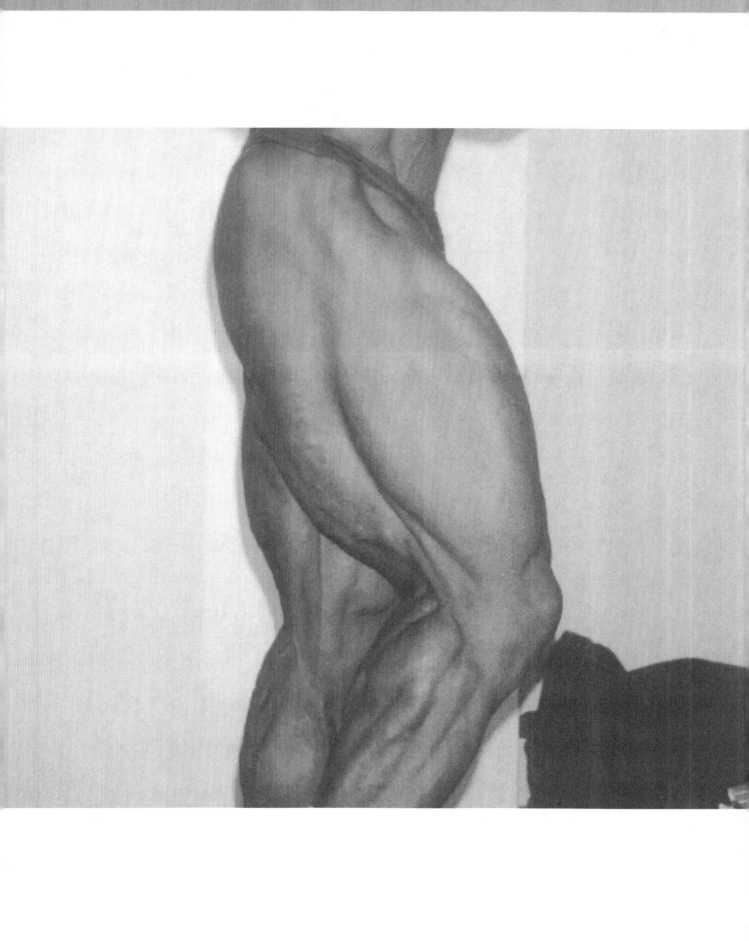

Chapter 18

FOCUS ON LEGS

I've yet to speak to any bodybuilder—pro or amateur—who actually enjoys training their legs. The reason is that leg training is the most demanding and strenuous form of exercise in all of bodybuilding. Consequently, many bodybuilders are outright scared of engaging in it properly. And, while it's very taxing and difficult, it's also—when you train with the Max Contraction protocol—the most productive form of training you can possibly perform.

Because Max Contraction Training is so demanding, and because the muscles that form the legs are so large, the energy debt created by Max Contraction Training is so great that the leg routine must be particularly brief in duration in order to ensure that the fine line between maximum growth stimulation and overtraining will not be crossed. The leg training routine presented in this chapter has been engineered in selection and sequence to provide maximum growth stimulation while allowing for only a minimum depletion of the body's energy reserves.

It is important to remember that with Max Contraction Training, maximum muscle growth can only be stimulated through maximum intensity of effort. You simply must be willing to fight through the discomfort that attends the proper performance of a Max Contraction leg training set.

ANATOMY AND KINESIOLOGY

Excluding the calves, there are 12 muscles that collectively make up the leg and that should be trained if complete leg development is your goal. On the frontal thigh resides a group of four muscles, known as the quadriceps. The quadriceps comprise the vastus lateralis, vastus intermedius, vastus medialis, and rectus femoris. The vastus lateralis is located on the outer side of the thigh; the vastus medialis on the inner (or medial) side of the thigh. Just above the kneecap and between both of these muscles are the vastus intermedius and the rectus femoris. All of the tendons attached to the quadriceps cross the knee joint; when they contract, the shin extends and the leg straightens. For this reason, a leg extension exercise is best for training these muscles and will be included in this particular specialization routine.

A total of five separate muscles comprise the inner thigh area. The largest of these is the adductor magnus, which originates on the pubis bone and inserts along the entire length of the femur (thigh bone). When the adductor magnus is contracted, it, along with the four medial thigh muscles, acts to draw the legs from a spread-out position to a position where the legs are crossed. Such a movement, from an open to a closed position, is called adduction, when referring to the function of these muscles. To my recollection, Nautilus was the first machine company to provide effective resistance for these five muscle groups with their Hip Adduction machine, which was introduced to the general public in 1980. Now, of course, myriad other machine companies have similarly designed machines of varying levels of quality that will train this muscle group. It is preferable to use one of these machines, as barbells and leg extension machines don't provide effective resistance to these muscles. However, if you don't have access to an adductor machine, Max Straps can be employed in concert with a floor pulley to great effect.

Finally, we come to the hamstring muscles, which compose the back of the thigh, probably the most underdeveloped area on all bodybuilders—including those in the professional ranks. The hamstrings comprise three separate muscles: the semitendinosus, the semimembranosus, and the biceps femoris (the tendons of which cross over the back of the knee capsule and cause the knee to bend when contracted). Traditionally, many bodybuilders have employed the stiff-legged deadlift exercise. While stiff-legged deadlifts do activate the hamstrings somewhat, it is not a direct enough exercise to serve the exacting standards of Max Contraction Training. Consequently, we are left with only one exercise that will effectively stimulate this extremely important muscle group. Fortunately, it is the best one in the book for hamstring development: the leg curl.

Now that we know the functions of these muscle groups and which exercises best serve them, we must now review the basic tenets of Max Contraction Training to ensure that our training is of the highest possible intensity.

MAX CONTRACTION TRAINING (THEORY REVIEW)

Bodybuilders from traditional training schools are forever counting repetitions as a gauge to their progress or relative lack thereof. "*Three more reps!*" screamed the headline of a popular trilogy of bodybuilding books co-authored by bodybuilder Rick Wayne some years back. For the most part, this is how bodybuilders have conditioned themselves to think about training. However, training doesn't need to be based on repetitions to be productive. Instead, bodybuilders should be intensifying their training efforts by utilizing Max Contraction Training. This would have them fully loading their muscles for 1 to 6 seconds and terminating their set—not at some arbitrary number of repetitions, but at the point of muscular failure. We need to generate progressively stronger muscular contractions to stimulate maximum increases in the size and strength of our muscles.

In order to ensure maximum contractions, the two preconditions mentioned back in 1971 by Arthur Jones must be met: (1) Since muscle fibers contract by reducing their length or shortening, a muscle needs to be in the fully contracted position if all the fibers are to be contracted simultaneously. (2) In order for all of a given muscle's fibers to contract simultaneously, a load needs to be imposed that is heavy enough to activate all of the muscle's fibers. At the point of full or maximum contraction, no further movement is possible and the maximum number of fibers have been activated. What makes Max Contraction Training so productive is that it is the only training system that engages a targeted muscle group in this fully contracted position for the full duration of a set. Other systems will work a muscle with a varying degree of intensity (as they must, given that movement is involved in their execution). However, results in bodybuilding are always proportionate to the level of intensity applied to the target muscle group, and with Max Contraction Training there is no way the intensity can be increased—100 percent is the top of the hill.

When you perform a Max Contraction set, you must take special caution not to "throw" or "thrust" the resistance into the position of full-muscular contraction. Instead, slowly initiate the lift utilizing only the contracting muscle fibers of the muscle group itself. Remember that any time outside forces, such as momentum, are brought into play to move the resistance, the involvement of the targeted muscle group is proportionately diminished. Once in the fully contracted position, hold the contraction for 1 to 6 seconds.

Leg extensions.

THE LEG SPECIALIZATION ROUTINE

Leg Extensions (2 Sets)

Sit down on a leg extension machine and place your feet behind the roller pads so that your knees are snug against the seat. Keeping your head and shoulders straight, slowly straighten both legs until you reach the fully contracted position and sustain this contraction for a full 1 to 6 seconds. As soon as you've hit a point of muscular failure in the contraction, reduce the resistance by 20 percent and repeat the movement for an additional 1 to 6 seconds. Immediately move on to your next exercise.

Max Straps Adductions (2 Sets)

When you pull one leg into or across the other using the Max Straps, you are putting a great deal of stress on the adductor muscles of your inner thigh. To perform the adduction movement, attach the Max Straps to the end of a cable running through a floor pulley to your left ankle. Step back and away from the pulley so that your left leg will have to travel inward to lift the weight stack. Stand erect so that your right leg is far enough away from the pulley so as to keep resistance on your left leg throughout the movement. Grasp a sturdy upright to help in retaining your balance and, using only the muscles of your inner thighs, slowly pull

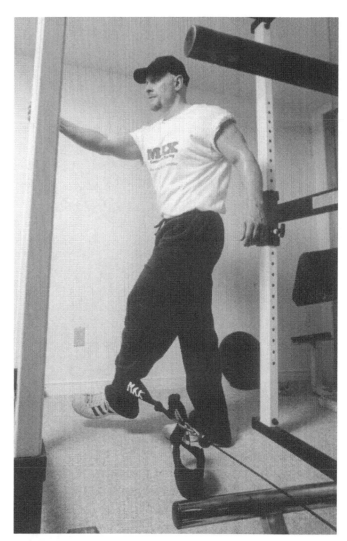

Max Straps adductions.

your left leg inward until it crosses over just in front of your right leg. Sustain this fully contracted position for 1 to 6 seconds. Then attach the Max Straps to your right ankle and repeat the exercise for 1 to 6 seconds.

Leg Curls (2 Sets)

Lie facedown on the leg curl machine. Place your feet under the roller pads with your knees just over the edge of the bench. Slowly curl your lower legs up until they're almost touching your buttocks. Once in this fully contracted position, sustain the contraction for a full 1 to 6 seconds. Then reduce the weight by 20 percent and perform a second set.

At this point in the routine, your legs are bound to feel rather wobbly—and with good reason. You've just exposed them to repeated bouts of nonstop maximum muscular contraction. Nevertheless, you still have the rest of your physique to deal with. We'll train it with only one Max Contraction set per bodypart, using the following exercises.

Standing Calf Raises (1 Set)

Sustain the full contraction for 1 to 6 seconds.

Lat Pulldowns (Incorporating Max Straps: 1 Set)

Sustain the full contraction for 1 to 6 seconds.

Pec Deck (1 Set)

Sustain the full contraction for 1 to 6 seconds.

Dumbbell Kickbacks (1 Set)

Sustain the full contraction for 1 to 6 seconds.

Chin-Ups (1 Set)

Sustain the full contraction for 1 to 6 seconds.

Max Straps Crunches (1 Set)

Sustain the full contraction for 1 to 6 seconds.

All of these exercises place a constant stress/tension on the target muscle groups from the start to the end of each individual set and are, therefore, the most productive exercises possible for the leg muscles owing to their extremely high-intensity threshold.

Your workouts should be structured to allow for adequate recovery to take place between workouts. With leg training, this can be anywhere from four days to two weeks—depending upon your own personal rate of recovery. If you follow this routine exactly as described in this chapter, you will be amazed at how quickly your legs will grow bigger and stronger. It is difficult, but very, very effective.

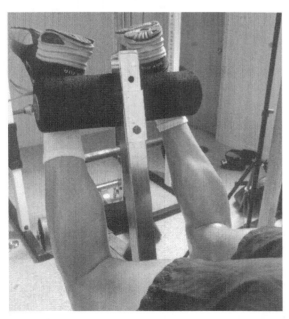

Leg curls.

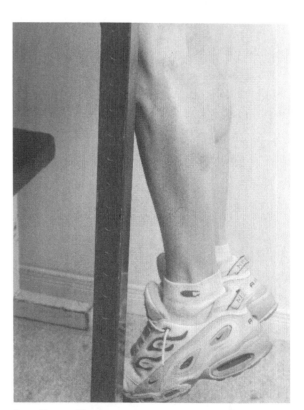

Standing calf raises.

Lat pulldowns.

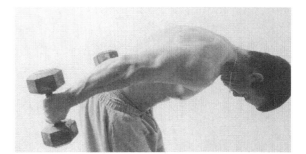

Dumbbell kickbacks.

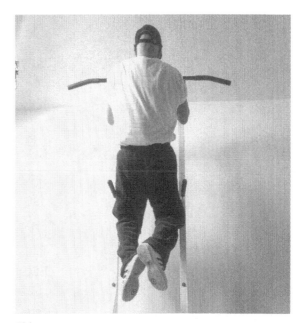

Chin-ups.

Pec Deck.

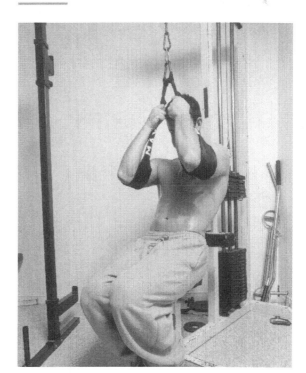

Max Straps crunches.

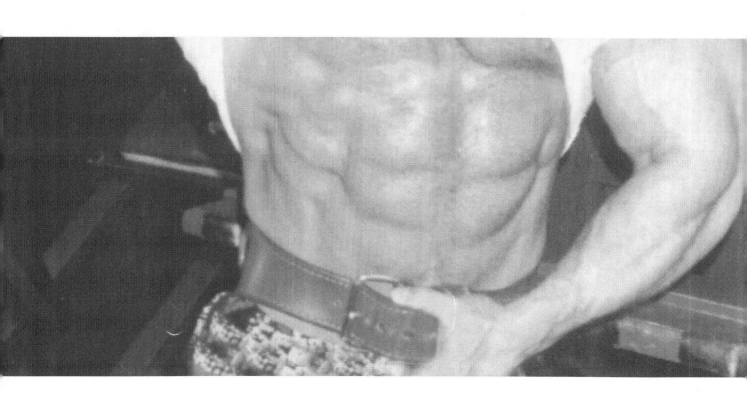

Chapter 19

FOCUS ON ABDOMINALS

Many bodybuilders, as well as laypeople concerned with trying to reduce their waistlines, have been known to perform hundreds of sets of hundreds of repetitions of various abdominal exercises in the misbegotten notion that by doing so they will be effectively removing fat from their midsections and developing their abdominal muscles.

However, a lean, muscular waistline has never been obtained by the performance of such high-set/high-repetition exercise. The appearance of the abdominals is affected by three factors, none of which involve high volume ab workouts. A striking set of abs is obtained via a low percentage of body fat, the development of the rectus abdominus and the external and internal oblique muscles, and—to a very large extent—genetics. In fact, just how and where a bodybuilder stores fat depends entirely upon his genetic makeup. In other words, whatever goes into your DNA before you're born and whatever goes into your mouth immediately after you're born are what will determine just how much and where you will store your body fat. The shape and pairing of the abdominal muscles are also based upon genetic inheritance, but your genetic predisposition and, indeed, your physical appearance can both be greatly enhanced by applying a sound understanding of anatomy and kinesiology of the abdominal musculature.

ANATOMY AND KINESIOLOGY

The abdominals are composed of front, back, and side muscle groups. From the front, the most visible is the "washboard" structure of the rectus abdominis, which is attached to the fifth, sixth, and seventh ribs. It extends across the pubis bone and its function is a simple one: to shorten the distance between the pelvic girdle and the lower section of the sternum. The two best exercises for this muscle group can be performed without any special benches or expensive abdominal machines: (1) Max

Straps crunches or (2) crunches performed on the floor with (if necessary) additional resistance provided by a simple barbell plate. To perform crunches, simply lie flat on your back on the floor and slowly roll both your shoulders and head up and forward while at the same time lifting your hips up and back towards your chest. When you reach a position of full muscular contraction, hold it for 1 to 6 seconds during each working set for the rectus abdominis.

The external oblique muscles are attached to the lower ribs and extend around the outer part of the waist until they attach to the hip bone. Their primary function is also simple: to bend the spine to one side and to rotate the torso to the opposite side. The internal oblique muscle resembles a sheath that runs beneath the external oblique. Its function is to produce lateral flexion to the side to which it is attached, in addition to providing torso rotation to the same side. The best exercise to train these muscles of the waist, utilizing conventional equipment, is the side bend with a weighted dumbbell or Max Straps Twists, which will be the exercise that we will employ to train both the external and internal obliques in this chapter's specialization routine.

THE AB SPECIALIZATION ROUTINE

Max Straps Crunches (2 Sets)

Attach the Max Straps to an overhead pulley (ideally on a lat pulldown machine that has a seat and knee pad). Sit down on the seat and place your arms through the Max Straps so that the pads are over the bends in your elbows. Lower your elbows down to a point and out to the sides so that the base of the Max Straps is touching the back of your neck. Now slowly bend your torso over while drawing your elbows downward until your elbows are almost touching your knees. Once you've hit the fully contracted position, sustain it for 1 to 6 seconds. When you can no longer sustain the contraction, reduce the weight and immediately perform a second set for 1 to 6 seconds. Move on immediately to your next exercise.

Max Straps Twists (2 Sets)

Attach the Max Straps to a floor pulley. Turning around so that your back is to the pulley, pick up the Max Straps and place your arms through the straps until the pads are resting on your upper arms or wrists (whichever is more comfortable). Keeping your feet planted firmly on the ground, twist your torso to the right as far as you can and sustain this fully contracted position for 1 to 6 seconds. When you can no longer sustain the contraction on the right side, slowly twist your torso to the left as far as possible and sustain this contraction for 1 to 6 seconds. When you have completed this, reduce the resistance by 20 percent and perform one more set for each side, making sure to sustain the fully contracted position for another 1 to 6 seconds.

It might seem like I'm unduly stressing the 1- to 6-second count, but it is a point that is crucial to your success with this method. Max Contraction Training could actually be called the "1- to 6-Second Contraction System" as it stresses each individual muscle group in the position that involves the maximum amount of muscle fibers over a 1- to 6-second time span. When using Max Contraction Training, you must throw out all preconceived training methodology. You no longer count repetitions because there are none. You don't need a variety of exercises to tax various muscle fibers because all of your available muscle fibers will be activated to sustain the contractions you're engaged in. Contracting a given muscle within the prescribed time frame of 1 to 6 seconds will ensure that each muscle has been sufficiently taxed and a higher level of growth stimulation will have been induced. If you're a beginner, you should perform this abdominal routine no more than three times a week. Advanced trainees should only train once a week—at the most.

The remaining bodyparts to be worked during this workout are as follows.

Leg Extensions (1 Set)

Sustain the full contraction for 1 to 6 seconds.

Leg Curls (1 Set)

Sustain the full contraction for 1 to 6 seconds.

Chin-Ups (1 Set)

Sustain the full contraction for 1 to 6 seconds.

Leg extensions.

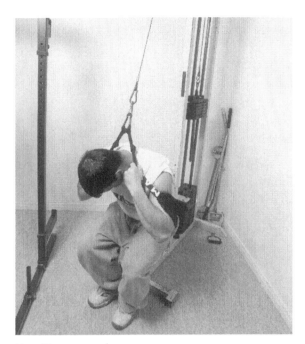

Max Straps crunches.

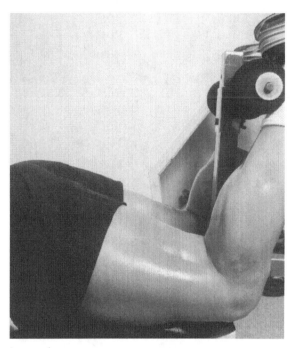

Leg curls.

Max Straps twists.

Chin-ups.

Cable Crossovers (1 Set)

Sustain the full contraction for 1 to 6 seconds.

Cable crossovers.

Lateral raises.

Lateral Raises (1 Set)

Sustain the full contraction for 1 to 6 seconds.

Max Straps Kickbacks (1 Set)

Sustain the full contraction for 1 to 6 seconds.

Steep-Angle Preacher Curls (1 Set)

Sustain the full contraction for 1 to 6 seconds.

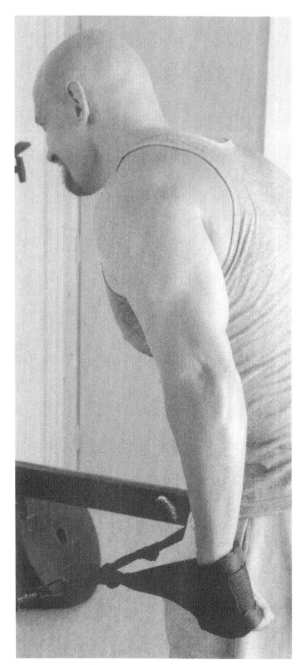

Max Straps kickbacks.

Wrist Curls (1 Set)

Sustain the full contraction for 1 to 6 seconds.

That is the specialization routine for abs. Don't let its seeming lack of volume lull you into thinking that this month's workout is a pushover. This routine properly performed will develop your abdominal muscles like no other system in bodybuilding and—when combined with a reduced calorie diet—will serve to "rip up" your midsection to such an extent that your abs could well become your best bodypart.

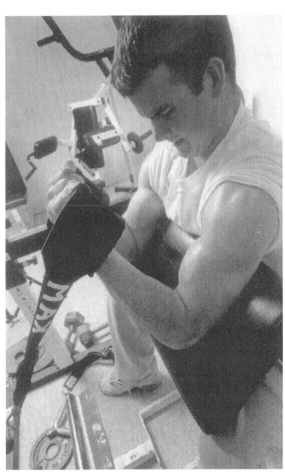

Steep-angle preacher curls.

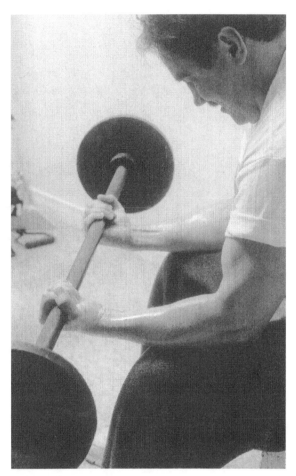

Wrist curls.

Part VI

ADDITIONAL CONSIDERATIONS

Chapter 20

MAX CONTRACTION FOR WOMEN

Many women still believe that if they engage in any kind of strength training they're going to end up with large, unfeminine muscles. Let us explode that myth right now. In Chapter 3 I touched upon the significance of genetics in determining the ultimate muscular potential of an individual's physique. Less than 1 percent of the male population has the capacity to develop a massive musculature like that of a professional bodybuilder; likewise, 99 percent of women lack the requisite genetics to develop a body like a male bodybuilder—even if they wanted to.

The reason men are, on average, bigger and stronger than women is also genetically based—because of the male hormone testosterone, which operates on the growth mechanism of the male body. The small percentage of women who have large muscles have either inherited a genetic predisposition toward inordinate levels of muscle mass or have an unusually high quantity of testosterone in their system. While the sex glands of women do secrete a small amount of testosterone, it isn't

enough to provide for the growth of massive muscles. However, even though the majority of women couldn't develop really large muscles if their lives depended on it, every woman can benefit from vigorous, intense weight training.

While the bodyweight of the typical male is approximately 15 percent fat, the typical female bodyweight is composed of 25 percent fat. This difference in body fat levels is due, in part, to the fact that female hormones—particularly estrogen—promote fat storage. It's also true, however, that women traditionally have been discouraged from participating in athletics and overloading their muscles vigorously. As a result, most women never develop much in the way of strength or muscle tone. This is unfortunate, because bodies of sedentary people, male or female, continue to change composition as they grow older, primarily through the addition of fat. This means that more of the total bodyweight will be fatty tissue and less will be lean body mass or muscle tissue; this progressive loss of muscle tissue makes it more and more difficult to lose fat. This results in a cycle that's hard to change—particularly for women.

Men naturally have more lean body mass and less fat to start with because of a higher basal metabolic rate (BMR)—anywhere from 5 to 20 percent higher than women. Although some of the male's leanness may be a sexual characteristic, it is the leaner people of either sex who have a higher BMR. This greater leanness means an ability to accommodate greater caloric intake without adding fat tissue to the body; it also serves to facilitate the burning of fat. Muscle tissue is much more active than fat tissue, burning more calories even at rest. So while low-calorie diets may result in weight loss, they are more effective when combined with exercise that strengthens and tones muscle.

Studies have revealed that 25 to 90 percent of the weight loss resulting from dietary restriction alone comes from muscle tissues, organs, and fluid—but not from fat. This loss of protein from muscles and organs is difficult to prevent even with a small caloric restriction in an inactive person and explains the wrinkling and sagging tissues that so often accompany weight loss by diet alone. For some, increased activity alone will turn the tide; one study found that overweight college women lost an average of 5.3 pounds in a two-month period during which they participated in a four-day-a-week, one-hour-per-session exercise program without any dietary restrictions. Skinfold measurements revealed that the weight loss was due to a much larger loss of fatty tissue and a simultaneous gain in muscle or lean body mass. Obviously then, the best procedure for promoting fat loss and altering body composition for improved appearance is a combination of diet and increased muscular activity.

OSTEOPOROSIS

Max Contraction Training yields another dividend: increased bone density. Studies have demonstrated repeatedly that physical activity increases the mineral content of our bones, and, more specifically, weight-bearing or resistance exercise has been associated with higher bone density. Sports medicine practitioners have universally concluded that weight training is beneficial in the prevention of osteoporosis, a condition that largely affects postmenopausal women in whom the density of bones decreases over time, often leading to fractures.

According to recent studies, osteoporosis currently afflicts 24 million Americans, and one out of every three women in her sixties is estimated to suffer a fracture in the spine because of it. The treatment of osteoporosis is by no means conclusive, but it's clear that lifestyle factors such as exercise influence the development of bone strength. An interesting fact regarding the significance of resistance on our bones was brought to light in the mid-1990s by the renowned aerobics guru Dr. Kenneth Cooper, who wrote:

> Along with many other exciting revelations from the NASA space program, the effect of weightlessness on bone mass reinforced the belief that exercise is important in the maintenance of bone strength. Using techniques which allowed scientists to measure the bone density of the astronauts of Skylab 4 both before and after space flight, it was discovered that weightlessness caused a marked loss of bone strength. In the absence of the pull of gravity, the bones were no longer required to support the weight of the body. As a consequence, the bones began to deteriorate rapidly. The calcium that was lost from the bones was eliminated from the body through the kidneys in such large amounts that there was actually concern that the astronauts might develop kidney stones in space! NASA's original plans for providing exercise for astronauts in space had centered around providing aerobic exercise to maintain cardiovascular fitness, which can easily be done in zero gravity. They are now working to devise forms of strength training that can be performed in order to protect the astronauts from muscle and bone deterioration.[1]

SELF-IMAGE

Of all the reasons women list for taking up an exercise and diet program, increasing sex appeal is uppermost in the minds of a great majority. After all, vanity is a strong motive for most of us. In a world where you present yourself to others daily, looking good seems to be of paramount importance.

A woman who has been sedentary for any length of time doesn't need reminders that she is losing her shape. There are certain areas that sag, dimple, and expand, serving as stark visible reminders of physical deterioration and potentially declining sex appeal. More often than not, the encroachment of the cellulite look and sagging tissues is due to poor muscle tone that results from inadequate training. Proper training, such as that found within the pages of this book, is part of the answer to regaining youthful form. Here are three trouble spots women need to watch, and some supplementary exercises that will help firm them.

THE WAISTLINE

Nothing seems to make a woman more painfully aware of her physical appearance than a bulging waistline. The first requisite in waist reduction is the elimination of excess fat. Reducing the fatty tissue circling the waist will come only from a reduction in the percentage of fat stored by the body, and this is best accomplished, most safely, by reducing daily caloric intake while at the same time eating a well-balanced diet.

Reducing calories below maintenance levels will result in fat loss over the entire body; if you're persistent with your diet, you will ultimately see a dramatic reduction in the fat that is presently deposited around your waist. But keep in mind that fat used for energy while on a diet comes fairly uniformly from the body's multiple fat stores, never from any one isolated area like the waistline. And since fat loss is a relatively slow process in the best of times, it will take a while before significant results are seen.

The degree to which you reduce daily caloric intake can be varied according to individual needs, but a minimum reduction of 500 calories per day is necessary to stimulate any meaningful fat loss. On the other hand, it's considered unwise for nutritional reasons to reduce one's daily intake to less than 1,200 calories. And while your diet is cutting into that unsightly flab, you'll have to turn to exercise in order to enhance your muscle tone and tighten your midsection. Don't think that you only have to target a problem area with one or two exercises to solve your problem. It's almost a natural tendency to think that spot reduction is possible. It isn't. Fat is general, and spot reduction simply does not occur. Exercise, of course, raises your activity quotient and metabolic rate so that some body fat is used for energy.

Intensive physical conditioning exercises can cause a decrease in fat deposits and an increase in lean bodyweight. In fact, it's possible to maintain the same weight but change your body's composition with a decrease in body fat and a balancing increase in muscular tissue. For example, a woman who weighs 140 pounds at 40 percent body fat will look much leaner and fit at 140 pounds and 20 percent body fat. Regardless of what changes in body composition and fat reduction result from your increased energy expenditure, your waist—or any bodypart for that matter—will trim down only in direct proportion to the loss of overall body fat.

A tight midsection, with firm, defined muscles, is a readily attainable goal for the average woman. Whatever your present condition, once you get started, don't be discouraged. The combination of diet and exercise, if you are faithful to it, will soon create a healthier and more toned and shapely appearance.

Max Straps Crunches (1 Set)

Since I've described this exercise in the previous chapter on abdominal specialization (see page 156), I won't go over its performance again here, except to say that Max Straps will help you immensely. Max Straps crunches will target your abdominal muscles directly. Other exercises that incorporate Max Straps, such as pulldowns, will further involve the abdominals in an indirect way because they are required to contract statically for the purpose of stabilizing your torso during these exercises. If you want to strengthen the oblique muscles at the sides of your waist, feel free to add the next exercise to your routine.

Max Straps Twists (1 Set)

Attach the Max Straps to a floor pulley. Turning around so that your back is to the pulley, pick up the Max Straps and place your arms through the straps until the pads are resting on your upper arms. Keeping your feet planted

Max Straps crunches.

Max Straps twists.

firmly on the ground, twist your torso to the right as far as you can and sustain this fully contracted position for 1 to 6 seconds. When you can no longer sustain the contraction on the right side, slowly twist your torso to the left as far as possible and sustain this contraction for 1 to 6 seconds. If you do not have a set of Max Straps, you may substitute the following exercise:

Dumbbell Side Bends

To perform this movement correctly, stand with your feet about shoulder width apart and clasp your right hand behind your head. Grasp a dumbbell in your left hand. Stand erect and slowly begin to bend laterally to your left, which will stretch your right oblique. Slowly ascend back to the starting position, but stop your ascent just before you raise yourself up to a completely vertical position. Hold this position for a full 1 to 6 seconds. Then switch the dumbbell to your right hand, place your left

Dumbbell side bends.

hand behind your head, and repeat the exercise. This exercise will tighten the sides of the waist by maximally contracting the oblique muscles.

THE GLUTES AND UPPER THIGHS

It is hard to get a good view of one's gluteus muscles, so it's easy to be unaware of their appearance. Because of a woman's naturally larger and broader pelvic girdle, in addition to her hormonal predisposition to fat buildup in the hips and buttocks, this area can quickly become out of condition. And the problem with the buttocks is that you can diet severely with little visible improvement.

The reason that diet alone can't turn the trick is that a sagging and deteriorating derriere is the result of diminished muscle tone in the gluteus muscles of the buttocks. While little can be done to change the shape of the female breast, there is always hope for the "glutes" (the name bodybuilders use in referring to the buttocks), as it is possible to train away that so-called cellulite and get rid of the dimples, pockmarks, and ripples that plague many women. Max Contraction Training will do the job. Combined with a sensible diet, Max Contraction Training can greatly tone and reshape the buttocks—you will find Max Straps helpful in training this area.

Properly toned muscle tissue gives your body shape and form. Fat has no tone or firmness at all. Since the buttocks problem is due to a loss of muscle tissue itself, the only solution is to strengthen the entire area, including the gluteus muscles, rear thighs, and lower back. High-repetition flexibility exercises, like those seen in so many women's magazines, will do little to help because the intensity of muscular output is simply too low.

Progressive resistance exercises provided by barbells or exercise machines are necessary to develop and tighten the glutes. You don't need to perform many sets of these movements. As a rule of thumb, stick with one to three sets of 1 to 6 seconds in duration. Make sure that when you reach your chosen time interval that this is the absolute *maximum* time you can sustain the contraction. In other words, don't simply select a modest weight and contract against it for an arbitrary number of seconds. For Max Contraction Training to be fully effective, the effort you put forth has to be the most you are momentarily capable of. No, it's not the easiest form of exercise, but it is the only type that consistently produces substantial results.

Stiff-Legged Deadlifts (1 Set)

This version of deadlifts is very effective in targeting the glutes. With the barbell set at knee level inside a power rack, and with your knees locked straight and head looking up, grasp the bar with one hand in an overhand position and the other hand in an underhand position (this will strengthen your grip and prevent the bar from rolling out of your

hands). Stand erect with the bar straight down at arm's length. Hold this contracted position for a minimum of 1 second and a maximum of 6. This exercise works the entire back side of the body from head to toe and will do wonders for tightening this problem area.

Hyper-Extensions (1 Set)

Lie down either crossways or lengthwise over a bench so that your torso is hanging over the edge of the bench. Have your partner hold, sit on, or in some way place resistance on your legs to counterbalance the weight of your torso. Place a weight (a modest one to begin) behind your neck and bend over at the waist. Slowly raise your torso (with your partner's assistance, if need be) using your lower back (or erector spinae) muscles until you have ascended as high as possible. At this point, you will have

Stiff-legged deadlifts.

Hyper-extensions.

activated the greatest percentage of muscle fibers. Try to hold this contracted position for 1 to 6 seconds.

Max Straps Thigh Kickbacks (1 Set)

This exercise will stress the glutes directly. Slip your right ankle into both of the Max Straps so that the pads are around your ankle. Then attach the end of a cable running through a floor pulley to the Max Straps. Stand erect and step back far enough from the pulley so that you have raised the weight from the weight stack. Draw your right leg straight back to the rear as far as possible. As soon as you have maximally contracted your right gluteus maximus muscle, sustain this maximal contraction for 1 to 6 seconds or until you can no longer sustain the contraction, and then lower the

Max Straps thigh kickbacks.

resistance. Now attach the Max Straps to your left ankle and repeat this exercise with that leg.

Leg Curls (1 Set)

You will need a special machine for this one, but it is well worth it. Leg curls are the most direct hamstring movement in existence, which is important if your desire is to firm up the rear portion of your thighs. Lying on your stomach, position yourself so your Achilles tendons make contact with the padded movement arm. Under control, bend your knees and curl the lower legs until the pad hits your buttocks. Sustain this fully contracted position for 1 to 6 seconds or until you can no longer sustain the contraction.

Leg Extensions (1 Set)

Again, you'll need a special machine for this movement (and you will for the next two as well). This movement thrusts the resistance directly onto the quadriceps muscles of the frontal thighs, which will help tremendously in firming up this area. Sit on the padded surface of the machine with your legs toward the movement arm of the apparatus. Slide forward until the backs of your knees are at the edge of the machine's padded surface. Hook your insteps under the lower set of roller pads. Sit erect and grasp the edges of the seat pad to

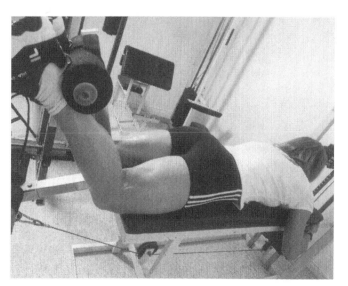

Leg curls.

Leg extensions.

steady your body in position during the movement. Slowly extend your legs until they are locked in a straight position and sustain this position for 1 to 6 seconds (or until you can no longer sustain the contraction) before lowering the weight.

Max Straps Hip Adductions (1 Set)

When you pull one leg into the other using the Max Straps, you are putting a great deal of stress on the adductor muscles of your inner thigh. To perform the adduction movement, attach the end of a cable running through a floor pulley to the Max Straps. Insert your left ankle into the Max Straps. Step back and away from the pulley so that your left leg will have to travel inward to lift the weight stack. Stand erect so that your right leg is far enough away

from the pulley so as to keep resistance on your left leg throughout the movement. Grasp a sturdy upright to help in retaining your balance and, using only the muscles of your inner thighs, slowly pull your left leg across until it just crosses over your right leg. Sustain this fully contracted position for 1 to 6 seconds. Then attach the Max Straps to your right ankle and repeat the exercise for a 1- to 6-second contraction.

Max Straps Hip Abductions (1 Set)

When pulling your leg away from the other leg against resistance, you will be stressing the muscles on the sides of your hips as well as the upper outer thighs. To perform the abduction movement, attach the Max Straps to your right foot (as you did previously for the adduction movement) so that your left side is closest to the floor pulley and the cable is running across your left ankle. Again, grasp a sturdy upright for balance during the movement and allow the weight of the apparatus to pull your right leg well across the midline of your body. Be sure to keep your right leg straight during the movement. Using only the muscles of your upper thighs and hips, slowly draw your right leg across your body and out to the side as far as possible and sustain this fully contracted position for 1 to 6 seconds. Then attach the Max Straps to your left ankle and repeat the exercise for another 1 to 6 seconds.

THE BUST

Women's preoccupation with the appearance of their bustlines has resulted in a multibillion dollar industry that purports to satisfy their "needs" in this department of anatomy. Gimmicks of all sorts can be found at the back of most women's magazines. There are exercises that promise added inches, and creams and massage treatments that are said to stimulate growth. My advice is to forget about these gimmicks and be realistic.

Be prepared to spend a little time on yourself. First, you'll have to accept the fact that the size and shape of your bustline are inherited

Max Straps hip adductions.

Max Straps hip abductions.

features and, therefore, not subject to dramatic alteration. Very little can be done to change the size and shape of the bust outside of drug treatments, surgery, implants, or large increases or decreases in body fat. However, having said that, you can bring your bust up to its genetic potential, which, of course, involves exercise. The Pec Deck exercise outlined in Chapters 12 and 16 is the best exercise for improving the size of your chest because it allows you to stimulate virtually every fiber in the chest region. It is also the safest chest exercise to perform. I would advise staying away from free weights, which can damage the shoulder joint and are not practical (for reasons already covered) for Max Contraction Training.

Pec Deck (1 Set)

This exercise hits not only chest muscles, but also your anterior deltoids and serratus muscles

Pec Deck.

as well. Adjust the height of the machine's seat so that your upper arms are perpendicular to your torso when you place your forearms against the resistance lever pads in front of you. Slowly draw your forearms together until they meet directly in front of your torso. Sustain this fully contracted position for 1 to 6 seconds or until you can no longer sustain the contraction. This exercise can also be performed to great effect by working one arm at a time.

THE BACK OF THE UPPER ARMS

Not long ago, I was training a woman who wanted to improve her golf game. She wasn't interested in "toning," or "firming." "I'm past that stage," she stated quite emphatically. "I just want to have more strength on the fairways." With this in mind, I devised a workout program for her based upon the principles of Max Contraction Training. It was a general program that covered the entire body, but with a little extra emphasis on the shoulders, back, and arms. My client's strength went up in every exercise in a very short time, and, to her delight, she was hitting the golf ball a lot farther off the tee and her short iron game also improved dramatically. However, I was most surprised one day when she came in for her biweekly maintenance workout and she told me, "I can't believe how toned my arms are! I used to have flabby skin at the back of my upper arms—that's all gone now! I feel 10 years younger!"

I hadn't really considered it at any great length before, but the triceps area (the back of the upper arms) really is a problem area for a lot of women. The older they get, the less exercise they tend to engage in that involves the triceps muscles. Their biceps, the muscle at the front of their upper arms, at least receive some stimulation by way of picking up things, carrying children, carrying groceries, and so on, but the triceps are all but ignored. To this end, if you happen to find your triceps area a little "wobbly," here is the best exercise to firm it up—and firm it up quickly: one-arm dumbbell kickbacks.

One-Arm Dumbbell Kickbacks (1 Set)

This exercise is more effective when performed on a cable machine with Max Straps. However, since most people have access to dumbbells, this is the variation of the exercise that I will feature here. Take hold of a dumbbell in one hand and, bending over so that your torso is at a 90-degree angle to your legs, extend your arm behind the midline of your body, all the while making a focused effort to keep the elbow of the arm holding the dumbbell completely locked straight. Sustain this fully contracted position for a full 1 to 6 seconds or until you can no longer sustain the contraction (whichever comes first). Then slowly lower the dumb-bell back to your hip and transfer the dumbbell to the other hand and repeat the exercise.

These exercises will serve to shape up the problem areas that are the concern of most women who embark upon a body-shaping or fitness program. Most women simply will not develop muscular mass no matter what they do, but lack of bulk doesn't mean that their strength and tone are not improving. And don't forget the other advantages of proper strength training, such as the reduced chances of developing osteoporosis in later years, reduced body fat levels, improved endurance, increased metabolic rate, and enhanced self-image.

One-arm dumbbell kickbacks.

A well-balanced diet—the only relevant nutritional factor in muscle building.

Chapter 21

NUTRITION: FACT AND FICTION

The common practice among some weight lifters, bodybuilders, and other power athletes of consuming liquids, powders, or pills of predigested protein is a waste of money and may actually be counterproductive.[1]

Supplements do not further improve a normal status.[2]

Normal people eating a well-balanced diet do not need to take additional vitamins.[3]

Active people and athletes do not require additional nutrients beyond those in a balanced diet.[4]

The above four quotes are taken from an exercise physiology textbook—a textbook that has no stake in the nutritional supplement business (obviously!) and that relates scientific facts regarding the human body, its energy and muscular systems, and its nutritional requirements. The statements are scientific facts—and yet, no doubt, they will have surprised and perhaps even have angered some people. Why is this? Because very few people have looked to the realm of nutritional science for the answers to their body's requirements in terms of food, preferring instead to look to diet gurus and muscle magazines, and to believe the blandishments of the marketers of nutritional supplements. And I would be angry too if I had spent thousands of dollars per annum on something that was "a waste of money and . . . actually counterproductive." But facts are facts.

I'm aware that these facts fly directly in the face of the propaganda that you read each month in the various muscle magazines, but it should be pointed out that bodybuilding magazines do not qualify as reliable guides as, quite frankly, there isn't one of them that isn't in the pocket of the nutritional supplement companies. In fact, I make no distinction between bodybuilding magazines and the supplement companies, as the lifeblood of the bodybuilding magazine business is advertising revenue, and the supplement companies are the heaviest advertisers in these publications. By extension, this means that should a supplement company that drops a lot of revenue per annum on advertising wish to have an article published that extols the virtue of their product or the merits of a particular ingredient found in their product, they command attention and their wishes are in most instances catered to.

"The customer is always right," says an old business adage, and the "customer" for the muscle magazines isn't the consumer who purchases the magazine every month, but rather the supplement companies that pay substantial ad revenues to the publishers of these magazines. It is the supplement companies—not the bodybuilders—who are the magazines' customers, and the more such customers they have, the bigger and more successful their magazines become. This explains why you see so many supplement advertisements within the pages of every muscle magazine; it is simply evidence of many "happy customers." And well they should be; according to a recent article by the Associated Press, the supplement business is a $19 billion dollar a year industry.

The bodybuilding magazines are notoriously behind the curve of most scientific training advances (as they are usually managed these days in consultation with accountants and lawyers rather than exercise scientists). However, they are absolutely cutting edge when it comes to knowing their consumer base, the disposable income of their consumer base, and the fact that supplements are "perishable" and, thus, the consumer—if he believes he must have them—will keep paying on a monthly basis so as not to be caught without his supply of a particular supplement. Valid training information, such as you have obtained with the purchase of this book, is what is known in business terms as a "one-off," a one-time sale. This means that you don't need to go out and buy this same book month after month; you've already obtained all the information it contains with your initial purchase of it. But supplements, so you're led to believe, must be consumed each month (which is why they are typically sold in one-month supplies) and require you to spend, in some instances, several thousands of dollars of your hard-earned money each year to obtain them.

Most magazines, recognizing the money to be made from the sale of supplements, now feature their own brands, usually under a different label so as not to appear too obvious about it to their readers. My point in mentioning the pervasive influence of the supplement companies in bodybuilding is to caution you that such influence is profound and it distorts the truth. Indeed, the prevailing worldview of most individuals in our culture is that supplements are an absolute necessity if health and fitness are your goals simply because that is what is reflected in the films (via product placement marketers) and the magazines. Unfortunately, most (in some cases all) of the "training" information that you read in the bodybuilding magazines is substantially biased in favor of what you are told you "need" to take in the way of supplements. This is not a knock against supplements per se, but rather a condemnation of the deliberate attempt to distort nutritional reality that the marketers of these supplements have chosen to engage in.

Supplements are intended to complete a diet that for whatever reason is unbalanced; that is, an individual is not getting the minimum amount of vitamins, minerals, or macronutrients that he requires in order to achieve a normal standard of health and thus develop properly. Supplements have also been touted from time to time as an alternative to the preferred choice of receiving adequate nutrition from the foods you eat. I'm in favor of choice; it's one of the benefits of living in a free society. And there is no question that we have made huge advances in our knowledge and creation of nutritional options. However, when the alternative is marketed as being superior when it is not, and essential and indispensable when it is neither, and when I see thousands of young or naïve bodybuilders being taken in by this, I feel a moral obligation to expose these enormous fallacies.

Whether you choose to derive your nutrition from a well-balanced diet or from nutritional supplements is just that: *your* choice. However, the marketers of these supplements have taken the morally reprehensible approach of attracting you to their product by simply carpet bombing you with propaganda condemning the supplement's alternative. They hope that if they can distill a fear in the consumer that he is not obtaining adequate nutrition from his regular diet, he will be more susceptible to their blandishments and, hence, more likely to purchase their company's particular brand of nutrition.

In the vast majority of cases (i.e., barring genetically based intolerance to certain foodstuffs), it makes no difference to your body whether the nutrition you ingest comes from a $45-a-month nutritional supplement or from a chicken breast, a T-bone steak, a Big Mac, or a glass of milk. A protein molecule is a protein molecule, and the molecules that form protein must bond in a specific fashion in order for your body to utilize them. Once your body ingests the protein molecule, it is put to work for growth and repair purposes as all protein molecules are—irrespective of their source. The problem with the supplement companies is that they want you to believe you can only get the nutrition you need for building muscles from supplements and, specifically, from *their* supplements—which is neither true nor ethical.

I'm not trying to be unduly critical of the bodybuilding magazines that promote these nutritional supplements; there are, of course, training principles advanced in these publications, some of which are quite effective, along with others that are grossly ineffective. And these are salted into the bodybuilding magazines with just the right regularity to convey the impression that the magazine deals with training, rather than merely being a catalogue for various nutritional supplements. Where the bodybuilding magazines have fallen ethically (not that many of them had much height to fall from) is in their willingness to comply with this nutritional deception, such as when their articles on training also indicate that the training principles work best in conjunction with a particular supplement. The fact that many of the champions featured in these publications extolling the merits of a particular nutritional supplement are loaded up with tens of thousands of dollars of contraband anabolic drugs is, of course, never disclosed.

I mention this as a caveat, as nutrition is a secondary concern in the muscle growth equation. (In fact, studies conducted at Harvard University indicated that muscle tissue can

grow on a starvation diet if the proper training stress is present, which indicates just how secondary the nutritional concern is.[5]) The first concern of the body in regard to growing bigger and stronger muscles is that the muscle be taxed or stimulated sufficiently by a high-intensity training stress (exercise)—something that no supplement can provide, for it is only accomplished via training. Yet, the vast majority of bodybuilding magazines would have you believe that bodybuilding is actually "85 percent nutrition." They have to distort nutritional reality; it's how they earn a living and has been since at least the 1960s.

The largest bodybuilding publications of that era were Bob Hoffman's *Strength & Health* and *Muscular Development* magazines and Joe Weider's *Muscle Builder* and *Mr. America* magazines. Both Hoffman and Weider sold protein powders, weight-gainers, and other such products, and all of the up-and-coming body-

Nutrition is actually a secondary concern in the muscle growth process. The most important factor is that the training stress is intense enough to stimulate an increase in muscle mass.

builders endorsed these various products as part of their entrance requirement into the world of big-time bodybuilding. Sometimes the bodybuilder got paid to publicly misrepresent the source of his muscular gains; more often he simply bartered his integrity for exposure in these publications.

And so the merry charade has continued, more or less unabated, since the 1960s; the magazines provide a little bit of information on training sandwiched in between a lot of hype for the latest supplement du jour. I said earlier in this chapter that you can derive your nutrition from a well-balanced diet or from supplements—or both—but that there exists no evidence whatsoever that nutritional supplements are superior or even a *preferred* source of nutrition for your bodybuilding needs. This isn't simply my opinion, but a fact of exercise science. You needn't take my word for it; the four quotes at the beginning of this chapter are simply a sampling of findings in this area.

Nutrition has been an area of bodybuilding that has been made unnecessarily complex and problematic. For thousands of years humankind has built muscle mass without "special formulas," "engineered foods," or "Mega-Mass" powders. Yet most newcomers to bodybuilding are under the impression that they need to spend up to $200 per month on food supplements if they want to realize their goals of a more muscular body. I'm here to tell you—after twenty-some years in this business—that the ads for nutritional supplements are, for the most part, complete and utter hogwash. The products they promote will do nothing—repeat, nothing—to stimulate your muscles to grow, nor will they allow the muscle growth you stimulate in your training sessions to develop any quicker than if you took no supplements at all. In fact, if you take the time to read the labels of most nutritional supplements closely, you will find a disclaimer similar to the following, which appears on a package of Weider Nutrition's Victory Anabolic Mass, and which is always posted in very small print:

> As with all supplements, use of this product will not promote faster or greater muscular gains. This product is however, a

nutritious low-fat food supplement which, like other foods, provides nutritional support for weight training athletes.

There it is folks—the black and white of it. These "Anabolic" (i.e., "tissue-building") "Mass" products "*will not promote faster or greater muscular gains*"—and the gains they won't promote can be yours for a few hundred bucks a year. The advertising for these products is governed by the Federal Trade Commission (FTC), which issues warnings to companies (if sufficient consumer protest is received) and, if the warnings are ignored, fines. However, it is the Food and Drug Administration (FDA) that is responsible for closely regulating false medical or scientific claims on products, and ignoring their "cease and desist" letters has serious consequences—from hefty fines to jail time. Supplement manufacturers can use seductive names, such as "Big Mass Builder" and "Super Muscle Maker," but if they make a claim that the product can't produce, they are subject to investigation and prosecution by the FDA. Thus the disclaimer—in very small print. The reason so many people think they need nutritional supplements is the fact that most newcomers to bodybuilding buy muscle magazines, and the muscle magazines are largely in the business of selling supplements—both their own brands and those of their advertisers.

This second bit of idol-breaking now out of the way, I'm not saying that nutrition isn't important for building muscle. I am saying that there is a difference between nutrition and nutritional supplements. I've known otherwise decent, ethical human beings who have completely sold out their integrity by lending their name or reputation to a supplement company in exchange for money—not giving a damn about the fact that their complicity would deliberately mislead thousands of consumers. Moreover, many of these same people—ranging from Ph.D.s to bodybuilding champions— never once in their lives used the supplement they were endorsing and telling their fans and followers to consume. This is a serious moral abdication. If they never used the supplement, how would they know what its effects are—

It isn't the supplements that professional body-builders take that make their muscles so freaky looking.

positive or negative? And if, as has on occasion turned out to be the case, the supplement causes health problems, how could they possibly in clear conscience recommend that others use it? They never seem to have such pangs of conscience; if the money is attractive, they are willing to have you believe that this inert and perhaps dangerous product played a huge role in developing their bodies.

If you don't know by now, the two factors responsible for most of the muscle mass you see on the bodybuilders in the magazines are genetics and drugs. Genetics, as we've seen, provides the foundation or raw materials that your training stimulates into growth; the more

of these raw materials you have in your genetic arsenal, the bigger and more defined your muscles will be. On the one hand, training will do nothing to improve upon your genetic predisposition to building mass, but, on the other hand, it is the only thing that will allow you to realize it. Anabolic steroids, on the other hand, are potent agents that serve to synthesize nitrogen in the muscles and also to store glycogen within the muscle, which, in turn, serves to retain the water of which muscle is largely composed. And the more water retained in the muscle, the bigger the muscle looks. And, of course, when you stop taking the drugs, you lose the additional nitrogen in the muscle along with the water it retained, and your muscles shrink back to mere "mortal" size.

I vividly recall an incident backstage at an amateur bodybuilding contest. A bodybuilder was so loaded up with nocuous contraband drugs that he actually passed out from an electrolyte imbalance caused by an inadvertent overdose on insulin—insulin, a potent diabetic drug, for God's sake!—and a medical team had to be called in to revive him. As this happened backstage, it went beneath the radar of the audience. Later that evening, after the "champion" had been brought back from death's door by the paramedics who arrived on the scene and had spent several hours in a local hospital, he ventured out onto the stage for the evening finals to a smattering of applause, as no one knew what had transpired earlier. He won no prize money, and today, eight years later, nobody in bodybuilding even knows his name. My point is that this man almost died—for nothing. I don't know what you would call such a spectacle, but please don't call it bodybuilding. Bodybuilding is, as the name would imply, an activity that actually "builds" one's "body"; what these morons are doing could rightly be categorized as "body destroying." This is not peculiar to amateur bodybuilding contests; in most professional contests the "winner" is the unhealthiest man in the show.

Incidentally, immediately after the amateur contest, the bodybuilder who nearly died had his photo taken by a magazine impresario. Told to hold up a can of the magazine's house brand of protein "mass builder," he complied. The ad appeared in the magazine several months later, and thousands of cans of this useless product were sold in the mistaken belief that its contents were in some way responsible for the "champion's" muscle size. In fact, he had never even seen the product until after the contest and most certainly never used it in building the physique that was in evidence that day.

NUTRITIONAL REALITY

There is such a thing as nutritional reality, and you will be pleased to know that in order to make maximum gains on Max Contraction Training, or any other bodybuilding system for that matter, you don't need to spend *any* money on contraband and dangerous drugs or nutritional supplements. High-intensity training of the Max Contraction variety places a demand on the body's biochemical reserves. These reserves include the amino acid pool (which is of vital significance, since amino acids are the very stuff of life and of big muscles); the elements sodium and potassium (the electrolytes needed for high-intensity muscle contraction); important minerals such as calcium and magnesium (which help maintain a steady-state nervous system); and, of course, vitamins (which transform our food into the enzymes responsible for energy metabolism).

The nutrients mentioned above sound impressive in isolation but in fact are easily attainable through a well-balanced diet. In fact, a well-balanced diet is the best way to obtain these amino acids. Many bodybuilders who were big on amino acids (some still are), owing to the huge amount of advertising they were exposed to about how significant they were to the muscle growth process, willingly spent thousands of dollars per annum on amino acid capsules. What does science have to say about this? Let's see for ourselves:

> The belief [was] that the simple amino-acid molecule is absorbed more easily by the body and in some magical way is available rapidly to facilitate the expected muscle growth brought on by training. This,

however, is not the case. Dietary proteins are absorbed by the body when they are part of the more complex di- and tri-peptide molecules compared to the simple amino acid molecule. The intestinal tract is better able to handle protein in its more complex form, whereas a concentrated amino-acid solution draws water into the intestines. This process can cause irritation, cramping, and diarrhea.[6]

These are exactly the symptoms of many of the bodybuilders who take amino acids. A well-balanced diet, on the other hand, does not cause such problems and allows the body to burn fat, build muscle, and create energy for high-intensity workouts just fine. In fact, this has been the case for thousands of years. Even fixating on one nutrient is undesirable; emphasizing protein, amino acids, creatine, B-vitamins, wheat germ, brewer's yeast—or the thousand other supplements that bodybuilders are told they "must have"—is pointless. To be healthy, eat healthy food and make sure all the basic food groups are represented in your daily diet. Without an ample supply each day of protein, vitamins, minerals, fats, carbohydrates, and water, your workouts will inevitably degenerate into pointless affairs, full of sound and fury perhaps, but ultimately signifying nothing.

A WELL-BALANCED DIET

A very important requisite for building a more muscular physique is good health. Along with adequate rest, maintaining a well-balanced diet is absolutely essential in developing your physique. Most reputable nutritional scientists indicate that a well-balanced diet consists of a ration of 60 percent carbohydrates, 25 percent protein, and 15 percent fats. Balancing your diet for health maintenance and for muscle gains requires over 40 different nutrients, but each of these various nutrients can be obtained from generous daily portions from six basic food groups. It may be simplistic to say that a well-balanced diet is "a little bit of everything," but in fact, that's exactly what it is. Nutritionists have divided foods into six groups based on similarities in nutritive value and their role in the diet. A well-balanced diet includes several servings from each group every day. Here's how they break down:

1. *Meat, poultry, dry beans, and nuts*: two or three servings of meat, fish, poultry, or eggs. Nuts and beans can be substituted. (Note: A serving size is average, e.g., three ounces of meat, and does not include gravies or sauces. The grains should not be included in cakes, pies, or other sweets. This does not mean that you shouldn't have gravy on your potatoes or cake for dessert, just that such items generally add only calories and are of little nutritional value.)

2. *Vegetables*: three to five servings.

3. *Fruits*: two to four servings.

4. M*ilk, yogurt, and cheese*: two or three servings of milk, cheese, butter, or ice cream.

5. *Breads and cereals*: four or more servings.

6. *Fats, oils, and sweets*: use sparingly.

These six groups are not the be-all and end-all of eating and nutrition, but they are a reliable guide to well-balanced consumption. They are analyzed in much greater detail in books devoted to nutrition (not diet books). Individual adjustments can be made to suit your basic needs, your additional needs for energy consumption (exercise and pregnancy can increase the total amount of food you eat and consequently the nutrients you ingest), products available in your part of the country, and your lifestyle. A person who eats a diet that includes most of the foods in these six groups each day should not need vitamin or mineral supplements of any kind. The various nutrients are classified within the six major categories already mentioned: protein, carbohydrates, fats, vitamins and minerals, and water. The following analysis will help you understand the role of each in your muscle building diet:

• *Protein*: the word *protein* is from the Greek word meaning "prime," or "of first importance." This does not mean, however, that protein is of *only* importance. But after water, protein is the primary constituent of muscle tissue, making up the bulk of the contractile element within muscle tissue.

• *Carbohydrates*: the primary fuel source for our muscles comes from carbohydrates in the simple form known as glucose. When we don't take in enough sugar through our diets to fuel muscular contractions, our bodies will transform the amino acid alanine into glucose (in other words robbing our muscle tissue to create glucose), so carbohydrates have a protein-sparing effect. In addition to supplying energy, carbohydrates supply deribose, which is found in RNA and DNA (two essential components of all living matter) and is a form of sugar derived from the carbohydrates we eat. Carbohydrates stored within our muscles in the form of glycogen are largely responsible for keeping water inside our cells. Bodybuilders who go on low-carb diets for any appreciable length of time experience a flattening effect on their muscles as the unreplaced glycogen sheds or releases the water it was bonded to in the muscle cell, and hence their muscles "deflate."

• *Fats*: fats are an important source of fuel which provides energy in low-intensity endurance activities once the anaerobic reserves have been depleted. Since certain vitamins are soluble only in fat, it is obvious that fats figure crucially in a well-balanced diet.

• *Vitamins and minerals*: all the various vitamins and minerals are referred to as "micronutrients," as they are required in such minute quantities each day. Recommended daily allowances of the micronutrients are measured in milligrams as opposed to the grams of the macronutrients. Vitamins and minerals combine in the body to form enzymes that serve as catalysts in innumerable physiological processes. If you are consuming a well-balanced diet, you could be getting all the vitamins and minerals you need.

• *Water*: all of life's complex chemical processes take place in a fluid medium provided by water. The fluidity of our blood and lymph is water; water keeps our joints lubricated and helps maintain a constant body temperature; and, not of least importance to the bodybuilder, water is the primary constituent of muscle tissue. Viewed thusly, water could rightly be said to be the most important nutrient for survival as well as for growth.

EATING MORE ISN'T THE ANSWER

While nutrition is important for maintaining good health, eating more nutrients than your body requires on a daily basis will not cause your muscles to grow at a faster rate. Most of us make the mistake of believing what we read in the muscle magazines, for example, that muscle is made up of protein, and conclude that we have to eat lots of protein in order to build bigger muscles. However, muscle is actually composed of 70 percent water, 22 percent protein, and 6–8 percent lipids and inorganic materials. The primary constituent of muscle is not protein—as the protein salesmen would have you believe—but water. However, this does not mean that we hasten the muscle growth process by drinking inordinate

amounts of water every day. Doing so would only result in your eliminating the excess water through urination. However, you don't have that same impunity with protein because protein contains calories: when you eat more calories than you need to maintain your existing condition, the excess (apart from that which can be excreted) is stored as fat. Protein can actually make you just as fat as carbohydrates or fats do because protein contains calories, and it is calories consumed in excess of maintenance levels that make you fat.

Contrary to popular belief, nutritionists find that heavy exercise requires little if any "extra" protein.[7] A running back and a desk clerk (of the same size), for example, have about the same protein needs. One study found that cross-country skiers used essentially the same amount of protein when they raced from 22 to 53 miles a day as they did while relaxing.[8] Muscle mass is not increased by eating more protein but through high-intensity exercise and good genetics. What we eat merely supplies the materials for the increase; it doesn't cause it.[9]

Contrary to popular belief, nutritionists have found that heavy exercise does not increase the body's need for extra protein.

Even the miniscule amount of protein that goes into building muscle that has been stimulated through exercise doesn't require "extra" amounts to develop, as the typical North American diet already provides all the protein that is required.[10, 11] The August 1997 issue of *The Physician and Sportsmedicine* reported the following:

> Based on a wide review of scientific data, current daily protein recommendations for serious strength trainers are about 0.6 to 0.8 grams per pound (1.4 to 1.8 g/kg).

Translated into bodybuilding terms, a 200-pound bodybuilder would only require from 120 to 160 grams of protein per day, while a 140-pound bodybuilder would need just 84 to 112 grams of protein per day. If you are trying to build muscle, you would be well advised to use the higher figure for determining your daily protein intake (i.e., 0.8 grams per pound), whereas if you have built sufficient mass and were, for example, dieting for a contest, you would probably be able to maintain your muscle mass by consuming the lower figure of 0.6 grams per pound of body weight. Female athletes, who typically carry less muscle mass than their male counterparts, would require less protein still. Nitrogen balance tests conducted on female endurance athletes revealed that they required only 75 percent of the protein that men did on a daily basis. However, female bodybuilders might require a higher amount (more in line with what male bodybuilders require) because they are carrying more muscle than most other female athletes.

EATING TO BUILD PURE MUSCLE

Let's assume that you're going to successfully apply the principles espoused in this book and train to stimulate 10 pounds of muscle growth over the coming year. Obviously nutrition must factor into creating those 10 additional pounds—but to what extent? How much food will you have to eat to gain 10 pounds of pure muscle without adding any body fat?

One pound of muscle tissue contains 600 calories. This is true in all human beings, whether we're talking about you or the current Mr. Olympia. If you were to surgically excise a pound of muscle tissue and place it in a device known as a calorimeter, it would give off 600 calories of heat. If you were to gain 10 pounds of muscle mass over the course of one year, you would have to consume 10 × 600 calories, or 6,000 a year over and above your maintenance need of calories (that is, the amount of calories consumed on a daily basis that are required to simply maintain your current bodyweight). You read that correctly: that's 6,000 extra calories a year—not 6,000 extra calories a day, a week, or a month, but 6,000 extra calories *a year*. And attempting to consume that amount within a day, a week, or a month will do nothing at all to hasten the muscle growth process. Again, your body has specific nutritional requirements, and any amount above these requirements is passed off or stored as fat.

Still, the tendency for most bodybuilders is to think of their nutritional needs in terms of days. And if we do the math on this, we find that the daily total of extra nutrition required to grow an extra 10 pounds of muscle comes out to approximately 16 extra calories a day (6,000 calories divided by 365 days) over and above your daily maintenance need of calories.

The actual process of eating contributes in a subsidiary capacity to the muscle growth process. The primary requisite for muscle growth is the stimulation you impart through your high-intensity workouts in the gym. Once this has occurred, nutrition becomes a secondary requisite in that you must provide adequate nutrition to maintain your existing physical mass and then provide 16 calories or so to allow for that tiny bit of extra muscle growth that might be taking place on a daily basis—and I emphasize "might be taking place."

The fact is that most trainees—regardless of their training preference—already eat more than they need to gain an additional 10 pounds of muscle over the course of a year. If you're not growing muscle mass to your satisfaction presently and you're eating sufficiently, then the reason you're not growing is that you're not

To build an extra 10 pounds of muscle per year, your daily caloric intake only needs to increase by a mere 16 extra calories, which can be accomplished by simply taking an extra sip of milk.

training with sufficient intensity to stimulate an adaptive muscular response. Again, the formula is:

1. Stimulate growth through your Max Contraction Training.
2. Eat enough to maintain your existing physical mass—your "maintenance need of calories."
3. And then, to assist in the growth of those additional 10 pounds, you've got to tack on 16 calories a day to your maintenance need of calories.

DETERMINING YOUR MAINTENANCE NEED OF CALORIES

Some of you reading this may be asking yourself, *What is a maintenance need of calories, and how do I determine it?* Your maintenance need of calories is simply that— the amount of calories required to *maintain* your present bodyweight. The method required to ascertain it is

a very simple one, taught to me by former Mr. Universe Mike Mentzer:

Every day for seven days write down every single thing you eat—from the ice cream bar you have for a snack at lunch to the teaspoon full of sugar you put in your coffee at work—and then, after each day is over, sit down with a calorie counting book and calculate your total number of calories for that day. At the end of the seven days, total your seven daily caloric totals, divide that number by seven, and—voila!—you have just computed your maintenance need of calories. Here's a hypothetical example of how this might break down:

Monday	2,500 calories
Tuesday	2,700 calories
Wednesday	4,500 calories
Thursday	1,500 calories
Friday	2,500 calories
Saturday	5,000 calories
Sunday	1,500 calories

Adding these seven daily totals from our hypothetical one-week period, we get 13,700 calories. Dividing this by seven, we come out with a daily average of 2,740 calories per day. This would be your maintenance need of calories (assuming of course that you neither gained nor lost weight during the time you recorded these figures). This simple method of computing your maintenance need of calories takes into account such diverse and highly individual factors as your Basal Metabolic Rate (BMR) and your voluntary physical activity output. It doesn't even matter how unique or fast your individual metabolism is—it's all taken into account with this formula. Once your maintenance need of calories has been determined, it becomes a relatively simple procedure to add 16 extra calories a day to your daily average in order to provide that extra nutrition necessary to assist in the growth of an extra 10 pounds of muscle. In our example above, this would mean that the daily average caloric intake would be increased from 2,740 to 2,756 per day. Those extra 16 calories can be obtained by simply taking a sip of milk!

All of this should underscore the fact that force-feeding yourself hundreds or even thousands of extra calories per day and thousands of dollars' worth of nutritional supplements a year will not hasten the muscle building process at all. In fact, the only thing that force-feeding will succeed in hastening is increasing the size of your waistline.

Bodybuilding nutrition is not infinitely complex. In fact, it's simple, straight-forward, and capable of being summarized in a single sentence: Eat a well-balanced diet.

Max Contraction Training will make you bigger and stronger—how much bigger and how much stronger is a matter that will ultimately be determined by your genetics.

Chapter 22

RATIONAL EXPECTATIONS

Now we come to the point where the proverbial rubber meets the road. After all this science, all this theory, and all these exercises, what sort of gains can you expect by training on Max Contraction?

I won't mislead you. I would be disingenuous if I told you that by following my system you'd develop 20-inch arms or a 50-inch chest, as no training method (mine included) is a guarantee for creating a championship physique. Nor will I guarantee that you will gain 5, 10, 15, or 30 pounds of muscle (even though there have been those who have accomplished this in a very short time while using the system). Since I do not know your physiology, your training experience, your age, your sex, or your ability to tolerate the stress of bodybuilding exercise, I have no means by which to assess your genetic potential ahead of time. However, the good news is that *you* have the means to determine your potential for bodybuilding success (the indices of which were covered in Chapter 3).

My caveat now out of the way, I will say that Max Contraction Training will substantially alter your appearance for the better; it will put more muscle on you than you might

Max Contraction will dramatically alter your appearance for the better.

have believed possible, and it will do this so quickly that it will shock you. And, if you have the genetic makeup to build 20-inch arms, then this training system will realize it in the quickest time possible. If your genetics aren't of such Godzilla-esque proportions, you needn't despair, however. After all, not every great bodybuilder has sported limbs of such super-human dimensions. Indeed, such time-honored bodybuilding champions as John Grimek, Steve Reeves, Frank Zane, Mike Mentzer, Chris Dickerson, Franco Columbu, Shawn Ray, and Lee Labrada—to name but a few—never built their arms up to 20 inches either, yet all of them possessed tremendously well-muscled physiques. Besides, as I indicated earlier, potential is simply the expression of a latent possibility (as an acorn is a potential oak tree) and can only be measured accurately in hindsight. You'll never know exactly what your ultimate muscular potential is (or might have been) unless you try.

IT WON'T HAPPEN OVERNIGHT

Gains in muscular mass—at least those derived from drug-free training—do not have to come slowly, but they won't happen overnight, either. While it is true that nobody gains muscle "too quickly," gains in muscle mass and strength can come quite rapidly if the correct stimulation to the muscles is present and an adequate period of time is allotted for rest and recovery from the workout. The key is to be realistic and far-sighted in your bodybuilding goals. If you train hard and eat properly, it won't take long (anywhere from six months to two years) to dramatically transform yourself.

How fast is the muscle growth process when you train with the Max Contraction method? Depending upon your genetic predisposition for building big muscles, as well as how underweight you are to begin with, you could gain anywhere from 10 to 30 pounds over the course of a year. Thirty pounds is a

The great John Grimek's arms never stretched the tape to 20 inches.

Size and strength gains come slowly but steadily—if you continue to raise your IOC.

huge amount of muscle, and would require *very* intense training to stimulate your body into producing—but it is possible. I've seen it happen. However, a more realistic expectation can be arrived at, not by looking at cases of tremendous success in isolation, but in looking at the average amount of muscle gained over a six-week period taken from a group of individuals of varying genetic endowment while training on this protocol.

For example, when I performed a study on 17 people doing Max Contraction Training during the summer of 2001, one individual gained 30 pounds of muscle, another gained 25, and another 18 pounds. These were the high-end gainers. Another trainee on the study gained 16 pounds, three gained 15 pounds, five gained 10 pounds, two gained 8 pounds, two gained 6 pounds, and one gained 5 pounds. Thus, the average gain was 12.5 pounds per person from one and a half months of training on Max Contraction.

Once an individual's bodyweight stabilizes to something closer to what would be considered normal for his genetic structure, gains in muscle mass are harder to acquire and require an ultra-high-intensity training stress and added periods of rest and recovery in order to manifest. Our figure of 12.5 pounds is a good average of what you can expect if you train on the Max Contraction method. This is actually well above the norm, as most exercise physiologists and seasoned bodybuilders would agree that gaining 10 pounds of muscle in a single year is a considerable achievement—not 10 pounds of bodyweight (i.e., including fat), but 10 pounds of *pure muscle.*

Admittedly, 12.5 pounds of muscle doesn't sound like much beef to someone hungry for muscle mass. However, looked at over a longer term, say five years (which is how you should look at your bodybuilding career), gaining at that rate of speed would see you packing on 62.5 pounds of rock-solid muscle, which would

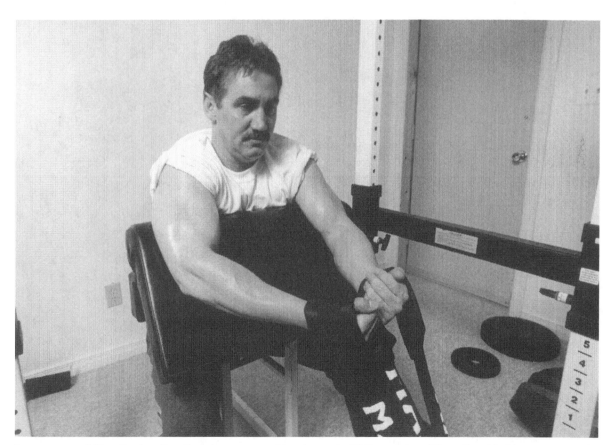

In one year of Max Contraction Training, you could gain up to 12.5 pounds, with noticeably bigger arms and shoulders.

represent a considerable change in your appearance. In fact, it would be enough to transform the average adult male weighing 155 pounds into a 217.5-pound competitive bodybuilder! Given that many competitive bodybuilders actually weigh much less than 217 pounds (despite many of their claims to the contrary) and the fact that these men are the genetic thoroughbreds of our species, an average of 12.5 pounds a year for five years might be beyond the reach of most of us lesser mortals.

"WHAT CAN I EXPECT?"

Let's assume that you are not grossly underweight, are in average to good health, and are willing to train on the Max Contraction method to the letter. Let's further assume that you are no stranger to weight training and that your bodyweight has reached a plateau of sorts after months and perhaps years of training conventionally. How much muscle can you expect to gain using Max Contraction Training? In considering all the data, I believe that you can gain at least 10 pounds of muscle over the course of one year. Granted, we don't like to think in terms of years; we prefer to think about *daily* progress! And with this in mind, many bodybuilders step on their weight scales every day eagerly looking to see if they're any heavier. Their silent query is, "What will I weigh today?"—as if 24 hours were sufficient time to suddenly morph into Mr. Olympia!

The reality is that 10 pounds of muscle growth spread over the course of a year is almost imperceptible if looked for on a daily basis. In fact, the projected muscle gain of 10 pounds in a year works out to 0.027 pounds of muscle gained per day. This is 12 grams, or less than half an ounce, not even of sufficient mass to register on a bodyweight scale—and yet many of us still continue to weigh ourselves everyday looking for some kind of weight gain. Believe me, if you're seeing weight gains every day when you step on the scale, then you're not gaining muscle, you're gaining fat.

We can see from the simple black-and-white mathematics of it that if you were to gain 10 pounds of muscle a year, you would not even be gaining a pound a month! So don't weigh yourself on a daily basis looking for muscle mass gains. A more reliable gauge by which to assess your bodybuilding progress would be your appearance. And this all rests on the assumption that your training efforts will be of sufficient intensity to stimulate 10 pounds' worth of muscle growth over the course of a year. As we have learned, muscle growth is a defensive mechanism of the body to adapt itself to the stress of intense exercise and, being such, time is required for it to take place, as with all other biological processes. However, bodybuilders have been duped into believing that "instant" muscles are just a supplement away; when they don't think they are gaining fast enough, they invariably conclude that they must be doing something wrong. This makes them immensely susceptible to the seductive pitches of the muscle magazines to increase their workouts, increase their intake of supplements, and follow a host of other unnec-

Hard, intense training is the key that will unlock your size and strength gains.

essary recommendations. Such things, however, don't hasten the muscle growth process; they actually slow it down.

The most important requisite in determining how much muscle mass you'll ultimately develop is the intensity of contractions you are willing to generate during your efforts in the gym. This must be balanced with adequate time off for recovery and growth. A third important factor is consuming a well-balanced diet that puts you in a slightly positive caloric balance (rather than a negative balance, such as dieters typically employ) that is, perhaps, 16 calories or so higher (per day) than your maintenance need of calories. Following these principles will result in your reaching the uppermost peaks of your genetic potential in the quickest time possible.

Train hard, get adequate rest, and eat a well-balanced diet—and you'll grow.

Chapter 23

COMMON QUESTIONS AND ANSWERS

I give numerous seminars each year in which I explain the principles underlying effective and scientific training. The following questions and answers were recorded during a recent seminar in Toronto, Ontario, on the new Max Contraction System.

MAX CONTRACTION VERSUS STATIC CONTRACTION

How is Max Contraction different from, say, a static contraction or isometric contraction?
Little: Max Contraction is a more precise term for the type of muscle contraction involved in this system. A position of Max, or "maximum," contraction—where the muscle has contracted maximally (or fully, or totally) is the only position in a given muscle's range of motion where maximum contraction can take place. And to get all of the fibers of a muscle to contract at one time, a load sufficient enough to activate all of a muscle's fibers must be imposed, since the well-known physiological principle of muscle contraction—the "all or nothing" principle—states that only the exact number of fibers required to perform a particular movement will be involved. Since a strong resistance in the fully contracted position is necessary for maximum stimulation in any muscle, it would seem logical that we practice only those exercises that incorporate this important feature. As all fibers are brought into play in this one position, substantially more fibers are stimulated into growth than would be if you simply held a weight at another point along the range of motion.

Since *isometric*, in physiology circles, means "same length" (*iso* = "same," and *metric* = "length"), an isometric contraction can take place at any point within a given muscle's range of motion and still, by definition, be an "isometric" contraction. Similarly with static contraction, which is just another term for a motionless "hold," you could, for example, perform a "static contraction" of the biceps muscle with the biceps in a position of full extension, as long as the muscle is simply holding the resistance statically in that position.

Max Contraction means just that—a contraction made in the maximally flexed or contracted position, and therefore it cannot be performed at any other point in a muscle's range of motion than the fully contracted position. It also happens to be the most important point in a muscle's range of motion, as it involves as many fibers as possible, whereas isometric or static holds are less specific and, therefore, less productive than maximum contractions that are held in the position of full muscular contraction.

MAX CONTRACTION VERSUS SUPERSLOW™ TRAINING

What are your thoughts on the high-intensity technique of Superslow™ training—and how does it compare with Max Contraction Training?
Little: Superslow™, created by Ken Hutchins, advocates having your muscles contract both

concentrically and eccentrically through a full range of motion with a very slow rep modality or tempo. In some respects, this is a good thing in that it creates additional tension to the muscle being trained, thereby raising the intensity of the exercise. In my opinion, the bad thing about this is that it is *synthetic* tension, by which I mean that the trainee must generate the tension himself, as the resistance selected is too light to cause sufficient tension within the muscle on its own as a result of it being far lighter than what the muscle is capable of contracting against maximally in its natural contractile ability.

As it is a step toward a maximum or Max Contraction, it is beneficial, as the Superslow™ protocol moves the muscle into the fully contracted position—the one position where all of the available fibers are brought into play—but it remains in this position very briefly, with the rest of the set dedicated to either moving away from (eccentric) or moving into (concentric)

Static contractions can take place at any point in a muscle's range of motion—including the position of full extension.

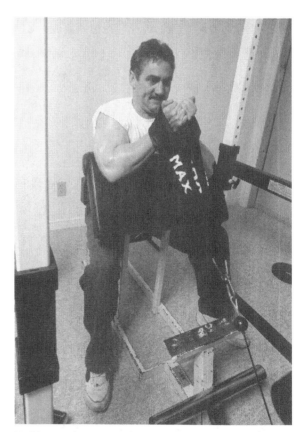

Unlike static contractions, Max Contractions can only be performed in a muscle's fully contracted position.

this optimal position. So, given that the majority of the Superslow™ set is spent out of this position, in addition to the fact that submaximal resistance is employed, it is largely inefficient. To simply make an exercise mechanically more difficult to perform does not necessarily mean you have made the exercise more productive. It is, for example, mechanically more difficult to perform a one-armed dumbbell concentration curl with your arm bent behind your back, but that does not make such an exercise productive.

To get back to my earlier point, when you train with a protocol such as Superslow™, you are limiting your muscles to contracting against resistance that is well below what they are maximally capable of moving—and force or overload is a major requirement in stimulating muscle growth. Superslow™ serves to "underload" a muscle, as the weights are much lighter than your muscles are capable of handling and do not require a maximum effort to contract against, with the result that you are not allowing the muscle to activate the maximum number of muscle fibers it is capable of—which are only recruited via the amount of force produced to overcome or move the resistance, not the range through which they are moved. Superslow™ is like tai chi with weights—an interesting concept, mind you, but unnecessary, and it makes training much longer and inefficient than it needs to be for the purposes of building muscle.

ARTHUR JONES AND MAX CONTRACTION

If a full range of motion isn't that important in building size and strength, why did Arthur Jones invent Nautilus equipment around it? Little: Jones, according to his own literature, invented Nautilus equipment to overcome the limitations he perceived as being inherent in barbells. To Jones, the problem with barbells were that they provided linear resistance, whereas most joints of the human body were rotational; in a barbell curl, for example, the resistance encountered by the muscles was always greatest at the 90 degree, or midpoint,

of the curl—where gravity made the resistance linear—whereas at the top of the movement, the resistance fell away completely, owing to the fact that the rotational axis had drawn the resistance away from the linear pull.

Jones acknowledged that the position of Max Contraction was the one spot in a given muscle's range of motion where maximum contraction of a muscle's fibers was possible, owing to the fact that a muscle contracted by shortening and it was at full contraction when it was shortest or fully contracted. He developed an offset cam for his machines that provided variable resistance, which is to say resistance that was constant throughout the range of motion, rather than simply huge in the middle as in the example of the barbell curl, and then falling off at the top, thereby removing the linear limitations of gravity and providing resistance in the one position where the muscle needed it most—the Max contracted position. Providing a piece (pieces, in fact) of equipment that would allow each bodypart to be trained in its fully or maximally contracted position was a positive boon to bodybuilders and strength athletes the world over.

However, Jones then fell back on the old tradition that a muscle had to be trained with many repetitions through a full range of motion and advocated those training on Nautilus to do just this. He had created a training tool to allow for resistance to be provided in the one spot in the range of motion where it needed it most—the Max Contraction position—and then, essentially, told bodybuilders that this position wasn't that important anyway and they should simply train their muscles through a full range of motion—from a position of full extension (where the fibers were not fully contracted and hence not fully stimulated) to full contraction (where the fibers were fully contracted and hence fully stimulated) and then back to full extension again.

In short, he had designed an extremely efficient tool for training and then counseled those to use it inefficiently. In fact, he actually built compound movements into some of his machines, such as bench presses on his Compound Chest machine, leg presses on his Compound Leg machine, shoulder presses on his Double Shoulder machine—which had little or nothing to do with rotary resistance and which had the same inherent linear limitations as the barbell. Not to say that such compound movements are without value—they most certainly are—but as with the isolation movements, that value is enhanced when the exercise is performed in its strongest range or maximally contracted position.

Jones would later go on to develop the MedX line of training equipment and direct his energies to solving the problem of "friction." However, as friction is a natural by-product of motion, when motion is eliminated, so too is the problem of friction. Jones knew the preconditions necessary to stimulate 100 percent of a given muscle's fibers—maximum contraction and sufficient resistance. Why he then opted to advise trainees to train into and out of this position, as opposed to sustaining this one position where 100 percent stimulation was possible, is lost on me.

EXERCISE SELECTION

How do you know that the exercises you have selected for Max Contraction Training are the absolute best for stimulating maximum muscle growth?

Little: The functions of the muscles dictate which exercises stress them most efficiently. For example, many bodybuilders perform bench presses in the mistaken belief that it is a direct chest exercise. But examining the action required of the limbs determines that the primary movement is an extension of the forearms from a position next to your chest to one directly above it. The extension of the forearms is the primary function of the triceps muscle—not the chest muscles. The primary function of the chest muscles is to draw the humerus, or upper arm bone, across the sternum. When this is understood, it becomes clear that the Pec Deck is a far more efficient exercise for the pecs, as it allows the muscle to more precisely fulfill its primary function.

Similarly, most bodybuilders possess the mistaken notion that the primary function of

Mike Mentzer bangs out a set of chest presses on the Nautilus Compound Chest machine. Arthur Jones was the first to alert the bodybuilding public to the importance of providing resistance to a muscle in the fully contracted position; he incorporated this feature into many of his machines.

the biceps is to draw the forearm up toward the shoulder. On the contrary, the primary function of the biceps is to supinate the hand, that is, to turn the palm upward. Only after the palm has been supinated will the biceps be able to contract maximally while fulfilling its secondary function—flexion of the forearm. You can see this for yourself: Pull your forearm up tight against your upper arm with your palm facing down in a gooseneck position. Then, place the tip of the forefinger from the opposite hand on the biceps of the goosenecked arm and feel what happens as you slowly turn that palm up; the biceps goes from an extended, relaxed position to a contracted position. This fact points to the necessity of keeping your palms up while doing any type of biceps exercise. The importance of keeping the palms facing up to activate the biceps while curling contraindicates the use of the EZ-curl bar for biceps training, as it places the biceps in more of a pronated position, thus denying its primary function.

Similarly, many bodybuilders with only a vague understanding of the function of the back or lat muscles have been led to believe that chins and pulldowns performed with an overhand or wide grip is a more efficient way to train their lats. However, it's better to use a palms-up position, since the palms-down, pronated position places the biceps in their weakest position, thereby compromising full stimulation of the lats. Because the biceps are smaller and weaker muscles than the lats, they will fail in the pulldown or chin before the lats get even close to a point of actual failure or full-growth stimulation. By turning the palms up into their strongest position, the biceps will help the lats get closer to a point of actual failure. That is why I invented the Max Straps: in fact, they bypass the biceps, directly placing the effective resistance on the lats. However, if you don't have a pullover machine or Max Straps, then close-grip, underhand chins and pulldowns are best for maximally productive lat work.

DRAWBACKS TO PLYOMETRICS

One of the strength coaches at my university has the football players training with plyometrics, where they jump with weights and perform their repetitions as quickly as possible. What are your thoughts on this method of training?

Little: The facts of the matter regarding impact forces and the nature of muscle fiber recruitment obviously fly in the face of what some of the bodybuilding and strength coaches have been preaching regarding plyometrics and other such "explosive" movements for developing strength and muscle size. Their theory, that the "fast-twitch" muscle fibers can only be activated by performing various exercises as fast as you possibly can, has been shown to be fallacious in light of what science has revealed regarding the principles of motor control and muscle fiber recruitment.

At the bottom position of a bench press performed throughout a full range of motion, the elbows are drawn away from the midline of the body, reducing the effectiveness of the exercise as a chest developer.

First off, if you train utilizing a very high rate of speed and ballistic movements, you will be forced to use light weights, as the heavier the resistance, the slower you can move it. If you use a light weight, the brain immediately picks up on the force required to move that weight and, obviously, with a light weight, the force required to move the resistance at a high speed would prove sufficient to engage the S and maybe the FO fibers. The FG fibers—the ones most important to high-speed movement and the ones contributing the most to increases in size and strength—are never activated in such a system because the resistance you will have restricted yourself to using will not be sufficient to warrant the brain sending the signal to recruit the FGs that would otherwise engage the full complement of muscle fibers. Not only does ballistic, or plyometric, training not stimulate the muscle fibers that its theory purports it does, but it only involves half of the muscle fibers available to be stimulated in any given set.

Obviously if you're only stimulating half the fibers you could be, your training system is only half as efficient as it could be, and certainly only half as efficient as Max Contraction Training, which engages all of the available muscle fibers (right down to the FG fibers). Any training system that is predicated on heaving weights up and down ballistically will not even come close to bringing the target muscle group into a position of full muscular contraction for any meaningful length of time and certainly will not engage anywhere near the full complement of available muscle fibers.

As if that wasn't enough, such training is highly traumatic to your joints and connective tissues. A barbell weighing 100 pounds, for example, if curled slowly in the conventional fashion will provide 100 pounds of resistance both concentrically and eccentrically (up and down). Holding 100 pounds in a position of full muscular contraction will do likewise. However, jerking and heaving that same 100-pound barbell up and down will magnify the trauma force on the joints to well over 1,000 pounds—and the impact to the joints which must suddenly stretch and then ballistically extend muscles, tendons, ligaments, and muscle fascia, can quickly add up to injury. Again, high-speed training is dangerous and far less productive than Max Contraction Training.

MIKE MENTZER AND MAX CONTRACTION

Did you ever share with Mike Mentzer your views on Max Contraction Training?
Little: Yes, I told Mike about it back in the late 1980s and again from time to time after we had published our books. Mike, as you may know, was very much influenced by Arthur Jones, who was a brilliant man in his own right, and it took Mike a while—many decades in fact—before he began to critically analyze some of Jones's theories with regard to high-intensity training. Up until this point, Mike accepted the "need" for a full range of motion as advocated by Jones as well as the "muscles will atrophy if you don't train them in 96 hours" belief advocated by people like Ellington Darden, Ph.D. However, near the end of his life—and you can read this yourself on pages 97–100 in his last book, *High-Intensity*

Training the Mike Mentzer Way—Mike not only advocated but trained many of his clients with great success utilizing static holds in the position of full (or maximum) contraction. He writes:

> Now I have most of my in-the-gym clients as well as my phone consultation clients perform fully contracted "holds" to failure . . . and the results are stunning, to say the least. I ascribe my clients' greater progress recently, in part, to the holds making a greater inroad into existing strength than do positives.[1]

Mike shared my view that this protocol was best employed with isolation exercises, or those exercises that, in his words, "involved rotary movement around one joint axis, and which provide resistance in the fully contracted position." For this reason, he had many of his clients perform static holds in the fully contracted position (i.e., the position of Max Contraction) on Nautilus machines, which took advantage of at least one of the reasons why the Nautilus machines were created in the first place: to overcome the paucity of effective resistance or load provided by the barbell when it came to the one position in the range of motion at which full contraction of the muscle was possible.

I even recall witnessing Mike put six-time Mr. Olympia Dorian Yates through a chest and biceps workout in 1993 in which Mike had him perform Max Contractions at the end of his sets. He had Dorian hold the resistance in a position of full contraction—on an Icarian Incline Chest Press machine and a Nautilus Multi-Biceps machine, respectively—for a period of 15 seconds, and Dorian loved the effect it had on his muscles. I don't know if he was experimenting with this technique as a result of our conversations or whether he simply came to a similar conclusion on his own; perhaps the latter, as Mike was constantly experimenting. Knowing what I know now, I would say that 15-second holds are gross overkill, as a 1-second hold works just as efficiently and will accomplish the desired effect.

Typically Mike would have his clients perform a static hold in the fully contracted position at the end of a regular set, but he even had them substitute the odd set of regular, full-range exercise on the leg extension, for example, with a static or, more accurately, "Max Contraction" set—I say "more accurately" because the quadriceps were in a position of maximum contraction for this set, and a static hold can by definition be performed at any point in the range of motion. I remember speaking about the success and rationale of Max Contraction with Mike many times over the years, and he, like me, saw the inherent potential of the protocol.

Where our approach differed was that Mike would then have his clients perform this incredibly efficient form of training only sporadically, as if—even when such issues as volume and frequency were well regulated—too much of a good thing (i.e., thorough muscle stimulation) was somehow a negative. It is true that high-intensity training can be a negative thing in terms of the demands it makes upon the body's energy systems (i.e., recovery ability), but this should never be allowed to become a negative if the frequency of training is adequately adjusted. And if this means that you are training but once every three weeks, so what?—as long as you are making progress. As Mike used to say, "Progress should not be an unpredictable, haphazard affair; you should witness progress every workout."

MAX CONTRACTION VERSUS NEGATIVE-ONLY TRAINING

Why is Max Contraction a more effective high-intensity training technique than, say, negative-only training or Superslow™?
Little: I've touched on the limitations of Superslow™ in relation to Max Contraction earlier, but in reference to negative-only training, Max Contraction Training generates the highest intensity possible, as it takes the muscle into the one place in its range of motion where all the fibers are activated and leaves it there for the duration of the set, thereby stimulating as many of a muscle's fibers as physiologically possible. Negatives do not allow for this; they

have the trainee release the full contraction almost instantly and lower themselves down to a position where less and less fibers are involved as the muscle extends.

Superslow™, as I mentioned, has the trainee utilize weights that are well below the trainee's maximum ability to contract against, and then, through a deliberate attempt by the trainee to make the resistance "feel" heavier than it is, they must move the muscles away from (negative) and toward (positive) a position of full muscular contraction. Yes, the intensity "feels" high in Superslow™, but "feel" is never an accurate gauge by which to determine intensity of effort. I could "feel" very fatigued during a workout in which I performed a leg extension with 75 pounds if I had the flu, or if I hadn't eaten properly the day before—or even if I am overtrained to the point where it requires tremendous volitional effort even to go to the gym to train—but that doesn't mean I have trained more intensely.

Intensity is simply observed and has to do with how much resistance you are making your muscles contract against. If the resistance is high, the duration of your set (or TOC) will be low—which is what it needs to be if you are looking to stimulate maximum gains in muscle strength and size. Remember, the higher the intensity, the briefer the duration. Remember also that you want your muscle building exercise to fall exclusively within the anaerobic pathways—which last from 1 to 60 seconds. By the 2-minute mark of a set of exercise, the aerobic system is responsible for 50 percent of your energy output, meaning that if your set lasts this long you are dividing the training stimulus between the aerobic and anaerobic systems, thus reducing the pure muscle building benefit. A Max Contraction set lasts between 1 and 6 seconds; a Superslow™ set lasts 2 minutes. I'm not knocking it as a fitness system or as a means by which to reduce momentum in exercise—both of which are good things. However, by virtue of the fact that it uses submaximal weights—thereby reducing the intensity of muscular contraction—and involves the aerobic pathways in each and every set, it is not as efficient as Max Contraction Training as a pure muscle building system.

PROTRACTED RECOVERY PERIODS

I'm still not clear on why it might take up to one whole week or longer to grow muscle after a workout. Can you elaborate on this?

Little: Certainly. This is one of the most frequently misunderstood and neglected facets of bodybuilding. Muscle growth is a tri-phasic process, and, even if even one of these three phases does not occur, you will never realize any progress—despite your greatest efforts in the gym. Let us assume that you have trained with sufficient intensity to stimulate muscle growth—and we'll call this Phase One.

Once your workout is over, you enter Phase Two, the stage of recovery. An individual muscle may, in some cases, recover fully within 24 hours and, in some extremely rare individuals, even within one hour. However, the recuperative subsystems that serve to mediate the recovery and growth processes—the kidneys, for example—require far more time to process the waste products and to obtain and direct nutritional matter to the various cells that require it. That is the only way one can fully recover from the exhaustive/depleting effects of a growth-stimulating workout, and the time it takes for this to happen will vary—in some cases quite widely—among individuals.

After identical workouts, for example, one person may be able to return to the gym in 48 hours and note muscular progress, while another person may need as many as eight weeks to go by in order simply to recover from his previous workout (recall the study by Drs. Howell, Chleboun, and Conatser)—and then another block of time must elapse in order to allow for the growth that was stimulated in that one workout eight weeks previously to manifest. Regardless of what your personal range of recovery happens to be, one thing is certain: the recovery period required after an intense muscle-growth-stimulating workout takes much longer than was initially thought, and training more than three days a week—at most—is going to be a mistake for most bodybuilders who are looking to increase their muscle mass. Should you opt to train again—even though your muscles "feel fine"—within the 48 to 72 hour time frame, then the only thing you will succeed in accomplishing will be an arrest of your progress. Recovery always precedes growth, and growth will not take place unless your muscles and the subsystems that replenish them have completely recovered. It is crucial to never let your enthusiasm work against your objectives.

Phase Three—the actual growth phase—will take place, so some exercise scientists report, within a 10- to 15-minute period after complete systemic recovery has taken place. It must be stressed that intense muscular contraction is a form of stress to the muscles and the overall physical system. When performed properly, such training will stimulate a compensatory buildup in the form of additional muscle size and strength, both of which aid the body in expending less energy in coping with a stress of like intensity in the future.

An ideal routine, then, would be of the highest possible intensity (and because of this fact, of the briefest possible duration) to stimulate maximum muscle growth and would occur infrequently enough to allow for full recovery and growth to take place after it had been stimulated. If, like some bodybuilders, you opt to train a different bodypart each day, the muscles you've trained in isolation may well have recovered by the time of your next workout, but your recuperative subsystems will not have recovered, and you will end up making daily inroads into your recovery ability, which ultimately feeds and dictates your future levels of muscle growth. This physiological fact reveals to us that daily training for muscle growth is a mistake, because it simply doesn't allow for recovery to take place, and, without recovery having taken place, there can be no growth production.

THE PROBLEM OF TOO-FREQUENT TRAINING

So you're saying that this is one of the reasons why bodybuilders who train up to seven days a week make little or no progress?

Little: It's precisely the reason that they don't make progress. Bodybuilders who insist on training six to seven days a week (whether on a three-days-on, one-day-off or a four-days-on, one-day-off system) will witness a catabolic effect, as the resulting drain on the energy systems of the body will actually result in the muscles becoming weaker and smaller owing to gross overtraining. In fact, all of the energy reserves will have to be called upon simply to attempt to overcome the energy debt caused by such overtraining. These facts strongly indicate that the less time spent in the gym, the better your results will be. You'll find that your results will be spectacular if you limit your total training time to one, two, or—at the very most—three workouts per week.

DO YOU NEED "THE PUMP"?

What about "the pump"? While my muscles feel a deep fatigue, I don't feel all that sore or pumped on Max Contraction, and I'm wondering why this is.

Little: Well, to begin with, a pump actually means nothing other than temporary edema of the muscle. You can get a great pump by pedaling your bike as fast as you can—but that won't stimulate much of anything in the way of muscle growth. I've seen bodybuilders training in Gold's Gym day after day—all of them getting tremendous pumps—but if a pump were the sine qua non of muscle growth stimulation, these same individuals would all have 28-inch arms by now. That isn't the case, however. In fact, these people make little or no progress in terms of muscle growth or strength increases.

The pump is illusory. Your muscles fill with blood, become temporarily larger as a result, and people think that this must be a sign that their muscles will remain bigger. But what happens an hour after you leave the gym? The blood dissipates from the muscle group you've just trained, and your muscles return to the same size they were before the workout. Simply pumping a muscle up will not stimulate muscle to grow; intensity of effort is what stimulates a muscle to grow, and the harder or higher your intensity of effort, the greater the growth stimulation. This has been verified by science as an absolute requisite for muscle growth; a pump has never been so verified.

And soreness is usually a sign that you've caused some microtrauma to the muscle or connective tissue, rather than an indicator that

you've stimulated growth. I remember speaking with Mike Mentzer—one of the most muscularly massive bodybuilders of all time—about this very topic and he told me that he seldom—if ever—got sore after a workout, and yet, again, he developed one of the most heavily muscled physiques in bodybuilding history.

DECEPTION AND THE MUSCLE MAGAZINES

Why do the muscle magazines publish articles that they know to be untrue?

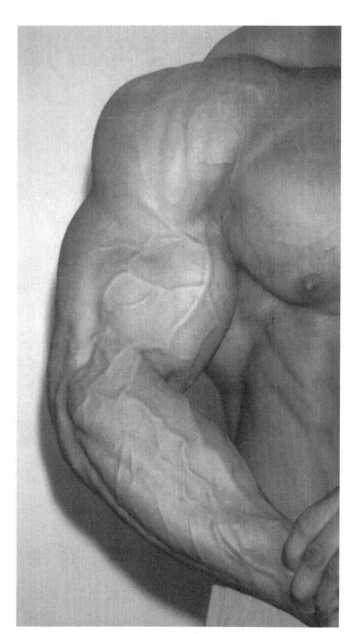

Getting a "good pump" in no way guarantees that you have stimulated muscle growth.

Little: Simply because it is in their vested interests to have you fail at your quest to develop a bigger, more muscular body. The reason being that if you fail, you are more receptive to their advertising claims that the problem must be with your diet or supplement regimen—"Hey, having trouble putting on muscle? It's probably because you're not taking 'brand X' muscle blaster!"—or whatever the supplement du jour may happen to be. They can then sell you more products (protein powders, exercise equipment, supplements, etc.) that, of course, you don't need.

In fact, in many cases the dietary indiscretions as well as the training errors bodybuilders make are the direct result of their failure to realize just how fallacious the claims made by the muscle magazines regarding muscle growth really are. Headlines scream, "My Olympia Training Program Can Work for You Too!" (which then lists a four-day program consisting of 45 exercises and 145 sets, which would lead to absolute overtraining and zero progress for the average trainee); "Double Your Gains Today!" (interestingly enough, this is about a bodybuilding supplement); and "Mr. Olympia's Max F—kin' Workout!" (which, apart from its juvenile title, indicates a training program of 6 days on, 1 day off, and 28 sets for back; 31 sets for arms; 11 sets for chest; 17 sets for shoulders; and 31 sets for legs—again, this is gross overtraining).

If a bodybuilder is expecting to "double" his gains "overnight" or even gain a pound of muscle a week or a pound of muscle a month —and realizes that he's not seeing those gains, then he typically becomes hysterical and begins training more often, utilizing different set/rep combinations, training routines, varying his hand spacings, utilizing more free weights, or increasing his protein or supplement intake— all the things the muscle magazines tell him he must do to overcome those "inevitable" plateaus and gain those muscular pounds that everyone displays so proudly in all of those flashy product ads and magazines. Sadly, all of this commercial hype cannot alter this fact of reality: muscle growth can be at times a slow, even arduous process.

But don't give up your dream of building a bigger, more muscular body just yet—because it *can* happen. And it can happen sooner rather than later if you don't buy into the hype that will cost you months and perhaps years (and perhaps it already has) of traveling down blind alleys and side streets, diverting you from your goals. If you can develop a firm grasp, if your mind can envelop—totally—a more realistic expectation of the nature of the muscle-growth process, then it's my firm belief that you will be less inclined to commit a lot of the ridiculous dietary and training errors that bodybuilders are so accustomed to committing.

WHY DON'T WE NEED SUPPLEMENTS?

How do you know that we don't need supplements? If we're building muscle with our workouts, how can our nutritional needs remain the same as, say, someone who is not building muscle? Haven't there been gains in our knowledge of nutrition that would enhance our efforts in the gym?
Little: Many bodybuilders feel that they require a superabundance—and certainly more than a balanced diet would allot—of the various vitamins, minerals, and other supplements. However, I will tell you categorically that this is simply not true. And for proof of this, you need look no further than the bodybuilding magazines of ten years back.

If you pick up a copy of *Muscle Builder/ Power* from the 1970s you'll read that the big "must-have" supplement of the era was milk-and-egg protein powder; in the 1980s it was amino acids that were de rigueur; in the 1990s it was MetRx. Presently it is creatine phosphate. In 10 years, it will be something else. How scientific. And with each passing decade, the must-have supplements from the previous decade drop from sight—so how must-have were they?

In the 1960s, for example, it was vitamin E capsules, which were being touted as wonder pills that would protect you from everything from smog and heart attacks to sexual problems. It was not uncommon then for their manufacturers to recommend up to 500 units of vitamin E to be taken after each meal. But what is the truth about how much vitamin E you really need to ingest on a daily basis? For this answer, we can't look to the vitamin E supplement salespeople, but rather to independent bodies such as the Food and Nutrition Board.

Going back to our example about vitamin E, we note that the RDA—or as it is known by its full name, the Recommended Daily Allowance, and which is busy being revised in a collaborative effort between the USA and Canada and is now called the Dietary Reference Intake or DRI—for vitamin E has dropped to 10 international units daily. In the early 1970s the RDA for this vitamin was 15 international units daily. Thus, the "1,500-units-a-day" supplement (500 after each meal) actually supplied over three months' worth of the RDA for this one vitamin. But ask yourself: "Is it likely that the RDA—or DRI—committee is grossly in error about the amounts of vitamin E needed for optimum health?"

Or, putting a sharper point on it, consider the fact that our species has been able to survive and evolve by eating food that we could readily obtain. Do you honestly think that there should exist large natural barriers to our ability to access the foods needed for the maintenance of our health? I mean, it's simple common sense—to obtain the "recommended" dosage of 1,500 I.U.s of vitamin E each day, our ancestors would have had to forage for foods rich in vitamin E, such as almonds. To get this amount of vitamin E would require *18 pounds of almonds a day.*

And wheat germ, which has also received much press as an excellent source of vitamin E, would require you to consume 27 pounds of it a day in order to obtain 1,500 I.U.s. This is an extraordinary amount of food! Just one tablespoon of wheat germ weighs six grams and provides 23 calories. Simple mathematics shows us that 27 pounds of wheat germ would require over 2,000 tablespoons a day! Which, in turn, would contain over 46,000 calories. Think about this. Is it really realistic to believe that a person can't obtain good health without either supplements or 27 pounds of wheat

germ? Don't be a health food fanatic—be a bodybuilder. They're two different things.

WHAT'S WRONG WITH THE RDAS?

You mention that a balanced diet is all that is required to build muscle beyond normal levels, but I've heard that what the Senate Subcommittee on Nutrition recommends—the Recommended Dietary Allowances, or RDAs—aren't set high enough for good health.

Little: I don't know where you heard that. The RDAs, or DRIs, are estimated to exceed the requirements of most individuals, which would thereby ensure that the needs of nearly all are met. I suppose a possible exception to this rule might be in the RDA estimates of calories, or energy—but even here, obviously, it would not be a good idea to set a generous excess, since obesity is a widespread problem.

The board responsible for formulating the RDAs, for those who don't know, was assembled under the auspices of the National Academy of Science's National Research Council and is composed of large numbers of America's more respected nutritional scientists. Moreover, its membership changes periodically, both to share the burden of the work and to broaden the variety of legitimately informed opinions. The Board's Committee on Dietary Allowances is composed of subcommittees for each nutrient, or in some cases, for groups of nutrients. And it is the job of the scientists on these subcommittees to constantly reassess what is known of the nutrients, and keep up to date on the latest research reports. They also study the quantities of nutrients in the American food supply, their effects on the body, and any additional relevant information about the public's health and eating habits.

Just about every five years, the Committee on Dietary Allowances publishes an updated report called "Recommended Dietary Allowances" (RDAs). This report sets out guideline recommendations for different population groups, according to height, sex, age, and weight. Thus a Recommended Dietary Allowance (RDA) for 17 different groups of people is estimated for every nutrient about which there is sufficient data to make an informed judgment.

A misperception has arisen over the years—largely promulgated by supplement companies—that the RDAs are minimums for survival, whereas in fact, they are set up to include generous safety margins. RDAs, under different names, are also set in other countries, such as Canada and Great Britain, and by United Nations agencies, and these are usually lower than the American RDAs for several nutrients. In practical terms, the committee you cited makes recommendations which should provide an excess of any given nutrient for at least 95 percent of people. Even this is very conservatively estimated, however. For example, back in their 1968 report the committee's RDA for vitamin C for the average adult male was estimated to be 60 milligrams a day. In 1974, based on revised information, the committee lowered this recommendation to 45 milligrams a day. So, by and large the RDAs are, if anything, overly generous, rather than inadequate.

HIGH BLOOD PRESSURE AND EXERCISE

I've heard that isometric-type exercises can cause an increase in blood pressure. If so, doesn't this make Max Contraction and other static-type exercise protocols more dangerous than regular training?

Little: The truth is that your blood pressure goes up during any vigorous exercise, including cycling, cross-country skiing, running, calisthenics, and weight training—of any sort. In the textbook titled *Exercise Physiology*, by Professors William D. McArdle, Frank I. Katch, and Victor L. Katch, they tested isometric, or motionless, exercise against two modes of isotonic exercise. The study was conducted at the University of Massachusetts, and the blood pressure of normotensive subjects was measured directly with a pressure transducer connected to a catheter that was inserted into the femoral artery. They then tested the blood pressure response of the subject performing four sets of isometric bench presses at 25, 50, 75, and 100 percent of maximal voluntary con-

traction in the same arm and body position as the two other protocols, which were free-weight bench presses performed at 25 and 50 percent of the maximum voluntary contraction and a hydraulic resistance bench press performed all-out for 20 seconds' duration at two settings: slow (for 11 reps) and fast (for 16 reps) carried through a full range of motion.

According to the textbook, all three forms of exercise produced dramatic elevations in blood pressure—even with relatively light exercise that required only 25 percent of the maximal effort. In looking over the data myself, I noted that the peak systolic and peak diastolic conditions were actually somewhat higher with the full-range exercises than with the isometric

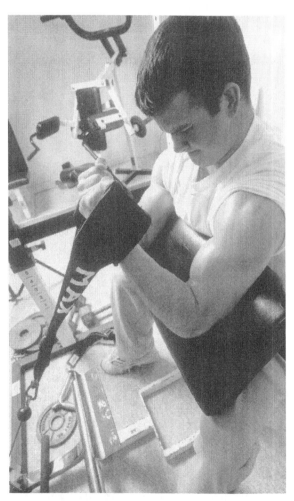

Any type of muscular contraction has the potential to raise one's blood pressure. It is always a good idea to get a thorough checkup by a qualified physician before embarking on any strenuous exercise program such as Max Contraction Training.

exercise (at 100 percent contraction isometrically, the peak systolic was 225 and the peak diastolic was 156, compared with 232 and 154 for the free-weight full-range bench press and 245 and 160 for the hydraulic full-range bench press).[2]

This makes sense, of course, because it doesn't take a maximal effort to cause an increase in blood pressure. In fact, your blood pressure is probably rising right now from the sodium in the soft drink you're drinking. Many common everyday tasks like carrying a briefcase and maintaining your posture are largely static or isometric and not considered dangerous. In fact, it's interesting to note that the increase in blood pressure from full-range weight training was one of the reasons that Arthur Jones designed his Nautilus equipment the way he did and why he also stressed that you should not grip the handles of the machines too tightly when training.

This is not to trivialize the concern: it is important that anyone beginning a vigorous weight training program get his or her physician's okay beforehand. But it's also a fact that any increase in blood pressure from weight training exercise, such as Max Contraction, returns to normal quite quickly after you complete your workout, provided your cardiovascular system is functioning normally. James Wright, Ph.D., in his article on motionless exercise—the same one that premiered my training system to North American audiences back in 1992—wrote that isometrics, or static, exercise did not cause blood pressure increases that were any greater than conventional forms of weight training, writing:

> There is no evidence that the transient elevations that occur during [isometric] exercise persist or influence the development of hypertension or cardiovascular risk. . . . The blood pressure changes are no more—and no different—than those that occur during any kind of heavy lifting. That's one reason some physicians in years past weren't too keen on weightlifting and bodybuilding. But who can say that transient elevations in blood pressure—which

only require the heart, which is a muscle, to pump harder for a brief period—is bad for you?[3]

This having been said, individuals with a precondition to heart disease would obviously be at risk by engaging in any activity that elevates blood pressure—from swimming to weight training. And if you are one of these people, then Max Contraction Training would not be a wise thing to do—but it's no more dangerous and causes no greater increase in blood pressure than any other bodybuilding exercise. In fact, according to the study I just cited, it causes less of a blood pressure increase than conventional training.

TRAIN LESS, GAIN MORE

The gains I've seen from people who are training on your system are impressive, but I'm still not clear on how less training can equal more muscle mass. Would you please elaborate on this?

Little: Well, I would point out that if conventional or long and frequent workouts were the sole factor responsible for the development of muscle tissue, then there would be a lot more Mr. Olympia–caliber physiques walking around these days, as the vast majority of bodybuilders train according to the approaches of the handful of men who have won the Mr. Olympia contest. That is to say, that they employ the multi-set, multi-volume approach.

Why aren't all of those who have trained in the same fashion—and the numbers are legion—developed to the same degree as these men, or even close to it? The answer is that it is not their training methods but their genetic endowment that accounted for the ultimate size of their muscles. Superior genetics is the prime determinant of bodybuilding success. Arnold Schwarzenegger, Lee Haney, and all of those who have achieved extraordinary levels of muscular development—including advocates of high-intensity training like Mike and Ray Mentzer, Casey Viator, and Dorian Yates—possessed an abundance of the requisite genetic traits, including long muscle bellies, greater-

Joe Ostertag (foreground) contracts his left pec against over 1,000 pounds of resistance, consisting of 585 pounds of weights, two riders weighing 190 and 195 pounds, and an additional 45-pound plate. Joe built up to his incredible feat after only five workouts of Max Contraction Training.

than-average muscle-fiber density, and superior recovery ability.

But to answer your question more directly, I think the best way to compare the efficacy of the two training approaches is to examine the results obtained by a genetically superior practitioner from each camp. From May 1 to May 29, 1973, Casey Viator increased his muscular bodyweight from 166 to 212 pounds as a result of training one half hour per workout, performing only three workouts per week. The exercise physiologists who observed Viator during this period discovered, using a sophisticated isotope machine, that Viator lost 17 pounds of fat during that month. Viator's actual lean bodymass gain was a whopping 63 pounds in one month, resulting from a total of six hours of training.

Now contrast Viator's achievement with what Schwarzenegger did to prepare for the 1975 Mr. Olympia contest that year. Starting in July of that year, when he weighed 200 pounds, Arnold trained four hours a day, six days a

week until that November, when he appeared in the contest at 225 pounds. In that four-month period, he trained for a total of approximately 288 hours, yet he gained only 25 pounds.

So there you have two individuals with superior genetics, who were gaining back previously held muscle mass—and yet Viator gained 38 more pounds of muscle than did Schwarzenegger. The only variable was the amount of time spent training—Viator trained for six hours and gained 63 pounds of muscle, whereas Schwarzenegger trained for 288 hours and gained 25 pounds of muscle. It was the intensity of Viator's workouts, coupled with their infrequency, which allowed for his greater recovery and growth.

RELATIVISM IN BODYBUILDING

I recently attended a top bodybuilder's seminar and he said that there "were no truths in bodybuilding" and that "we each had to find out which bodybuilding routine worked best for us." Could you comment on this?
Little: There are, of course, relativists in bodybuilding; the ones who hold that "what is true for you [in terms of training] isn't true for me, and what is true for me may not be true for you." In other words, that truth in training matters is purely a matter of subjective opinion and that there are no objective or universal principles by which one can determine a superior course of action. In fact, Arnold Schwarzenegger once made the statement to me and approximately 70 other people at a seminar in downtown Toronto that "what I do might not work for you, and what Mike Mentzer does might not work for you—because we are all so different." He then advised us to "buy all of the books and courses of all of the bodybuilders to find out which training approach works the best *for you.*"

We all applauded his profundity at the time, but later, when I got home and had time to reflect on what he said, I realized that it was tantamount to saying nothing at all. It is the equivalent of asking someone the most efficient way to get from Los Angeles to New York, and being told, "Well, the most efficient way I get to New York may not get you to New York, and the most efficient way someone else gets to New York might not get you to New York; you have to experiment with all of the ways of all modes of travel (e.g., airplane, car, bus, motorcycle, helicopter, horseback, horse-drawn carriage, walking, jogging, sailboat, cruise ship, canoe, etc.) and see which one of these methods is the most efficient *for you*." In other words, to such a person exact knowledge in such matters is impossible.

However, simple logic reveals that if exact knowledge is impossible, his statement is meaningless. He purported to offer you a statement of certainty, but if certainty, that is, exact knowledge, is "impossible," then it contradicts itself; that is, if his statement is true, then his statement is false. Such statements always implode—if truth is merely subjective opinion and "what is true for you is true for you" and "what is true for me is true for me," then my reply would be, "Truth is absolute, not opinion, and the bodybuilder who told you this is absolutely in error." Since this is my opinion, then he would have to grant that it is true.

Proper bodybuilding training, however, is not subjective but objective—based on immutable facts of human physiology. It's not "true only for me" that muscles grow bigger when subjected to a progressive overload or higher intensities of muscular contraction. It's an objective fact. It's not "true only for me" that the more intensely you do something, the shorter the time you can engage in that something. Again, it's an objective fact. Being a product of science and logical thought, Max Contraction Training advances a position that there is an absolute "best" way to train and that the truth of the matter is knowable and objective—not relative and contradictory.

THE MYTH OF "SPOT REDUCTION"

I would like to lose fat from the area around my chest and entire waist area without losing size anywhere else. Can I spot reduce these areas with Max Contraction?

Little: Sorry to disillusion you, but spot reduction isn't physiologically possible; it is a bogus concept perpetrated by business interests sell-ing spot-reduction devices and supplements. When you go on a diet, fat will be mobilized from all of your body's multiple fat cells, not from isolated areas, such as those in the areas you might be exercising. Once fat has been broken down and mobilized, it is transported by the blood to all the individual active cells in the body and burned for energy. You would be better advised to go on a general reducing diet in conjunction with Max Contraction Training, working all of your muscle groups in a single workout performed once to three times weekly. This will lower your overall percentage of body fat and build muscle at the same time, thereby causing a reduction in the areas you desire, while maintaining muscle size in all body parts.

MUSCLE DOES NOT TURN TO FAT

I like the idea of growing bigger and stronger muscles, but I've been told that should I ever stop training, all of my muscles will turn to fat. What do you say to that?

Little: I say it's a supposition contrary to fact. Muscle and fat are two totally different types of tissue and one won't magically transform into the other any more than a peach will transform into a watermelon. Viewed under a microscope, muscle is seen as long fibrous strands, known as myofibrils, while fat comprises little spherical globules. A chemical analysis of muscle and fat reveal the former to be made up of over 70 percent water, 6 percent lipids, and about 22 percent protein. Fat, on the other hand is only 15–20 percent water, 70 percent lipids, and approximately 15 percent protein.

It's been a long-standing falsehood that muscle turns to fat later in life, most likely arising from the fact that oftentimes uneducated or just noncaring athletes would often continue eating the same quantity of food after they'd stopped competing as they did when they were competing. I knew many hockey players in Canada who were very lean when they were practicing several times a week and playing high-level hockey twice a week on top of this. Such a regimen required them to consume thousands of calories each day simply to maintain their bodyweight and fuel their training and game sessions.

However, after their competitive careers ended, they weren't nearly as active and thus didn't burn as many calories as they did when they were training and competing, with the result that a good many of them are now very fat. That doesn't mean that playing hockey will make you fat—and neither will bodybuilding training. As long as you match your calorie consumption to your energy expenditure, you needn't worry about your muscles "turning to fat."

MAXIMUM CONTRACTION IS NOT MAXIMUM CONTRACTION?

I read somewhere that a position of maximum muscle contraction does not necessarily activate all available muscle fibers. This author indicated that a static contraction performed anywhere in a muscle's range of motion will activate the same amount of muscle fibers within a given muscle. Could you comment on this?

Little: Well, I will say that this gentleman is mistaken. The position of full muscular contraction is just that—the position of "full muscular contraction." Following his logic, you could simply hold onto a weight in the fully extended position—where the fibers are not activated to any great degree, such as the starting position of a leg extension, where your shin is at a 90-degree angle to your thigh—and you would be recruiting the same amount of muscle fibers. Some muscles, such as the vastus medialis muscle of the quadriceps, don't even come into play until the last one-third of extension. You can determine this for yourself: Simply place your hand on your vastus medialis and slowly extend your leg. You will actually feel it "kick in" once you enter the last one-third of extension. It won't kick in at any point below this.

Again, the idea is "Maximum Contraction"—not simply "static contraction." There's a big difference. Why is your biceps, for example, harder when you flex it maximally than when you attempt to flex it with your arm extended, if not for the fact that more muscle fibers are engaged? Polemics against anything

new is to be expected, but there's simply no scientific basis for this gentleman's assertion.

STRENGTH EQUALS SIZE

I notice that you keep referring to "size and strength" increases—as if the two go together—when I've always thought that they were two separate processes.

Little: Well, if they were two separate processes, it would be possible for your muscles to get bigger and you to get weaker, or you would get stronger and your muscles would become smaller—and that's simply not the way it happens; as you get bigger, you get stronger and when you get stronger, you get bigger. The vast majority of bodybuilders don't realize that a proper bodybuilding routine is—or should be—essentially a strength-building program.

It was discovered a long time ago that muscular size and strength are related. More precisely, the strength of a muscle is proportional to its cross-sectional area. If you want to grow larger muscles, then you must become stronger. For many, strength increases will precede size increases. This means that you will grow stronger for a time with little in the way of visible mass or bodyweight increases. But as your strength increases continue, they will eventually turn into muscle mass increases.

This explains why certain powerlifters, including Olympic champions, have been forced into heavier weight classes. As they set records and grow stronger, they gain muscular bodyweight and no longer qualify for their customary weight class. If you are imposing a sufficiently intense training stress on your musculature with your Max Contraction workouts and you train neither too long nor too frequently, you should witness a strength increase—as indicated by lifting more weight or holding the weight you are using for up to six seconds—as a result of each workout, or at least on a very regular basis.

STEROIDS AND SUPPLEMENTS

I know a guy who has been taking a supplement that does the same thing as steroids. It's called a "natural steroid." However, as steroids have side effects—both positive and negative—I was wondering what you could tell me about this.

Little: I can tell you that your friend is being sold a bill of goods. There is no such thing as a "natural steroid." Steroids are drugs—not food supplements—being composed of chemical compounds that exist within the body naturally or can be manufactured in a laboratory. The steroid's chemical structure is of a specific organic nature that makes it a very powerful anabolic agent. Because steroids are so potent, they are available by prescription only, and buying them on the black market is against the law. What your friend is buying is not a steroid and will not cause any of the effects that real steroid compounds do—whether positive or negative, and I'm not sure what the "positive" effects are that you're thinking of, by the way. What your friend is buying most likely won't have any effect at all. People selling so-called natural steroids or steroid-like supplements are simply taking advantage of gullible consumers and cashing in on all the recent hype involving anabolic steroids. They promise you the same benefits, presumably faster growth, without the negative side effects. This is not only misleading but fraudulent. My advice to your friend would be to stop wasting his money on these useless supplements and get on a Max Contraction Training schedule and a well-balanced diet. If he trains hard, eats a well-balanced diet, and gets adequate rest, he will be doing all that he can to increase his muscle mass.

RECOVERY VERSUS SLOTH

A bodybuilding trainer who claims to specialize in high-intensity training recently told me that we should stay out of the gym for a month after each workout and that our goal should be to work out only once every six to eight weeks. Do you agree with this?

Little: Recovery ability is such a personal thing that you can't simply assert an arbitrary time period; it all depends on your personal rate of progress. If you are making progress, then obviously your muscles have had adequate time

to recover and adequate time to grow. If your muscles are staying the same, that is, not getting bigger and stronger, then you are recovering from the workout, but not allowing enough time to elapse for growth to take place. And, of course, if you are getting weaker, then you are not even allowing enough time for recovery to take place. This issue of the frequency of training must be seriously factored into the formulation of any high-intensity training equation, and as Max Contraction Training is so intense, the recovery periods are longer than with conventional training protocols—typically, if not categorically—one application of the Max Contraction Training stress every 4 to 14 days.

This being said, I don't—save for individuals who are grossly, chronically overtrained—subscribe to the theory that it is desirable to stay out of the gym for months at a time, as it is too easy for the average trainee to stay out of the gym entirely, fall into old habits, and slip into a state of terrible health and fitness. Training your muscles is not only necessary, particularly as you get older, but desirable, effecting a host of benefits to the body, from increased blood flow to the extremities, less stiffness to joints, relief of stress and tension, and more efficient mobility, among others.

The logic that you should try your best to stay out of the gym as long as possible seems to me a lazy man's prescription for staying lazy, in addition to being a sure-fire way to ruin your health and physique. You should stay out of the gym long enough to recover and grow—not as long as possible. To add weeks and weeks of doing nothing as a means of compensating for each strength increase, however incremental, were you to follow this logic to its invariable conclusion, could, theoretically, see you training your body but once every 10 years—or perhaps one workout for the rest of your life.

The muscles of the human body, however, aren't geared for inactivity; they require use, and sometimes daily use, in order to not only grow larger, but to operate at peak efficiency and to help with other "noncosmetic" functions such as blood circulation. The muscles of the body operate on the premise of "use it or lose it," and it's a sad fact that more people become old prematurely by rusting out than by wearing out. I think that many of us in the high-intensity community have been guilty of maligning exercise as negative and touting recovery ability as positive to an unnecessarily large extent and to the point where we are distorting the reality of an otherwise very simple relationship.

Yes, recovery ability is important, but too many high-intensity theorists have glorified off-days to the point of elevating sloth into a training method. Recovery ability is crucial, however, and shy of Mike Mentzer, I've probably written more on this facet of exercise science than any other advocate of high-intensity training. And it may be that for the purpose of building size and strength, one may only be required to train once a week or once every two weeks for 9 seconds—or 18 to 32 seconds of total training time per month. But 32 seconds of high-intensity training does not require three weeks to recover from, let alone months, as the exposure to the training stress is too brief to disturb more than the bare minimum of reserve ability. Had one been exposed to it repeatedly or more frequently, then, perhaps, an argument could be made to support staying out of the gym for a greater length of time.

But the way this topic is discussed, doing one set of a lat pulldown exercise is tantamount to being hit by a bus, requiring extensive "recovery" periods of up to several months and intake of special amino acid formulas and "recovery enhancers." Hey, folks, this is exercise—not surgery—we're talking about here. Training your body, working out—[this is] not a tropical disease or a virus that you need to

Rest just long enough between exercises to catch your breath—and then hit your next exercise as intensely as possible.

guard against. You must train hard to gain, but not so long or so hard as to put you out of commission for several weeks. Sounds like common sense, doesn't it?

The good news is if you train intelligently and purposively, you can accomplish your bodybuilding goals in under 10 minutes of training a month. The whole world of bodybuilding is constantly falling prey to this appeal to the lazy man's approach. New techniques, new supplements, new drugs—it's all predicated on "an easier way," on wishes rather than on reality.

REST IN BETWEEN SETS

How much time should I take in between Max Contraction sets?
Little: You should allow just enough time in between sets so that you can resume the next set and still reach a point of muscular failure.

If you are forced to terminate the set because your breathing is too labored, you didn't rest long enough. How long your workout should take will be an individual matter contingent upon your physical condition.

Follow the routine I outline in *Max Contraction Training* and go at a casual pace initially. Work at progressively reducing the workout time by shortening the rest periods between sets. You should make a concerted effort to reduce those rest periods, but don't allow your workouts to become a race against the clock. Your breathing will be very labored upon cessation of any Max Contraction set and should still be heavier than normal when resuming the next set. The length of the rest between Max Contraction sets will depend upon the size of the muscle you're working and at what point in the workout you're at—the beginning or the end—as well as your existing physical condition.

NOTES

Chapter 1

1. Will Durant. *The Life Of Greece* (New York: Simon and Schuster, 1939) 211, 298.
2. J. A. Symonds. *Studies of the Greek Poets* (London: Adams & Charles Black, 1920) 187.
3. Homer. *The Odyssey*, trans. A. T. Murray (Cambridge, Mass.: Harvard University Press, Loeb Classical Library, 1984) viii, 146.
4. Xenophon. *Conversations of Socrates*, trans. Hugh Tredennick and Robin Waterfield (London: Penguin Books, 1990) 3.12.3; 171–72.

Chapter 4

1. B. Morpurgo. *Ueber Activitats-hypertrophie der wikurlichen Muskeln* (Sienna: Virchows Arch.: 1897) 150, 522–44.
2. Arthur Steinhaus. "Training for Strength in Sports" in *Toward an Understanding of Health and Physical Fitness* (Chicago and Crawfordsville, Ind.: R. R. Donnelley, 1963) 322.
3. H. Petow and W. Siebert. "Studien ueber Arbeitshypertrophie des Muskels," *Zeitschrift fuer Klinische Medizin* 102 (1925): 427–33.
4. Lange. *Ueber Funktionelle Anpassung* (Berlin: USW, Julius Springer, 1917).
5. H. Petow and W. Siebert. "Studien ueber Arbeitshypertrophie des Muskels."
6. W. Siebert. "Untersuchungen ueber Hypertrophie des Skelett-muskels," *Zeitschrift fuer Klinische Medizin* 109 (1928): 350–59.
7. T. H. Hettinger and E. A. Muller. *Muskelleistung und Muskel-training, Arbeitsphysiologie* 15 (1953): 11–126.
8. Steinhaus. "Training for Strength in Sports," 323.
9. E. A. Muller. "The Regulation of Muscular Strength," *JAPMR* 11 (1957): 5, 41–47; and T. H. Hettinger. *The Physiology of Strength* (Springfield, Ill.: C. H. Thomas, 1961).

Chapter 5

1. H. S. Milner-Brown, et al. *Journal of Physiology* 230 (1973): 350.

Chapter 9

1. Ralph N. Carpinelli and R. M. Otto. *Master Trainer*, December 1997.
2. Ibid.
3. Ibid.
4. R. A. Berger. "Comparison of the Effect of Various Weight Training Loads on

Strength," *Research Quarterly* 36 (1963): 141–46.

5. K. J. Ostrowski, et al. "The Effect of Weight Training Volume on Hormonal Output and Muscular Size and Function," *Journal of Strength and Conditioning Research* 11 (1997): 148–54.

Chapter 10

1. Ellington Darden. *The Nautilus Advanced Bodybuilding Book* (New York: Simon and Schuster, 1984) 11–12.

Chapter 11

1. Herbert A. DeVries. *The Physiology of Exercise* (Dubuque Iowa: WCB: Wm. C. Crown Company Publishers, 1980), page 53.

2. James E. Wright. *Muscle & Fitness*, May 1992, 192.

Chapter 20

1. Kenneth H. Cooper and Syndey Lou Bunnick. "Aerobic Exercise, Strength Training, and Bone Mass" in *The New Fitness Formula of the 90s* (Excelsior, Minn.: The National Exercise for Life Institute, 1990).

Chapter 21

1. William D. McArdle, Frank I. Katch, and Victor L. Katch. *Exercise Physiology* (Philadelphia, Pa.: Lea & Febiger, 1986) 23.

2. Ibid., 35.
3. Ibid.
4. Ibid., 55.
5. A. L. Goldberg, et al. "Mechanism of Work-Induced Hypertrophy of Skeletal Muscle," *Med. Sci. Sports* 7 (1975): 185–98.
6. McArdle, et al. *Exercise Physiology*, 23.
7. N. Smith. *Food for Sport* (Palo Alto, Cal.: Bull Pub., 1976).
8. R. Hedman. "The Available Glycogen in Man . . . etc." *Acta Physiologica Scandinavica* Vol. 40, 1957, pp. 305–9.
9. *Nutrition for Athletes* (Washington, D.C.: American Association for Health, Physical Education and Recreation, 1971).
10. J. Bergstrom and E. Hultman. "Nutrition for Maximal Sports Performance," *Journal of the American Medical Association (JAMA)* 221: 999–1006.
11. Food and Nutrition Board. *Recommended Dietary Allowances* (Washington, D.C.: National Academy of Sciences, 1974) 43.

Chapter 23

1. Mike Mentzer. *High-Intensity Training the Mike Mentzer Way* (Chicago: Contemporary Books, 2003) 97–100.

2. William D. McArdle, Frank I. Katch, and Victor L. Katch. *Exercise Physiology*, (Philadelphia, Pa.: Lea & Febiger, 1986) 251–52.

3. James E. Wright. *Muscle & Fitness*, May 1992, 191–92.

INDEX

ABOUT THE AUTHOR

John Little is the author of more than 30 books on bodybuilding, martial arts, history, and philosophy. He is the creator/innovator of the Max Contraction Training method of bodybuilding/strength training and has worked alongside the biggest names in bodybuilding from Mike Mentzer to Steve Reeves. Little's books have sold over 600,000 copies and are published in several languages. He is a monthly columnist for *Ironman* magazine, and his articles have been published in every major health and fitness publication in North America. He is also an award-winning documentary filmmaker.

If you would like more information on Max Contraction Training and Max Contraction products (including audios, videos, and Max Straps), you're encouraged to visit the official Max Contraction website at maxcontraction.com.

Made in the USA
Lexington, KY
04 April 2010